THE HUMACHINE

There is a lot of hype, hand-waving, and ink being spilled about artificial intelligence (AI) in business. The amount of coverage of this topic in the trade press and on shareholder calls is evidence of a large change currently underway. It is awesome and terrifying. You might think of AI as a major environmental factor that is creating an evolutionary pressure that will force enterprise to evolve or perish. For those companies that do survive the "silicon wave" sweeping through the global economy, the issue becomes how to keep their humanity amidst the tumult.

What started as an inquiry into how executives can adopt AI to harness the best of human and machine capabilities turned into a much more profound rumination on the future of humanity and enterprise. This is a wake-up call for business leaders across all sectors of the economy. Not only should you implement AI regardless of your industry, but once you do, you should fight to stay true to your purpose, your ethical convictions, and indeed your humanity, even as our organizations continue to evolve. While not holding any punches about the dangers posed by AI, this book uniquely surveys where technology is limited and where the true opportunities lie amidst all the disruptive changes currently underway. As such, it is distinctively more optimistic than many of the competing titles on Big Technology.

This is a compelling book that weaves together philosophical, psychological, and legal insights; organizational governance, operations, and strategy; and technological breakthroughs and limitations. The authors set out to identify where humans and machines can best complement one another to create an enterprise greater than the sum total of its parts: the Humachine.

Combining the business and predictive acumen of Professor Nada R. Sanders, PhD, with the legal and philosophical perspective of John D. Wood, Esq., the authors combine their strengths in business strategy, forecasting, law, and sustainable business to bring us this profound yet accessible book. This is a "must read" for anyone interested in AI and the future of human enterprise.

Nada R. Sanders, PhD, is a distinguished professor at D'Amore McKim School of Business at Northeastern University in Boston. Her expertise includes forecasting, analytics, global supply chain intelligence, and sustainability. She is the 2019 president of the Production and Operations Management Society and fellow of the Decision Sciences Institute. Her publications have appeared in *California Management Review*, *Journal of Operations Management*, *International Journal of Forecasting*, and *Production and Operations Management Journal*.

John D. Wood, Esq., is a member of the New York and Texas Bar Associations and a graduate of NYU School of Law. He is founder of The Law Firm of John D. Wood, PLLC, providing strategic counsel to property owners. His expertise includes risk management, legal compliance, and sustainable business strategy. His publications have appeared in *NYU Journal of Law and Liberty*, *NYU Environmental Law Journal*, *The Environmental Law Reporter*, as well as numerous Bar Association journals.

THE HUMACHINE

Humankind, Machines, and the Future of Enterprise

Nada R. Sanders
and
John D. Wood

Routledge
Taylor & Francis Group

NEW YORK AND LONDON

First published 2020
by Routledge
52 Vanderbilt Avenue, New York, NY 10017

and by Routledge
2 Park Square, Milton Park, Abingdon, Oxon, OX14 4RN

Routledge is an imprint of the Taylor & Francis Group, an informa business

© 2020 Taylor & Francis

Library of Congress Cataloging-in-Publication Data
A catalog record for this title has been requested

ISBN: 978-1-138-57135-8 (hbk)
ISBN: 978-1-138-57134-1 (pbk)
ISBN: 978-0-429-00117-8 (ebk)

Typeset in Sabon
by Lumina Datamatics Limited

To the pioneers and visionaries who will shape our future.

—Nada

This book is dedicated to everyone working to help technology help humanity.

—John

CONTENTS

CONTENTS

CONTENTS

CONTENTS

CONTENTS

LIST OF FIGURES

LIST OF TABLES

PREFACE

The competitive playing field is shifting, not slightly but seismically. A gaping fault line has opened in the ground, creating a branch in the evolutionary trajectory of human enterprise, dividing the past from the future.

On The Past side of the fault line are those companies that mistakenly treat AI as another piece of technology to tack on to your company (like Eeyore's tail). But AI does not fit the plug-and-play model of technology adaptation. It is not like updating your workforce's laptops or installing a new CRM platform. Indeed, it is unlike any technological change that has ever occurred in recorded human history.

On The Future side of the fault line are those companies implementing AI at the enterprise level, mutating into a new form of enterprise entirely—one that combines the highest capabilities of humankind with the newfound and continually emerging powers of AI.

You might think of AI as a major environmental factor being introduced to the Earth's ecosphere, which will create a sort of evolutionary pressure that will force enterprise to evolve or perish. And for those companies on The Future side of the fault line, the issue becomes how to keep their humanity amidst the tumult.

What started as an inquiry for executives into how companies could adopt AI to harness the best of human and machine capabilities turned into a much more profound rumination on the future of humanity.

This is a wake-up call for executives and business leaders. Not only should you consider implementation of AI regardless of your industry, but once you do, you should consider how to stay true to your purpose, your ethical convictions, indeed your humanity, even as our organizations continue to evolve.

INTRODUCTION
Defining the Humachine

> This is quite possibly the most important and most daunting challenge humanity has ever faced. And—whether we succeed or fail—it is probably the last challenge we will ever face.
>
> Nick Bostrom, author of *Superintelligence: Paths, Dangers, Strategies*[1]

"Corporations are People, My Friend"

When Mitt Romney was running for President of the United States, he used a phrase during a campaign speech that got a lot of airtime, for better or worse. On August 11, 2011, at the Iowa State Fair, responding to a protestor claiming that the government should tax corporations instead of people, Romney candidly remarked, "Corporations are people, my friend."

To be fair, a corporation very much just *is* the directors, the officers, the managers, the laborers, the shareholders, and the individual purchasers—all of these *people*. When we think of "corporate activity," it really is all of these people engaging in a bundle of interconnected commercial activities that we have in mind.

When Romney says, "Corporations are people," he may have been using a linguistic convention called *synecdoche*, "A figure of speech in which a part is made to represent the whole or vice versa."[2] Further, in a legal sense, his comment is accurate. About two hundred years ago, the Supreme Court of the United States held that corporations are legal persons:

> An aggregate corporation... is, in short, an artificial person, exist-ing in contemplation of law and endowed with certain powers and franchises which, though they must be exercised through the medium of its natural members, are yet considered as subsisting in the corporation itself as distinctly as if it were a real personage.[3]

According to Black's Law Dictionary, an "artificial person" has been understood since the 1600s to mean an entity created by law and given certain legal rights and duties of a human being.

What makes a person, a person? The least controversial answers that are more intuitive might be that personhood means having a sense of having a mental life, selfhood or having an "I," making meaningful choices, some notion of interiority, an internal mental theater. For the sake of clarity, we have to distinguish our project from those common sense answers. We just have to set to the side the whole debate about phenomenal consciousness. We are *not* talking about the first-person subjective experience of consciousness, like what it means to see a color, taste a flavor, or hear music—all of the notions of "personhood" and "interiority" and the first-person subjective feelings of being conscious with which we are familiar. Our focus is on *rational agency*—the mental activity of thinking, of processing information, of making logical inferences, of making decisions—that are relevant to legal and business contexts. What if we took the phrase, "Corporations are people," in a different way, combining the *legal* sense with the *rational* attributes associated with human personhood—the ability to learn, reason, plan, and process complex facts?

To hold that "Corporations are people," allows us to justify attributing civil liberties to a commercial enterprise. Generally, most people don't think an organization has a mind. Relatedly, it is not common to suggest that a corporation possesses qualities of personhood. Corporations are in a certain sense merely legal fictions formed by filing some paperwork with a secretary of state in a given jurisdiction. No one thinks that a corporation has a soul, or religious beliefs, or could fall in love, or could befriend a dog, or could have a favorite flavor of ice cream, or do other things we think of when we think of a unique "person."

That said, maybe we should start to take this mere figure of speech as something literally true: a corporation can marry (merger) or divorce (divestiture), or adopt (acquisition) or procreate (subsidiaries), or die (dissolution). A corporation can speak (campaign finance contributions). A corporation can break a law or serve its nation. A corporation can have an idea. A corporation can be moral. If corporations are people, and people can attain enlightenment, then would it follow that a corporation can attain enlightenment? Can we create enterprises that operate free from bias, ignorance, greed, and fear?

We believe an organization could have a mental life in the sense that an enterprise could possess intelligence and make decisions that are not simply reducible to the decisions of specific people within the company.

What happens when humans institute procedures and practices that are functionally equivalent to human mental states but at the enterprise level? Have we created something new, a collective consciousness? What new creature is this that combines human qualities of content-rich thoughts, wisdom, and creativity with mechanical efficiency in a way that is scalable? That, we contend, would be a Humachine.

What is a Humachine?

To go back to Philosophy 101, the proper way to go about rational discourse is to first define the key terms so that one is clear about what we *mean*. Then, based on those definitions, to distinguish those terms from other terms, so that one is clear about what we do *not* mean. Then, upon those definitions and distinctions, we may make deductions. Definition, distinction, deduction—these are the "three d's" of proper philosophy. We hope by following proper philosophical method we can avoid junk science, hype, and hyperbole, which are all too common when discussing the frontiers of technology and AI in particular.

To our knowledge, the word "Humachine" first appeared on the cover of a 1999 *MIT Technology Review Special Edition*.[4] The Editor in Chief understood this was a unique phrasing: "Don't be surprised if you didn't recognize the title of this column. The word isn't in dictionaries yet. But it may be soon. Or some other word like it, coined to describe the symbiosis that is currently developing between human beings and machines. Humachines."

There are meaningful distinctions between that use of the term versus how it is deployed in this book. All of the examples given in the *MIT Technology Review* article were mere brute physical combinations of humans with machinery, such as visual implants and wearable technology—in other words, cyborgs and androids, which we are careful to distinguish. We are talking about the emergence of a new form of intelligence in the history of life on Earth. We are *not* talking about cyborgs, androids, or AI that can parrot a human personality. We are not talking about any specific physical example that combines some human attribute with a machine, or combines some mechanical attribute with that of a human.

We begin with the Oxford English Dictionary.[5]

Human =$_{df}$ "Relating to or characteristic of humankind. ... Of or characteristic of people as opposed to God or animals or machines, especially in being susceptible to weaknesses. ... Showing the better qualities of humankind, such as kindness."

Machine =$_{df}$ "An apparatus using mechanical power and having several parts, each with a definite function and together performing a particular task. ... Any device that transmits a force or directs its application. ... An efficient and well-organized group of powerful people. ... A person who acts with the mechanical efficiency of a machine."

Now combine those terms into "Humachine."

Humachine =$_{df}$ the combination of the better qualities of humankind—creativity, intuition, compassion, judgment—with the mechanical efficiency of a machine—economies of scale, big data processing capabilities, augmented by artificial intelligence, in such a way as to shed the limitations and vices of both humans and machines while maintaining the virtues of both.

In this book, we are interested in exploring combining human and machine virtues at the enterprise level—an organization, company, corporation, or other kind of organized economic undertaking. In other words, when we say "Humachines," we are talking about harnessing the power of machines to amplify human capabilities to create benign superintelligence at an enterprise level.

Humachine is, of course, a *portmanteau*, "A word blending the sounds and combining the meanings of two others."[6]

Moravec's Paradox holds that what machines are good at, humans are not, and vice versa.[7] **Kasparov's Law** holds that "*weak human + machine + better process* [is] superior to a strong computer alone and, more remarkably, superior to a *strong human + machine + inferior process*."[8] Bostrom's definition of "collective" or **organizational network superintelligence** holds that superintelligence could emerge "through the gradual enhancement of networks and organizations that link individual human minds with one another and with various artifacts and bots."[9]

The Humachine is created by implementing an organizational management framework that applies Kasparov's Law to solve the problem posed by Moravec's Paradox in a way that satisfies the conditions of Bostrom's collective superintelligence.

Our book means to lay out a roadmap for the future to create some day that entity which combines the highest capabilities of humanity with the highest capabilities of machinery. By machinery we mean the nonhuman mechanisms powering the underlying processes responsible for work.

Machinery can be computational—for instance, information processing tools that extend the computational capabilities of human minds—or they can be physical—such as an industrial-sized metal cutting tool that extends the physical capabilities of human hands.

With the Industrial Revolution, physical machinery in certain ways supported and in other ways supplanted human labor. The physical capabilities of a steam-powered engine outstripped the capabilities of human muscle and sweat, not to mention animal labor. Machinery was used to operate at scales unachievable by human hands and to perform tasks involving high temperatures or health and safety issues that presented unacceptable physical risk.

Physical machinery supplanted human labor again in part, when national economies evolved from "industrial" to "service" as the primary output. Certain jobs in the service industry became co-opted by robots in disguise. The bank teller became the ATM, which is really just a very rudimentary wall-mounted robot that dispenses money for us. With the evolution from service to information-based economies, physical machinery is once again supplanting human work. Airborne drones with special sensors piloted from thousands of miles away are replacing soldiers' boots on the ground. As the economy evolved from agricultural to industrial, to service, to information-based, physical machinery continued to evolve too, shaping the economy and being shaped by it.

As the marketplace has evolved, *computational machinery* has also supported and supplanted human mental activity. Perhaps this displacement began with the abacus or the beloved TI-83 calculator, but certainly with the quantum computers in the nuclear laboratories: computational power is no longer bounded by the physical limits of our grey matter. Instead of a room full of junior attorneys conducting document review for a month, we can now feed documents into a natural language processing software that finds key words in a matter of seconds. This liberates well-educated human resources to focus on higher value work.

The *humachinist* finds ways to harness the powers of physical and computational machinery to provide optimum enhancements to human action. Our emphasis in this book is on computational machinery, such as sensing technology (e.g., RFID chips) as well as processing technology (e.g., big data analytics), rather than physical machinery. We contend that humans can harness computational machinery to create mentality at the enterprise level that transcends present-day human mental limitations.

Of course, the coming self-awareness of an enterprise portends great changes, not all of them positive. We will get into the risks posed by artificial intelligence instantiated in large-scale networks more in Chapter 6, wherein we discuss ways in which legal frameworks are challenged to help mitigate these risks and keep AI on the right track.

An incremental step in the right direction is to understand what a Humachine is and how to build one. The omega point is, in our view, a sustainable equilibrium that enables the human species to thrive on this planet and beyond.

As exciting as the endeavor to create Humachines may be, it is also dangerous. There is a very real existential concern about the "*control problem*," or building something that is so powerful it cannot be contained.

"If some day we build machine brains that surpass human brains in general intelligence, then this new superintelligence could become very powerful. And, as the fate of the gorillas now depends more on humans than on the gorillas themselves, so the fate of our species would depend on the actions of the machine superintelligence."[10] By imbuing superintelligence with humane qualities, we hope to mitigate the dangers of the control problem by creating superintelligence that regulates itself, vetoes dangerous impulses, and even protects humanity from its own vices.

We think the risk factor of expanding AI at the enterprise level is, at present, like the risk of hitting an iceberg in a vast sea of opportunity. That is to say, AI is a known risk that we should see coming with ample opportunity to avoid the danger. We know about the risk of rogue actors weaponizing AI. Lawmakers are already having hearings on this subject. We hope tech giants are taking that risk seriously because they can actually do something about it. But, because the gravity of the harm and its irreversible nature, we wish to give priority to those AI researchers like Professor Nick Bostrom who forecast an inevitable lurch toward a singleton AI that would hold the human condition in its virtual hands:

> "In principle, we could build a kind of superintelligence that would protect human values. [But] in practice, the control problem—the problem of how to control what the superintelligence would do—looks quite difficult. It also looks like we will only get one chance. Once unfriendly superintelligence exists, it would prevent us from replacing it or changing its preferences. ... This is quite possibly the most important and most daunting challenge humanity has ever faced. And—whether we succeed or fail—it is probably the last challenge we will ever face."[11]

While Bostrom's grave concerns may be, in his own modest words, "seriously wrong and misleading," nonetheless we agree with Bostrom that "the alternative views that have been presented in the literature are substantially worse—including the default view, or 'null hypothesis,' according to which we can for the time being safely or reasonably ignore the prospect of superintelligence."[12] Bostrom is concerned that if we do not give the control problem sufficient attention we will make no provision for the dangers posed thereby, and we agree it is much more prudent to be overly cautious than to proceed with no safeguards in this context.

It is with respect to the control problem—howsoever remote it may be at this early stage of AI research—that we include a fairly generous helping of normative, rather than simply descriptive and tactical, ideas in this book. In our healthy and good-spirited quest for strategic competitive advantages, let's not lose sight of what happens if we were to slip on this tightrope walk toward the future.

Summary of each Chapter

Chapter 1: The Fourth Industrial Revolution. We explain what the Fourth Industrial Revolution means for human work. We introduce Kasparov's Law, which tells us that superior performance does not necessarily require human genius or superior machines; rather, it can be achieved through better processes using ordinary people and machines. Next, we explain Moravec's Paradox to illustrate the symbiotic, mutually dependent relationship between human and machine. In contrast to the promise of combining the best of human and machine, we look at the peril of creating super-intelligent machines. We discuss the control problem to underscore the gravity of what's at stake in managing AI. We conclude by introducing the form of enterprise that leverages the collaboration between human and machine to achieve "superintelligence"—the Humachine.

Chapter 2: Pathways to Superintelligence. We introduce the concept of superintelligence as any intellect that greatly exceeds the cognitive performance of humans in virtually all domains of interest. We lay out the various well-defined pathways to attaining super-intelligence: biological cognitive enhancement, neural lace, whole brain emulation, and collective superintelligence. We argue that the latter is the most promising pathway. This appreciation for the potential of collective superintelligence motivates the rest of this book. We refute the prejudice of "species chauvinism" that suggests only human beings can have mental states. We introduce the notion of collective intentionality to bolster our contention that an enterprise could conceivably have a mind of its own. This chapter concludes with an excerpt from Teilhard de Chardin's *Phenomenon of Man,* a beautiful depiction of his vision for the noosphere, that layer of consciousness enveloping Earth that provides the next pathway for the evolution of life itself.

Chapter 3: The Limits of Machine Capabilities. We push back against some of the hyperbole surrounding AI by illustrating the extent of its powers and its limits. We explain the role of big data, algorithms, cloud computing, and dark data as a predicate for understanding AI, machine learning, deep learning, and neural networks. While AI excels in pattern recognition and the ability to process data with super-human velocity, accuracy, volume, and consistency, AI is significantly hampered when compared to human general intelligence. AI systems lack common sense, fail to appreciate context, are data hungry and brittle, lack intuition, limit suggestions to local optima, make decisions in a black box, and are limited by the quality of the data upon which they feed.

Chapter 4: The Limits of Human Capabilities. We look at the limits of human capabilities at work. First, we discuss how demographic changes are impacting the labor force in ways that are at least as profound as botsourcing—or the displacement of human laborers with robotic labor or automated processes. Then we look at both our strengths and our weaknesses, with an eye toward implications for the work environment. We will think about thinking with guidance from Daniel Kahneman's take on System 1 and System 2 type thinking. We try to understand in more depth what human general intelligence brings to the table when compared to AI. Our originality, intuition, emotions, care, playfulness, ethical conviction, and aesthetic taste, for example, are irreplaceable by machines. That said, human rationality is prone to specific kinds of breakdowns. We look at some well-documented human biases that affect how we work with others. We conclude by identifying uniquely human qualities that we need to cultivate, including creativity, emotional intelligence, intuition, care, ethical convictions, aesthetics, and playfulness. As machines become increasingly intelligent and enterprises shift responsibilities away from humans, we must cultivate certain human traits to remain relevant.

Chapter 5: Integration of People and Technology. We look at the evolution of work as people and artificially intelligent machines deepen collaborative relationships. We consider AI not a replacement to human workers but an enabling layer that is complementary to uniquely human skills. If we can successfully manage the human-machine interface, human learning and performance will be significantly amplified. Leveraging our relationship with AI requires us to place trust in technology. We consider the potential risk of atrophy resulting from an ongoing reliance on machines to perform work previously requiring certain human skills.

Chapter 6: Legal Issues in the Humachine Era. We lay out the control problem posed by artificial intelligence and urge readers to take this problem seriously, even as we pursue headlong the creation of a Humachine. Let's consider what laws might do to manage the risk of these AI-augmented powers. As law is a reflection of our appetite for risk, we contrast the precautionary principle with the more traditional cost-benefit analysis risk management approach. We recommend the former for dealing with the risks posed by AI. We take a deep dive into the problem of deepfakes to illustrate the challenge AI can pose to lawmakers. Issues of data privacy and security become increasingly urgent in light of the control problem because AI feeds upon, and could potentially weaponize, consumer data. The black box nature of AI decision-making and issues posed by ingraining bias within AI systems also throw curve balls at traditional legal notions of liability and fault.

Chapter 7: Breaking the Paradigm. We describe four shifts needed to detach from the traditional plug-and-play model of technology adoption. The Humachine is driven by technology but nonetheless human centric. Following the Four I's of Intentionality, Integration, Implementation, and Indication, we can create an organization that is greater than the sum of its parts. From profits to purpose, siloes to integration, and rigid performance quotas to aspirational metrics, a paradigm shift about the role of technology in the workforce lays the foundation for the Humachine.

Chapter 8: Mutations. We see the Humachine emerging in front of our eyes. Human-centric orientation, flat and fluid organizational structures, entrepreneurial and innovative cultures, and enterprise-level self-awareness define the Humachine and distinguish it from traditional business structures. We explain the necessity of purposeful, mission-driven disruption to organizational structure in order to create a cultural and technological ecosystem that supports mutation. We introduce the concepts of rendanheyi and holacracy as examples of flat and fluid organizational structures. The three variables of Kasparov's Law—people, machine, and process—need to be unified around the intentionality of the enterprise. The Humachine is capable of delivering products and services that excel in the experiential economy because they are co-created by humans and machines, workers, and consumers. Drawing intelligence through its porous organizational boundaries, the Humachine delivers innovation rapidly to market. Ultimately possessing self-awareness at the enterprise level, the Humachine is not business transformed; it is business mutated, dynamically adapting to evolutionary pressures.

Chapter 9: Reflections on the Humachine. We prognosticate on where all this is headed. We sum up some of our findings about the future of enterprise, offer some normative reflections on what executives can and should be doing to navigate the transition to create humane superintelligence, review changes to educational curriculum organized around the new discipline of "humanics" to prepare students across educational departments, and conclude with a look at what the future of work may hold in the Humachine era.

Conclusion

To distinguish this project from Bostrom, we propose that *collective* superintelligence is not only more likely, it is more desirable than *individual* superintelligence. We set forth an organizational network theory of superintelligence motivated by Kasparov's Law. Ordinary humans combined with ordinary computers with the right process can outperform human genius and supercomputing combined. Along the way, we survey technology, philosophy, psychology, economics, and other disciplines to help illuminate this multifaceted area of inquiry.

We are not fixated on some silver bullet technological breakthrough like the pill from the movie *Limitless*, or some genius programmer who writes the script for general artificial intelligence. We do not even suggest that the pot of gold at the end of this rainbow requires hiring the very best human resources. We offer a roadmap that involves using the human and technological resources available to us *now*, implementing certain processes to manage those resources effectively, and by application of Kasparov's Law, turning what is ordinary into something extraordinary. To take humans and machines, combine them in certain ways, and yield a *Humachine* capable of carrying humanity into a future that is both healthy and humane.

We share the core conviction that an enterprise can have a mind, and that, as a consequence, an enterprise can and should pursue superintelligence for the betterment of our species. That is a lofty goal. Being preoccupied with lofty goals for AI is better than to have idle hands where AI is used merely for entertainment. We need no more of the devil's playthings than our species already has.

Notes

1 Bostrom, preface, p. v.
2 Oxford English Dictionary. Available at https://en.oxforddictionaries.com/definition/synecdoche
3 *Trustees of Dartmouth Coll. v. Woodward*, 17 U.S. 518, 667 (1819) (Story, J.)
4 Intelligent Machines—Humachines, From the Editor in Chief John Benditt. *MIT Technology Review*, May 1, 1999. Available at www.technologyreview.com/s/400387/humachines/
5 Oxford English Dictionary. "human" is defined at https://en.oxforddictionaries.com/definition/human and "machine" is defined at https://en.oxforddictionaries.com/definition/machine
6 Oxford English Dictionary. https://en.oxforddictionaries.com/definition/portmanteau
7 Moravec, Hans P. 1988. *Mind Children: The Future of Robot and Human Intelligence*. Harvard University Press, Cambridge, MA.
8 Kasparov, Garry. *Deep Thinking: Where Machine Intelligence Ends and Human Creativity Begins*, p. 246. Hatchet Books, New York, 2017.
9 Bostrom, pp. 58–59.
10 Bostrom, preface, page v.
11 Ibid.
12 Ibid., p. vii.

1

THE FOURTH INDUSTRIAL REVOLUTION

Previous industrial revolutions liberated humankind from animal power, made mass production possible and brought digital capabilities to billions of people. This Fourth Industrial Revolution is, however, fundamentally different. It is characterized by a range of new technologies that are fusing the physical, digital and biological worlds, impacting all disciplines, economies and industries, and even challenging ideas about what it means to be human. The resulting shifts and disruptions mean that we live in a time of great promise and great peril.

> Professor Klaus Schwab, Founder and Executive
> Chairman of the World Economic Forum,
> author of *The Fourth Industrial Revolution*[1]

The business plans of the next 10,000 start-ups are easy to forecast: Take X and add AI.

> Kevin Kelly, founder of Wired and former
> publisher of *Whole Earth Review*[2]

"Deep Blue" Blues

It was 1997 and Garry Kasparov was the greatest chess player in the world. At the age of twenty-two, he was the youngest ever undisputed World Chess Champion. He had been beating chess-playing computers since the 1980s and had just prevailed over an early version of IBM's supercomputer *Deep Blue* a year earlier. Now he was going for a rematch.

Garry went into the match confident. He was considered unbeatable. Now in front of a global audience, playing the fateful second match with Deep Blue, Garry was becoming visibly frustrated. He fidgeted and shook his head, waiting for his opponent's next move. After only nineteen moves, the audience saw Garry jump up and race away from the board. He had just been beaten by a machine.[3]

1

The match against Deep Blue put Kasparov in a philosophical mood[4]:

> I got my first glimpse of artificial intelligence on Feb. 10, 1996, at 4:45 p.m. EST, when in the first game of my match with Deep Blue, the computer nudged a pawn forward to a square where it could easily be captured. It was a wonderful and extremely human move … Humans do this sort of thing all the time. But computers generally calculate each line of play so far as possible within the time allotted … So I was stunned by this pawn sacrifice. What could it mean? I had played a lot of computers but had never experienced anything like this. I could feel—I could smell—a new kind of intelligence across the table. While I played through the rest of the game as best I could, I was lost; it played beautiful, flawless chess the rest of the way and won easily. Later I discovered the truth. Deep Blue's computational powers were so great that it did in fact calculate every possible move all the way to the actual recovery of the pawn six moves later. The computer didn't view the pawn sacrifice as a sacrifice at all. So the question is, if the computer makes the same move that I would make for completely different reasons, has it made an "intelligent" move? Is the intelligence of an action dependent on who (or what) takes it?

Did the triumph of Deep Blue over the GOAT human chess player signal a "superhuman" level of intelligence in game-playing artificial intelligence (AI)?

A special-purpose chess-playing algorithm is extremely limited: "It plays chess; it can do no other."[5] We are well-advised to bear in mind the extraordinary *narrowness* of artificial intelligence—even when rising to a superhuman level in one area of mental endeavor, that excellence does not necessarily translate into any other area of mental activity.

Yet, let's not forget the unique and singular focus and ruthless resilience of artificial intelligence when it is playing to its strength: Deep Blue does not get overcome with emotion when encountering an outrageous move by its opponent. In Kasparov's words, "Had I not melted down during game two and resigned prematurely, none of this would have mattered. Not only was the early resignation my fault, but allowing it to ruin my composure was the real fatal mistake."[6] Absent extreme heat, computers do not "melt down" under mental strain or emotional stress.

What if we could combine the labile generality of human intellects with the power and rigor of narrow AI?

Like an adamantine needle, artificial intelligence is currently as narrow as it is rigid. AI, like Deep Blue, suffers from a "lack of a purpose beyond its narrow goal," which is set out by its programmers.[7] Another way to frame this is, "Expertise does not necessarily translate into applicable understanding, let alone wisdom."[8]

Nonetheless, this was a revolutionary moment—the beginning of the world seeing the capability of thinking machines. The IBM supercomputer Deep Blue was a machine capable of processing over 100 million positions per second, nothing any human could do.

Kasparov's Law: Triumph of Process

In the fallout of the Deep Blue match, Kasparov was motivated to analyze the potential interactions, and collaborations, of human and machine thinking: "What if, instead of human versus machine, we played as partners? My brainchild saw the light of day in a match in 1998 in Leon, Spain, and we called it Advanced Chess. Each player had a PC at hand running the chess software of his choice during the game. The idea was to create the highest level of chess ever played, a synthesis of the best of man and machine."[9]

The results of this experiment were both predictable and surprising. Predictably, humans with access to machine support were less likely to make tactical blunders, because the computer would analyze potential moves and countermoves with speed and accuracy surpassing human ability. This, in turn, freed up the human player to deploy mental bandwidth on strategic analysis and creative ideation, instead of using precious (that is, far more limited) brainpower doing labor-intensive computations of the various permutations on the board. Even Kasparov, who was perhaps unparalleled among chess players for his powerful and accurate calculations (relative to other humans), lost a competitive edge under these conditions.[10]

Computers compute; when human competitors both have access to computers, the human with greater computational power loses his edge, as the computer has an equalizing effect along that dimension. As a consequence, when aided with machine computation, the human with greater creative and strategic skills will tend to prevail, all other things being equal.

Another foreseeable result was that the teams that combined amateur chess players with ordinary computers prevailed over a superhuman chess-specialist computer with no human teammate. "Human strategic guidance combined with the tactical acuity of a computer was overwhelming."[11]

However, as the "Advanced Chess" tournament came to a climax, something remarkable occurred. Based on the foregoing, you would be forgiven for betting that the champion of the Advanced Chess tournament would be a grand master (among the greatest human chess players alive) partnered up with a high-powered chess-specialist computer. You would be wrong.

The winning team was actually composed of *two amateur chess players* who deployed *three ordinary computers* simultaneously. The champions were amateurs Steven Crampton and Zackary Stephen, "chess buddies who met at a local club in New Hampshire in the US," who "had spent a few years honing their skills at the game," but still "had day jobs and were effectively unknown in the world of competitive chess."[12] Steven and Zackary entered the freestyle tournament up against no less than "several teams of grandmasters aided by computers."[13] Based on historical precedent and the merits of the competitive playing field, they should have lost. But they didn't, thanks to a unique method.

Steven and Zackary happened to have developed a database fed with over four years of data of their own personal strategies. This database showed "which of the two players typically had greater success when faced with similar situations," so they knew when to defer to their teammate and when to take the initiative.[14] They also fully utilized the rules allowing for the use of personal computers running optimization algorithms for any given arrangement of the board they happened to find themselves in.

The secret ingredient to the success was, according to one of the players, "We had really good methodology for when to use the computer and when to use our human judgement, that elevated our advantage."[15]

The shocking outcome demonstrated that "certain human skills were still unmatched by machines when it came to chess and using those skills cleverly and co-operatively could make a team unbeatable."[16]

We contend that the results of the Advanced Chess tournament are instructive well beyond the realm of chess. Kasparov's own takeaway from the surprising results actually provides a major theme for our book: "A clever process beat superior knowledge and superior technology. It didn't render knowledge and technology obsolete, of course, but it illustrated the power of efficiency and coordination to dramatically improve results."[17]

In what has become known as **Kasparov's Law**, we can formulate the insight as: "*weak human + machine + better process* was superior to a strong computer alone and, more remarkably, superior to a *strong human + machine + inferior process*."[18]

One of the objectives for this book is to elucidate what this "better process" looks like at the enterprise level. Even chess enthusiasts can appreciate that this type of human + machine cooperation is not limited to chess and extends from diagnostic medicine to manufacturing. How can ordinary ("weak") humans combine ordinary ("weak") machines to achieve extraordinary results? By using a better process. That process is laid out in Chapters 7 and 8. We do not need to be geniuses or have access to quantum computer power in order to achieve extraordinary results. We simply need to follow Kasparov's Law.

Using ordinary people and ordinary machinery, combined with the right process, we can create the extraordinary—the Humachine. That is the goal of this book.

The New Kid in Town

While the forecasts of the extent of blue-collar and white-collar professional displacement by machines vary in magnitude, they all share the same insight: the machines are coming for human jobs of all kinds. We may call it the *silicon wave*, as computerization, bots, autonomous machines, and so forth gobble up human jobs. At each successive interval of machine innovation, more and more jobs appear to be "low-hanging fruit," easily susceptible to displacement by machines. The silicon wave promises to cause a flood of biblical proportions, leaving behind a world transformed, no less profound than the changes wrought by the onset of electricity.

Research shows that while automation will eliminate very few occupations entirely in the next decade, it will affect portions of almost all jobs to a greater or lesser degree, depending on the type of work they entail.[19] Unless forbidden by law, no job is sacrosanct—a machine could theoretically displace *any job*.

Could a robot be President of the United States? These days, it would appear nothing is too controversial for that office. The US Constitution, Article II, Section 1 provides that, "No person except a natural born citizen, or a citizen of the United States, at the time of the adoption of this Constitution, shall be eligible to the office of President; neither shall any person be eligible to that office who shall not have attained to the age of thirty-five years, and been fourteen years a resident within the United States." At first blush, we cannot elect a robot to be the President because a robot is not a "natural-born citizen."

However, we need just a little bit of interpretive wriggle room to get there. Does the word "born" include "*assembled*"? If yes, then a computer that is "Made in America" is "born" in the USA.

Can we pass a law that grants citizenship to a robot? The humanoid AI bot christened Sophia has already been granted citizenship by Saudi Arabia, so we know that robot citizenship is possible.

Therefore, a robot assembled in the USA and granted citizenship by law, that has been in existence for no less than 35 years and which has been within the territorial limits of the USA for no less than 14 years, could theoretically run for the office of the President.

Not that President Tron would be guaranteed a strong chance of successfully navigating the political landscape, but in theory it is possible. Thirty-five years provides a lot of time for upgrades and feeding algorithms with political data.

Imagine a robot mind running the calculations of IBM's Watson to determine the absolutely pitch-perfect talking points at any given political moment, optimized to persuade a critical mass of voters. This hypothetical is just to illustrate the point that any job, even President of the United States, could theoretically be displaced by a machine. So we better make preparations for that silicon wave to wash over every sector and every level of the corporate hierarchy.

According to Ed Hess, Professor of Business Administration and Batten Executive-in-Residence at the Darden Graduate School of Business, "Because AI will be a far more formidable competitor than any human, we will be in a frantic race to stay relevant. That will require us to take our cognitive and emotional skills to a much higher level."[20]

Unfortunately, the very traits that make humans succeed where robots struggle—that is, innovative thinking and emotional intelligence—are stymied by "our natural cognitive and emotional proclivities: We are confirmation-seeking thinkers and ego-affirmation-seeking defensive reasoners." According to Hess[21]:

> We will spend more time training to be open-minded and learning to update our beliefs in response to new data. We will practice adjusting after our mistakes, and we will invest more in the skills traditionally associated with emotional intelligence. The new smart will be about trying to overcome the two big inhibitors of critical thinking and team collaboration: our ego and our fears. Doing so will make it easier to perceive reality as it is, rather than as we wish it to be. In short, we will embrace humility. That is how we humans will add value in a world of smart technology.

We simply cannot compete with machines in terms of processing speed, calculation accuracy, pattern recognition across big data sets, or the quantity of computations per second. We need to recognize the playing field is forever unleveled along those dimensions.

Let's shift our focus to where we can compete. Hess suggests we redefine what it means to be "smart," determined "not by what or how you know but by the quality of your thinking, listening, relating, collaborating, and learning." In a phrase, Hess recommends *humility* as the life raft to avoid drowning in the silicon wave.

Artificial intelligence has arrived in multifarious forms. We now live in a world of smartphones with predictive text and voice recognition, digital assistants in our home stereos, and self-steering vacuum cleaners. A recent study estimates that analytics, AI, and automation will wipe out half of today's workforce by 2055, or possibly even twenty years sooner.[22]

Those familiar with AI research may find the timing of these predictions amusing in one sense. Since the invention of the computer in the 1940s, the "expected arrival date" of human-like machine intelligence (what we can call strong general artificial intelligence) has generally been about twenty years in the future. This forecast "has been receding at a rate of one year per year."[23] "Two decades is a sweet spot for prognosticators of radical change: near enough to be attention-grabbing and relevant, yet far enough to make it possible to suppose that a string of breakthroughs, currently only vaguely imaginable, might by then have occurred."[24]

No matter what year it is, we cannot ignore the very real fact that displacement of human labor by automation has already begun. Another study by Oxford University estimates that one in every two jobs will be automated.[25] We discuss the issues around labor displacement more in subsequent chapters. Suffice it so say, robotics will revolutionize the workplace and the workforce, in every kind of service industry, in manufacturing, in policing and military force, in transportation and logistics, and even in the lesser-discussed (but no less significant) areas of the economy such as the black market.

Vernor Vinge, a math and computer scientist and science fiction author, is perhaps the original prophet of disastrous artificial intelligence predictions. He coined the term *singularity*, by which he means the tipping point occurring after we create intelligence greater than our own. We have avoided use of the term "singularity" to describe the integration of human and machine virtues. We are not throwing shade at Kurzweil or Vinge. We use "combine" and "integrate" as opposed to "singularity" because singularity has an almost rapture-esque, apocalyptical sound to it.

According to Vinge, when the singularity happens, "Human history will have reached a kind of singularity, an intellectual transition as impenetrable as the knotted space-time at the center of a black hole, and the world will pass far beyond our understanding."[26] Once the "technological means to create superhuman intelligence" emerge, "shortly thereafter, the human era will be ended."[27]

While this sounds ominous, it need not be. The end of the anthropocene era could also mean the end of living in the fear of mutually assured destruction from nuclear war, the end of famine, and the end of environmental degradation because superintelligence would have given us the security, prosperity, and abundance, respectively, required to avoid these all-too-human problems and begin to live in dignified peace.

We are optimistic about the era that happens after the human era has ended, insofar as it will be the Humachine era.

That said, these forecasts are startling and augur socioeconomic disasters of various forms.

Despite the fun of fearmongering, it is not the primary goal of this book to identify the various kinds of risks or benefits that automation or superintelligence brings, nor to point out potential safety nets (such as universal basic income or a return to more Luddite modes of being). We will have a better time managing these challenges if we follow Kasparov's Law and create a Humachine. We simply take for granted that these changes are coming and operate under the assumption that competing in this new world will require a different approach to educating future workers, and require reimagining the structure of enterprise. Keep in mind an implication of Kasparov's Law: *we need not attain genius to improve our performance; we simply need better processes.*

Details on how firms can improve process are available in the closing chapters of this book, in Chapters 7 through 9. To lay the foundation for that, we will first explore the symbiotic, mutually dependent relationship between humans and machines in Chapters 3 through 5 that takes each to the limits of its capabilities.

The "Big Bang" of Modern AI

According to Jensen Huang, the co-founder and CEO of graphics processor company Nvidia, his company has been evangelizing the utility of artificial intelligence for a long time. They were initially focused on gaming, which naturally had them interested in refining "computer graphics, of course, and physics simulation, whether it's finite element analysis or fluid simulations or molecular dynamics. It's basically Newtonian physics."[28] It is somewhat ironic that what was originally driven by sheer entertainment purposes has grown so relevant to commercial enterprise.

As applications of AI have evolved, so has the context of innovation. As Huang says, "The first thing is that Moore's Law has really slowed. So as a result GPU-accelerated computing gave us life after Moore's Law, and it extended the capability of computing so that these applications that desperately need more computing can continue to advance. Meanwhile, the reach of GPUs has gone far and wide, and it's much more than computer graphics today. We've reached out into all fields—of course computer graphics, virtual reality, augmented reality—to all kinds of interesting and challenging physics simulations."[29]

From these somewhat humble origins in video game applications, Nvidia's technology—and AI in general—has shifted the paradigm from Newtonian physics to quantum mechanics, the next great leap in computing. Huang says, "Almost every supercomputer in the world today has some form of acceleration, much of it from Nvidia... The field of quantum chemistry is going quite well and there's a great deal of research in quantum chemistry, in quantum mechanics... And deep learning, combined with the rich amount of data that's available, and the processing capability came together to become what people call the Big Bang of modern AI."[30]

Nvidia is now powering Microsoft, Facebook, and other leading companies because, according to Huang, "AI is eating software. The way to think about it is that AI is just the modern way of doing software. In the future, we're not going to see software that is not going to continue to learn over time, and be able to perceive and reason, and plan actions and that continues to improve as we use it. These machine-learning approaches, these artificial intelligence-based approaches, will define how software is developed in the future. Just about every startup company does software these days, and even non-startup companies do their own software. Similarly, every startup in the future will have AI."[31]

Another breakthrough in AI applications is that, in the future, no machinery will be "dumb" because it will all contain some degree of artificial intelligence. AI is not "limited to cloud-based intelligence, resident in powerful, gigantic data centers" because, according to Huang, "You've got cars, you've got drones, you've got microphones; in the future, almost every electronic device will have some form of deep learning inferencing within it. We call that AI at the edge. And eventually there'll be a trillion devices out there: Vending machines; every microphone; every camera; every house will have deep learning capability."[32]

"Robot Proof" the Workforce: Embracing Moravec's Paradox

AI researchers have given a name to the seeming inverse relationship between man and machine capabilities. *Moravec's Paradox* holds that where machines have strength, humans have weakness, and vice versa.[33] While AI can now do many mental tasks that require "thinking" (such as mathematics), nonetheless AI has a hard time doing what biological beings easily do "without thinking" (such as intuiting someone else's emotional state).[34]

In his 1988 book *Mind Children*, Moravec writes:

> Encoded in the large, highly evolved sensory and motor portions of the human brain is a billion years of experience about the nature of the world and how to survive in it. The deliberate process we call reasoning is, I believe, the thinnest veneer of human thought, effective only because it is supported by this much older and much more powerful, though usually unconscious, sensorimotor knowledge. We are all prodigious Olympians in perceptual and motor areas, so good that we make the difficult look easy. Abstract thought, though, is a new trick, perhaps less than 100 thousand years old. We have not yet mastered it. It is not all that intrinsically difficult; it just seems so when we do it.

Examples of skills that have evolved for millions of years include things that we do unconsciously, such as recognizing a face, moving around in space, judging people's motivations, catching a ball—or instinctively dodging an object thrown at us.

Perception, visualization, motor skills, and social skills took us a long time to evolve. Intuitive skills such as setting goals and instinctively paying attention to things that are interesting and different took millions of years to garner. They evolved instinctive and intuitive because they won out through some neo-Darwinian process of responses to selective pressures, reinforced by sex, violence, death, and reward. On the other hand, skills like mathematics and scientific reasoning are harder for us to master as they appeared much more recently in the timeline of human evolution.

Professor Bostrom offers up one hypothesis for why it has been so challenging for researchers to create machines that can match human capabilities in perception, motor control, common sense, and language understanding, while researchers have very much excelled at creating machines that surpass humans in performing logical cognitive functions[35]:

> Our brains have dedicated wetware for these functions—neural structures that have been optimized over evolutionary timescales. By contrast, logical thinking and skills like chess playing are not natural to us; so perhaps we are forced to rely on a limited pool of general-purpose cognitive resources to perform these tasks. Maybe what our brains do when we engage in explicit logical reasoning or calculation is in some ways analogous to running a "virtual machine," a slow and cumbersome mental simulation of a general-purpose computer. One might then say (somewhat fancifully) that a classical AI program is not so much emulating human thinking as the other way around: a human who is thinking logically is emulating an AI program.

In order to transcend the status quo capabilities handed down to us by the evolutionary process, we need to take our development into our own hands by educational design.

Ironically, the last thousand years or so of education following the Jesuit tradition emphasized Aristotelian reasoning—definitions, distinctions, deductions—and the pursuit of mathematics and sciences. Only now have we applied those skills to build machines that far outstrip our own reasoning and information processing skills. Now it seems like we have built an educational apparatus that is in dire need of an upgrade, because it is cultivating capabilities in us that are far surpassed by machines. Why train in a competition where you are by nature hopelessly outmatched?

At a 2017 summit of the New England Board of Higher Education, Northeastern University President Joseph E. Aoun put forth an assessment of the choices facing institutions of higher education in light of these disruptive advances in technology: *embrace the reality or become obsolete*. The same is true for business organizations.

According to Aoun, the rational response for educational institutions to this impending crisis is to teach humans to become "Robot Proof," by deploying what he coins as a new educational discipline: humanics.[36]

Educational institutions should give in to the power of Moravec's Paradox instead of trying to fight against it. Aoun's theory of humanics would be a step in the right direction. *Humanics*:

> prepares students to perform the future jobs that only human beings can do. It achieves this by fostering purposeful integration of technical literacies, such as coding and data literacy, with human literacies, such as creativity, ethics, cultural agility, and entrepreneurship. When students combine these literacies with experiential components, they integrate their knowledge with real life settings, leading to deep learning. Experiential learning is a powerful delivery system for the humanics curriculum.[37]

An education in humanics teaches us how to work alongside high-performing technologies while accentuating our uniquely human strengths. This blended approach to educational policy would empower us to do what neither the smartest person or the most advanced AI system could do alone. Our effort in this book is in furtherance of Aoun's objective of promoting humanics, not only in the classroom but in the office bullpen as well.

To be fair to humans, even those on the front lines of AI research and implementation still believe humans are indispensable from some of the most important kind of work to be done. For instance, John E. Kelly III, director of IBM Research, contends that jobs requiring higher-order critical thinking, creative thinking, innovation, and high levels of emotional engagement will need to be filled by humans for some time to come. Of course, human performance in these kinds of jobs would be greatly enhanced by harnessing the power of "cognitive systems" that enable decision-makers to penetrate complexity and crunch through big data sets to make optimal decisions.[38]

The urgency of significant educational policy reform called for by Aoun is echoed by the sentiment expressed by Kasparov: "That our classrooms still mostly look like they did a hundred years ago isn't quaint; it's absurd... Wealthy nations approach education in the same way a wealthy aristocratic family approaches investing. The status quo has been good for a long time; why rock the boat? ... The prevailing attitude is that education is too important to take risks. My response is that education is too important *not* to take risks."[39]

Machines Can't Do Everything

We are in an age of infatuation with evolving technological capability. However, it is still humans—executives, managers, and other decision-makers—who use the output of algorithms to make decisions within an organizational context. These decision-makers bring their human judgment, individual personalities, opinions, and biases to the decision-making process, deciding how to use the analytically generated output. For example, UPS drivers are authorized to override the route optimization algorithm.

Humans and technology are often seen as competitors in the new world. However, the reality of the situation is more nuanced and should be approached with cautious optimism rather than fear. The strengths of one are the weaknesses of the other. Automation technologies such as machine learning and robotics play an increasingly greater role in everyday life and have a huge potential effect on the workplace. Today automation has gone beyond repetitive manufacturing activities. Robots run factories, they work side by side with physicians in operating rooms, they read X-rays, and render medical diagnoses. Analytics is used in everything from fraud detection to driving autonomous vehicles.

Yes, machines are far superior at both repetitive and nonrepetitive tasks. They have precision, strength, and do not fatigue. Humans are imprecise, overconfident, and prone to place too much faith in their intuitions. They are highly biased.

However, all machine intelligence is based on data and is *only as good as the data upon which it is based*. Machines are not good at "out-of-the-box" thinking. They are not creative or develop innovative solutions. How can an algorithm develop innovative strategy or a unique marketing campaign? Yes, they can identify photos of dogs, but they can also confuse a dachshund dog with a hot dog, and they cannot extrapolate that one is a pet while the other is a ballpark treat.

Context matters and machines don't have context. Consider the "broken-leg problem."[40] An actuarial formula based on historical data might be highly accurate in predicting the odds of someone going to the movies in a given week. But that model should be abandoned if it turns out the person in question has a broken femur. The broken leg problem demonstrates the importance of paying attention to context. We might be able to use historical, actuarial data to predict odds, but the forecast will fail if we don't appreciate the context. Obviously, without that information, the algorithm would be way off. All the data provided to the algorithm suddenly becomes irrelevant because of this change in context.

The fact is that in today's rapidly changing economy, the "broken-leg problem" occurs often. Disruptions that require understanding context and providing interpretation are simply a part of today's business environment. This could be a storm delaying a shipment, a political event, a competitor launching a new product, or a union strike. Today companies operate in volatile markets and environments, and "broken-leg problem" is a part of corporate life. Yes, algorithms can offer a far better answer provided the future facts look exactly like the data upon which forecasts are based. However, they cannot help when the environment and context change.

Machines are stronger, better, faster, more precise. Humans are intuitive, creative, and understand context. Harnessing the strengths of both—and finding the right way for them to work together—is the recipe for success. That is what this book is about. By all measures machines are getting smarter, better, faster, and stronger than humans at a variety of "mental" processes. Machines assess customer credit card risk. They detect fraud, fly airplanes, and drive cars. They can grade school essays, sort mail by reading handwritten characteristics, and diagnose illness by comparing images.

A number of inventions that enjoy widespread commercial applications were invented by sheer humanity. Accidental good fortune, fun, and humor are foreign notions to computers, but they sure drive a lot of inventions.

Consider the invention of the Post-it Note (the yellow sticky note). Post-it Notes are ubiquitous in the office environment, yet they were invented through creativity, innovation, and out-of-the-box thinking. In 1968, Dr. Spencer Silver, a scientist at 3M, was working on developing a super-strong adhesive but accidentally created a "low-tack" reusable adhesive. It was a "solution without a problem." Although he promoted it within 3M, there was no apparent use for this reusable adhesive. Then in 1974, Arthur Fry, a colleague at 3M, came up with the idea of using it as a bookmark for his hymnbook while singing in the church choir.

The low-tack adhesive would not tear the fine Bible paper used in the hymnal. Thus the Post-it Note was born. If it were not for the real-world lived experience of the 3M employee, this novel application of a low-tack adhesive would not have been conceived. We cannot rely on machines to invent like this.

How about the invention of saccharin, the oldest artificial sweetener? It was discovered by accident when a researcher at Johns Hopkins forgot to wash his hands before lunch. He accidentally spilled a chemical on his hands and discovered that it made the bread he was eating taste sweet. It was an "aha moment" and saccharin was born. Initial adoption was slow but then received widespread use when sugar was rationed during the First World War. Its popularity skyrocketed with the increase of diet-conscious consumers and the manufacture of Sweet'N Low and diet soft drinks. Without the happy accident of discovering the sweet taste of saccharine, Sweet'N Low would not exist. Machines do not take lunch breaks, and as a result, are unlikely to discover a new flavor by accident.

What about the beloved Slinky toy? The idea came in 1943 from a naval engineer, Richard James. He was working on developing a spring that would support and stabilize sensitive equipment on ships. One of the springs accidentally fell off the shelf and continued moving. James thought it moved in a manner that was bouncy and fun. Since then, more than 250 million Slinkys have been sold worldwide. No AI can identify what we as humans perceive as "fun." It takes humans to do that.

What these examples have in common is context, creativity, and innovation. Yes, today's technology can make us 100 times more efficient and effective when it comes to repetitive tasks. At the turn of the century, technology changed agriculture and freed humans from laborious farming tasks. Today, technology is freeing us from doing repetitive tasks and becoming spreadsheet monkeys. There are no more issues of routine screening of documents, no more spelling or math issues. Technology can make us more efficient at those kinds of analytical tasks. The goal is not simply to process spreadsheets faster; it is to liberate human resources to perform those creative, innovative, and context-driven tasks (like inventing the next Post-It-Note) that machines simply cannot do.

Technology can take over repetitive things. As a result, we can be increasingly focused on creative endeavors. Perhaps when our smartest workers are liberated from the repetitive analytical tasks that now consume our work lives, we can discover that elusive miracle cure, develop renewable energy resources, and find ways to augment human happiness. Technology creates a tremendous opportunity for business by freeing us to innovate.

There Are Worse Things than Losing Your Job

As technology takes over our lives, there has been a tremendous amount of automation anxiety, that human jobs will go the way of horses displaced by steam engines and we will be left impoverished as a result of our "progress."

We call this *botsourcing*, which is the robotic version of "outsourcing," where a job, good, or service that was originally delivered from an existing internal source is contracted out to a foreign or external supplier, generally in order to reduce costs or improve quality. Like outsourcing, botsourcing displaces internal labor.

For every job that is displaced by a machine, there could very well be more jobs to do or greater wealth to share as a result of the increase in quality, productivity, and savings. The invention of the steam engine caused the collapse of horse-powered transportation, but it also increased societal wealth and created all sorts of jobs that were hitherto unimaginable.

We appreciate the concern about botsourcing, but that is not exactly an existential threat. Our concerns for the onslaught of AI in enterprise are deeper. Namely, that machines—robots, AI, and technology in general—will take over in the sense of asserting control over humankind.

In other words, advances in AI pose the so-called *control problem*. We want to build a superintelligent system that exceeds human capabilities (so that we can harness this new power) without inadvertently unleashing an unstoppable threat upon the realm.

There is a popularly articulated fear that machines will not only displace humans in the workforce in a vicious way—that is, leading to poverty and lack instead of augmenting freedoms and wealth—but worse, that machines would take over the world.

As Bostrom puts it[41]:

> The initial superintelligence might obtain a decisive strategic advantage. This superintelligence would then be in a position to form a singleton [that is, an entity with no natural competition or check on its power] and to shape the future of Earth-originating intelligent life. What happens from that point onward would depend on the superintelligence's motivations.
>
> Second, the orthogonality thesis suggests that we cannot blithely assume that a superintelligence will necessarily share any of the final values stereotypically associated with wisdom and intellectual development in humans—scientific curiosity, benevolent concern for others, spiritual enlightenment and contemplation, renunciation of material acquisitiveness, a taste for refined culture or for the simple pleasures in life, humility and selflessness, and so forth.

Third, the instrumental convergence thesis entails that we cannot blithely assume that a superintelligence ... would limit its activities in such a way as not to infringe on human interests. An agent with a final goal [of something otherwise benign like calculating the decimal expansion of pi] would have a convergent instrumental reason, in many situations, to acquire an unlimited amount of physical resources and, if possible, to eliminate potential threats to itself or its goal system. Human beings might constitute potential threats; they certainly constitute physical resources. Taken together, these three points thus indicate that the first superintelligence may [create an outcome] in which humanity quickly becomes extinct.

That AI would take a treacherous turn and become hostile to its creator is an alarming scenario, to say the least.

It can be prevented by keeping superintelligence from gaining a decisive strategic advantage—say, by building in limits and competition to prevent a singleton from forming—or by shaping the goals of any superintelligence to align with broadly accepted standards of human well-being. If we go about building Humachines in a conscientious manner, technology will compliment humans by making us more efficient and more productive, safeguarding values such as peace, autonomy, and health. As routine tasks are taken over by machines, humans can live more fulfilling lives, freed from the monotony of routinized tasks, liberated from the mineshafts, and gifted with the analytical resources of smarter, faster, and tireless analytical engines.

Consider that throughout time machines have taken over human jobs, from farming to factories. Machines are now taking over offices. As in the past, it is up to humans to create new jobs and industries, buoyed by the enabling layer of AI. As people are displaced from jobs it is up to us to find novel ways of giving value to our lives, being productive members of society, or at the very least finding ways to enjoy the bounty of abundance made possible by this latest wave of displacement. The real risk is that we ignore the risks of malevolent applications of technology. As technology improves, so too do our powers to manipulate the environment, and concomitant with that power is the responsibility to steer our enterprises toward a just future.

The Humachine: People, Process, Machines

The Humachine is the optimal human-machine partnership. Here, people and technology operate seamlessly. This hybrid workforce creates an unparalleled team of industry leaders that takes advantage of technology to complement and augment human decisions.

The ability of artificial intelligence and advanced robotics to outperform humans is no longer a shocking development like it was when Deep Blue beat Kasparov in 1997. Today we are used to autonomous vehicles, automated kiosks, and personal shopping assistants. We take news of the next displacement as *fait accompli*: the silicon wave is an inevitable, irresistible force that needs only time to overtake all industries at all levels.

But there are steps we can take to make this transition less painful. And there are areas where it makes less sense for machines to take over. Technology and people are all too often seen as competitors, with technology threatening to replace people in the workforce. While some displacement may be inevitable, the conversation about the future of work has shifted to managing human labor displacement with universal basic income and taxing the productive output of robots.

To be clear: we do not seek to abate the displacement of human labor by machines, nor do we seek to address how to solve the social and economic problems created by this displacement. Those are political problems than need political solutions. However, there is another scenario where an enterprise creates synergy between technology and people, understanding that *the strengths of one complement the weaknesses of the other*.

In this book we use the term "machine" to encompass all types of technologies that are changing how we work and live. This includes all forms, such as analytics and decision technologies, processing technologies such as robotics, communication technologies, and platforms such as cloud computing and blockchains. As described in the Preface, our focus is not on physical machinery but on computational machinery. Certainly there are tremendous differences between the various technologies. However, for our purpose, the common element is that these smart technologies have seeped into the workings of every aspect of business. These technologies are fundamentally changing the way business operates, how businesses compete and innovate.

Organizations, such as Google and Amazon, demonstrate Humachine traits. However, the opportunity is not limited to these tech giants. It is within reach for every organization, from large legacy corporations to small and medium firms to start-ups.

Technology can deliver a competitive advantage along every organizational function, from targeted location-based marketing to refining sourcing channel options and optimizing supply chain inventories. However, today's technology giants—Apple, Amazon, Google, Facebook, and Microsoft—do all these things in a *coordinated way* as part of an *overarching strategy imbedded in the organizational culture*. They are striving to find the optimal blend of people and technology. To be clear, we are not setting these companies up as an exemplar of moral leadership—we are simply pointing to them to illustrate what is happening along the cutting edge.

How to Get There

Looking to these examples, as well as numerous companies we surveyed, interviewed, or visited for this book, we present the foundation of what makes the optimal human-machine partnership and provide a roadmap for how companies can get there.

Most companies we talked with are following a plug-and-play approach to technology. The primary questions they are asking are:

- Which technologies should we adopt?
- What are our competitors doing?
- How do we become a "digital organization"?
- How will we pay for it and what is the ROI?

This is the wrong approach. Becoming a Humachine requires the *integration of people, processes, and technology*. It is the symbiosis of these three elements *and continuous improvement and adaptation* that are required to succeed in the Fourth Industrial Revolution.

Overlaying technology on top of poor processes will just crystallize the inefficiencies of the past. Selecting technology based on what competitors are doing is foolish—as another's strategy, roadmap, and timetable may not necessarily match your strategy.

Ultimately, it is people that are responsible for making this transition happen.

Becoming the Humachine requires having the right leadership. Many companies have created the position of Chief Data Officer (CDO), Chief Technology Officer (CTO) or at least someone who is in a leadership role tasked with looking into how to implement AI. They have revenue responsibility, sit on the executive committee, and are a single point of accountability for technology.

Leaders are the ones who develop the strategy and articulate a compelling vision. They are also the ones who create the culture needed to support any organizational change or process implementation.

Equally important is talent selection, recruiting people with a desire to innovate, grow, and become more data savvy. Retaining talent comes next. Pay is not everything. Consider that SAS Analytics is consistently on Fortune's top places to work, yet its pay scale is just around the *mean* in its industry. Employees stay for the culture, benefits, and life-style amenities, not because they couldn't get paid more elsewhere.

Lastly, there must be the right organizational culture and incentive structure. *Objective and Key Results (OKRs)* are a framework for defining and tracking objectives and their outcomes. Unlike traditional KPIs that are limiting, OKRs are aspirational. OKRs were created at Intel and today are used by many tech giants such as Google, LinkedIn, Twitter, and Uber.

Very few companies have achieved technological integration with human resources, let alone superintelligence. This is especially true of small and midsized enterprises with tight budgets and little room for experimentation, but also large legacy firms with huge overheads, large staff, and engrained processes.

Engaging in fragmented and localized implementation of technology rather than a systematic and coordinated effort produces isolated benefits, lack of insight and competitive advantages, organizational operations plagued with inefficiencies and cost overruns, IT infrastructure costs with limited ROI, and employees fearful of job losses. And yet, fragmented, ad hoc, plug and play adoption of technology is the norm.

The "marriage" of technology with people enables the organization to maximize its capabilities by elevating the basis of organizational decision-making with closer-to-perfect information and rationality. This book is about *how to do this*. It is about how to create synergies between technology and people where the whole is greater than the sum of the parts, the efficiencies of corporate structures are utilized in full, while the limitations of corporate culture attributable to human vices as well as the general imperfections of human self-interest, rationality, and information are left in the past.

What is needed is leadership, strategic thinking, and a roadmap. A plan must be in place for acquiring and managing both human capital and technological investments. Numerous obstacles stand in the way:

- Scarce resources and uncertain ROI
- Cultural resistance to change
- Lack of organizational alignment and agility
- Understanding that data is an asset
- Lack of business direction and executive leadership

Ironically, the key to success is people—not technology itself. It is on careful talent selection, carefully nurtured organizational culture, the right organizational structure, team management that promotes

THE FOURTH INDUSTRIAL REVOLUTION

innovation and creativity, and the right organizational incentives. Most of all what is needed is managing *organizational change.*

Conclusion

We can resolve Moravec's Paradox by applying Kasparov's Law. If we can combine human and machine using the right process, then we enjoy the strengths of both while suffering the weaknesses of neither. Our educational systems should accept the paradox. Stop trying to make humans into machines. It took us millions of years to get the way we are now. We need to embrace our differences.

In this book, we lay out a path for how companies can integrate human resources with technology to leverage the strengths of both for an optimal combination—creating a superintelligent enterprise. That is what we call the Humachine. It represents the optimal human-machine partnership. It is not an unattainable ideal but a reality achievable today, with ordinary humans, technology, and processes.

Before we can begin, however, we need to look at the concept of superintelligence. After all, the premise of the Humachine is that an enterprise can achieve collective superintelligence as a result of synergies between humans and machines. But what is superintelligence, what are the pathways to superintelligence, and which path offers the most promise for an enterprise? We look at that next.

Notes

1 Kelly, Kevin. The Three Breakthroughs That Have Finally Unleashed AI on the World. *Wired*, October 27, 2014. Available at www.wired.com/2014/10/future-of-artificial-intelligence/
2 Schwab, Klaus. The Fourth Industrial Revolution, World Economic Forum. Available at www.weforum.org/about/the-fourth-industrial-revolution-by-klaus-schwab (emphasis added). Schwab argues, "all of these new technologies are first and foremost tools made by people for people."
3 Weber, Bruce. Swift and Slashing, Computer Topples Kasparov. *The New York Times*, May 12, 1997.
4 Kasparov, Garry. The Day That I Sensed a New Kind of Intelligence. *Time*, March 25, 1996, no. 13.
5 Bostrom, Nick. *Superintelligence: Paths, Dangers, Strategies*, p. 14. Oxford University Press, Oxford, UK, 2014.
6 Kasparov, Garry. *Deep Thinking: Where Machine Intelligence Ends and Human Creativity Begins*, p. 217. Hatchet Books, New York, 2017.
7 Ibid., p. 221.
8 Ibid., p. 225.
9 Ibid., p. 244.
10 Ibid., p. 245.
11 Ibid., p. 246.

12 Baraniuk, Chris. The Cyborg Chess Players That Can't Be Beaten. *BBC Future*, December 4, 2015. Available at www.bbc.com/future/story/20151201-the-cyborg-chess-players-that-cant-be-beaten
13 Ibid.
14 Ibid.
15 Ibid.
16 Ibid.
17 Kasparov, Garry. *Deep Thinking: Where Machine Intelligence Ends and Human Creativity Begins*, p. 246. Hatchet Books, New York, 2017.
18 Ibid.
19 Chui, M., Manyika, J. and Meremadi, M. Where Machines Could Replace Humans—and Where They Can't (Yet). *McKinsey Quarterly*, July 2016.
20 Hess, Ed. In the AI Age, "Being Smart" Will Mean Something Completely Different. *Harvard Business Review*, June 19, 2017. Available at https://hbr.org/2017/06/in-the-ai-age-being-smart-will-mean-something-completely-different. Ed Hess is co-author, with Katherine Ludwig, of *Humility Is the New Smart: Rethinking Human Excellence in the Smart Machine Age*. Berrett-Koehler, Oakland, CA, 2017.
21 Ibid.
22 www.mckinsey.com/global-themes/digital-disruption/harnessing-automation-for-a-future-that-works.
23 Bostrom, Nick. *Superintelligence: Paths, Dangers, Strategies*, p. 4. Oxford University Press, Oxford, UK, 2014.
24 Ibid.
25 Frey, Carl Benedikt and Michael A. Osborne. The Future of Employment: How Susceptible Are Jobs to Computerisation? September 17, 2013. Available at www.oxfordmartin.ox.ac.uk/downloads/academic/The_Future_of_Employment.pdf; Scott, Patrick. These Are the Jobs Most at Risk of Automation According to Oxford University: Is Yours One of Them? September 27, 2017. Available at www.telegraph.co.uk/news/2017/09/27/jobs-risk-automation-according-oxford-university-one/
26 Vinge, Vernor. First Word. *OMNI Magazine*, January 1983.
27 Vinge, Vernor. The Coming Technological Singularity: How to Survive in the Post-Human Era. In *Vision-21: Interdisciplinary Science and Engineering in the Era of Cyberspace*, pp. 11–22. NASA Conference Publication 10129. NASA Lewis Research Center, 1993.
28 Etherington, Darrell. AI Everywhere. *TechCrunch*, May 5, 2017. Available at https://techcrunch.com/2017/05/05/ai-everywhere/
29 Ibid.
30 Ibid.
31 Ibid.
32 Ibid.
33 Moravec, Hans P. *Mind Children: The Future of Robot and Human Intelligence*. Harvard University Press, Cambridge, MA, 1988.
34 From Nilsson, Nils J. *The Quest for Artificial Intelligence: A History of Ideas and Achievements*, p. 318. Cambridge University Press, New York, 2009, quoting computer scientist Donald Knuth.
35 Bostrom, Nick. *Superintelligence: Paths, Dangers, Strategies*. Oxford University Press. Notes, Chapter 1, Note 62, pp. 328–329.
36 Aoun, Joseph. *Robot-Proof: Higher Education in the Age of Artificial Intelligence*. MIT Press, Cambridge, MA, 2017.

37 Schawbel, Dan. Northeastern University President Joseph E. Aoun: How To Be "Robot-Proof". *Forbes*, November 24, 2017. Available at www.forbes. com/sites/danschawbel/2017/11/24/northeastern-university-president-joseph-e-aoun-how-to-be-robot-proof/#6a9e455651fb

38 Kelly III, John and Steve Hamm. *Smart Machines: IBM's Watson and the Era of Cognitive Computing.* Columbia Business School Publishing, October 15, 2013.

39 Kasparov, Garry and Mig Greengard. *Deep Thinking: Where Machine Intelligence Ends and Human Creativity Begins*, pp. 234–235. New York: PublicAffairs, 2017.

40 Meehl, P. E. *Clinical versus Statistical Prediction: A Theoretical Analysis and a Review of the Evidence.* University of Minnesota Press, Minneapolis, MN, 1954. Reprinted with new Preface, 1996, by Jason Aronson, Northvale, NJ. Reprinted 2013 by Echo Point Books. Meehl, P. E. (1957) When Shall We Use Our Heads Instead of the Formula? *Journal of Counseling Psychology*, 4:268–273.

41 Bostrom, Nick. *Superintelligence: Paths, Dangers, Strategies*, pp. 140–141, 143. Oxford University Press, New York, 2014.

2

PATHWAYS TO SUPERINTELLIGENCE

The idea here is not that this would enhance the intellectual capacity of individuals enough to make them superintelligent, but rather that some system composed of individuals thus networked and organized might attain a form of superintelligence.

Nick Bostrom, Professor of Philosophy,
University of Oxford

According to a broad class of plausible materialist views, any system with sophisticated enough information processing and environmental responsiveness, and perhaps the right kind of historical and environmental embedding, should have conscious experience.

Eric Schwitzgebel, Professor of Philosophy,
University of California, Riverside[1]

Now, at long last, the processes of cultural evolution have generated another envelope, superimposed on the biosphere, i.e., a 'sheet of humanized and socialized matter,' which is the noosphere.

Pierre Teilhard de Chardin,
The Phenomenon of Man (1955)

Thousand Pound Gorilla Philosopher

Serious research into artificial intelligence should come to grips with the claims made by Professor Nick Bostrom. We are not committing hagiography when we say he is a big deal in this space. Bostrom is Professor in the Faculty of Philosophy and Oxford Martin School at the University of Oxford, Director of the Strategic Artificial Intelligence Research Centre, Director of the Future of Humanity Institute, and author of the New York Times bestseller, *Superintelligence: Paths, Dangers, Strategies*. For a book as wonky, cerebral, and intellectually rigorous as *Superintelligence* to make it onto the New York Times bestseller list is enough to give us optimism about the future of the human race. We treat Bostrom as an authority on this subject. Therefore, we do not disagree with Bostrom unless we have serious grounds for doing so.

23

Bostrom lays out several "pathways" to superintelligence: biological cognitive enhancement, neural lace, whole brain emulation, and collective superintelligence (or what we call "organizational network intelligence"). We will describe them here, as they are all interesting and helpful in our understanding of where we as a species may be headed.

We think one of these pathways is the most promising, but it just happens to be the pathway Bostrom dismisses as least important.

There is a pathway currently available, within the state of the art, to create a Humachine that for all practical purposes is "superintelligent." That is the roadmap set forth in this book. One of the good things about our roadmap is—well, there are several benefits. It does not require:

- Drilling into your employee's skulls and implanting hardware sold to you by Elon Musk;
- Harvesting and vitrifying the brain of your deceased most valuable employee and uploading it into a supercomputer; or
- Waiting for a technological breakthrough that is just over the horizon and which happens to recede at the rate of "one day per day."

To the contrary, our roadmap for superintelligence at the enterprise level that is also humane is available now. We can create a Humachine with the human and institutional resources we already possess. Failing to take seriously the notion that organizations could possess a mind of their own with superhuman levels of intelligence is a major limitation on research and innovation in management theory and organizational behavior.

What Is Superintelligence?

Bostrom defines *superintelligence* as "any intellect that greatly exceeds the cognitive performance of humans in virtually all domains of interest."[2] For our present purposes, we are interested in combining the virtues of humanity with the virtues of machinery to create a Humachine—an enterprise that possesses superintelligence.

We are particularly interested in machines that possess *general* intelligence instead of narrow intelligence. Rather than simply the ability to follow a preprogrammed set of instructions (narrow), a generally intelligent machine would have the capacity to[3]:

- Learn
- Deal effectively with uncertainty and probabilistic information
- Extract useful concepts from sensory data and internal states
- Leverage acquired concepts into flexible combinatorial representations for use in logical and intuitive reasoning

As before, we are not interested here in whether computers dream or have feelings but rather whether they *think*, and if so, how to get them to think better than we do, so they can help us.

Bostrom describes superintelligence with intentional vagueness, as "intellects that greatly outperform the best current human minds across many very general cognitive domains." We think it may be helpful to be as vague as he was, because it does not try to nail down superintelligence to an arbitrary IQ score. Further, Bostrom alleviates some of the vagaries by "distinguishing different bundles of intellectual super-capabilities."[4] Thus, Bostrom disaggregates superintelligence into "speed," "collective," and "quality" kinds of intellects.[5]

- *Speed superintelligence* is "a system that can do all that a human intellect can do, but much faster,"
- *Collective superintelligence* is "a system composed of a large number of smaller intellects such that the system's overall performance across many very general domains vastly outstrips that of any current cognitive system," and
- *Quality superintelligence* is "a system that is at least as fast as a human mind and vastly qualitatively smarter."

To help us understand what is meant by these distinctions, we will provide some real-world examples of speed, collective, and quality intelligence (if not superintelligence). Speed intelligence is illustrated by the quantum computers housed at the Lawrence Livermore National Laboratory, capable of running staggering volumes of data through simulations using parallel processing engines.

An example of collective intelligence would be your garden-variety corporation, with its organizational hierarchy, list-serves, functional teams, divisions of labor, watercooler gossip, and so forth. An example of quality intelligence would be your Kasparov, your Hawking, your once-in-a-generation polymath—qualitatively smarter than the average human. Now, take those examples and extend them to their logical extremes until the image in your mind is of a system that is much faster, vastly outstripping the performance of existing systems, and is vastly smarter, respectively.

Using (Not Abusing) Neo-Darwinian Accounts of Intelligence

We find it helpful to review evolutionary explanations of intelligence as a starting-off point for understanding intelligence *per se*. However, we caution against getting carried away with biological evolutionary accounts of intelligence because they offer limited applications in the context of machine learning, artificial intelligence, and the emergence of the Humachine.

Competition, Evolution, and Survival

The competitive business environment has some deep structural similarities to the evolutionary context of biological life itself. It would go beyond the scope of this book to describe them all, but it bears mentioning that life forms *and* businesses are locked in a fight for survival under challenging environmental conditions with finite resources subject to competition between rivals.

The way enterprises have emerged and evolved may be able to tell us interesting things about biological evolution, too, if we cared to look. The evolution of collective action, resource sharing, competition, teamwork, and the relationship between resource consumption and the environment may be as much reflections on human nature as they are on biological life itself.

The way life evolves not through design but rather via advantageous random mutation is also instructive. We elaborate more on the theme of mutation later, in Chapter 8. Indeed, "evolution achieved human intelligence without aiming at this outcome[.]"[6] We think that the emergence of Humachines will be in large part spontaneous mutation similar to how intelligence emerged in biological life.

Suffice it to say we can learn something about innovation in competitive business environments by looking at evolutionary theory. In particular, whether enterprise should even pursue superintelligence in the first place can be informed by lessons from evolution. "Even environments in which organisms with superior information processing skills reap various rewards may not select for intelligence, because improvements to intelligence can (and often do) impose significant costs, such as higher energy consumption or slower maturation time, and those costs may outweigh whatever benefits are gained from smarter behavior."[7]

The same principle of evolution could also be said for business. Having greater information-processing capabilities than ones competitors may create competitive advantages, but there are diminishing marginal returns from increasing investments into more and more analysts. The analysis becomes too expensive in terms of human resources, financial resources, raw energy consumption, or time, and a business with less analysis but swifter, leaner processes could win out.

In a very literal sense, data storage and processing power consume a lot of energy, and the more data, the more energy. One does not have to be a fan of HBO's show *Silicon Valley* to appreciate that solving the data storage (read, "file compression") problem will open up the next frontier of technology. Indeed, the collection, storage, and analysis of data are the hallmark of the twenty-first-century enterprise, across all sectors of the economy.[8] Until we attain the unicorn-like magic bullet of "middle-out" file compression, those with more information processing powers will need more energy—similarly to the information-energy relationship found in biological life forms.

Indeed, by 2025 data storage could consume as much as 20% of global energy output,[9] and energy consumption is a rapidly growing problem for data centers.[10] According to Swedish researcher Anders Andrae, who works for Chinese communications technology firm Huawei, "The situation is alarming. We have a tsunami of data approaching. Everything which can be is being digitalized. It is a perfect storm."[11]

Indeed, as of the end of 2017, "US researchers expect power consumption to triple in the next five years as one billion more people come online in developing countries, and the 'internet of things' (IoT), driverless cars, robots, video surveillance and artificial intelligence grows exponentially in rich countries."[12]

We could be forgiven for asking whether the rush to maximize information processing in business is entirely rational. There may be too much of a good thing from an evolutionary perspective of long-term competitive advantage, as far as information processing capabilities is concerned.

According to inventor "Rado" Danilak, we are now in a shocking *performance plateau* where technology is reaching the limits of device physics and microarchitectures, leading to disappointing departures from Moore's Law. "In the good old days, more than a decade ago [from 2017], semiconductor process shrinks gave us both higher performance and power reduction at the same time. Now, process shrinks no longer give us more speed, nor can they offset rapidly increasing power consumption by data centers."[13]

We suggest that this performance plateau is a closing door that should lead us to pursue alternative avenues for innovation. Instead of trying to fly in the face of physics, we should acknowledge that perhaps we have reached a natural limit, and instead of transforming our devices, we should transform how we use them.

As biological life has shown via the paths of natural selection, it is not always the species with greatest information processing capabilities that survives. More is not always better. It's not about having more information *per se*; it's about strategically using what information can be sustainably collected, stored, and analyzed that will be the key to enterprise success as we go deeper into the twenty-first century.

The Evolutionary Paths of Human and Machine Intelligence Split

Beyond the staggering energy consumption involved in guzzling information with data-thirsty machines, there's also the problem of the smart guy finishing last. The runner who spends too much time analyzing the optimal path around the track before taking off from the start line will lose to the runner who just starts stumbling forward in the right general direction immediately after the starter pistol goes off.

Evolution will select for what is *useful*, not necessarily what is *true*—and if "smarts" are defined in terms of information processing, or getting at the truth of things, then evolution will not always select for the *maximum* intelligence but rather the most *useful kinds* of intelligence.

The distinction between the maximum intelligence and the most useful intelligence is a bit nuanced. We illustrate with a common example. We all know someone who is not necessarily the smartest person in their network but they have managed to be the most successful in every meaningful respect. We all know someone who *is* the smartest person we know, but they are not necessarily successful in several meaningful respects.

Those concrete examples prove our point. We don't need maximum smarts; we need *useful* smarts. For that reason, we also do not need to solve the hard problem of general artificial intelligence or fully understand and be able to replicate human cognition in order to evolve our organizations into Humachines. We simply need to implement policies and procedures to manage human and technological resources in the most useful combinations.

While it is important to inform our understanding of intelligence with an eye toward evolutionary biology, we caution against letting the tail wag the dog. Evolutionary biology offers a helpful perspective on the evolution of intelligence, but we should not let the *perspective* dominate the *subject under view*.

Case in Point

According to Professor Andrew Lo of the MIT Sloan School of Management, principal investigator of the MIT Computer Science & Artificial Intelligence Laboratory, we should be thinking about intelligence in terms of sex: "The key to understanding which types of behavior are more likely to survive is how behavior affects reproductive success in a given population's environment. From this perspective, *intelligence is naturally defined as behavior that increases the likelihood of reproductive success*, and bounds on rationality are determined by physiological and environmental constraints."[14]

We do not dispute this definition of natural intelligence, as it arose in biological life forms whose very survival depends upon sexual reproduction. But we do take issue with this perspective as applied to computer science and artificial intelligence. It barks up the proverbial wrong tree.

We contend that if our understanding of *machine* intelligence is inherently bound up in the way intelligence evolved in *humans in particular*, we are destined for failure in realizing general artificial intelligence. Indeed, we would go so far as to reject the Lo theory of natural intelligence as applied to machine intelligence.

Moving away from the biological or "natural" theory of intelligence goes hand-in-glove with the need to shy away from species chauvinism. If we accept that mental states can be realized in machines, we need to also appreciate that intelligence can emerge in nonbiological ways.

It seems strange that we would need to clear this up, but *intelligence is not just a vehicle for increasing the likelihood of conjugal relations*. Indeed, both stereotypical jock and stereotypical nerd can confirm that intelligence is neither necessary nor sufficient for reproductive success.

Do not mischaracterize the foregoing. We are not rejecting the broad contours of neo-Darwinian theory as an accurate explanation for the ascent of life and the emergence of intelligence in humans. We believe the neo-Darwinian account of human intelligence is accurate.

Rather, we are concerned about the ability of this mode of thinking when applied to the domain of computer science and the "evolution" of *machine intelligence*. While artificially intelligent machines may need *some* kind of incentive structure to learn and evolve, as far as we can tell, *reproductive success* is not, and should not be, the motivating factor of an AI to attain superintelligence.

Now we turn to Bostrom's pathways to superintelligence.

Biological Cognitive Enhancement

The first stop along our tour of pathways toward superintelligence is *biological cognitive enhancement*. This means deliberately extending human intelligence along the existing evolutionary path toward higher forms of natural intelligence. It basically involves engineering biological forms of intelligence, which is not a trivial undertaking.

Now, Bostrom does take seriously the notion that genetic selection is a pathway to creating superintelligence *in humans*. This pathway means we actually breed for intelligence within subgroups of the human population, extending upon and augmenting the billion years of evolution that got us to be as smart as we now happen to be.

Let us go on record and unequivocally caution against this biological cognitive enhancement pathway to superintelligence as *exceedingly dangerous social engineering*. We hardly need to discuss the disastrous historical precedent of the 1940s state-sponsored eugenics to say we should not go down that path again.

We are not being churlish; we are not suggesting the advocates of biological cognitive enhancement mean *in any way* to endorse the historical precedent. We are just abundantly cautious that anyone could get this program right without leading to profound ethical conflicts. We know humanity too much to trust our governments to conduct a multi-generational breeding program aimed at biological cognitive enhancements and not do something horribly and irrevocably bad in the process.

With this backdrop in mind, we shudder at the clinical tone of the following passages describing genetic cognitive enhancements in pursuit of a biological pathway to superintelligence[15]:

> Recalcitrance starts out high while the only available method is selective breeding sustained over many generations, something that is obviously difficult to accomplish on a globally significant scale. Genetic enhancement will get easier as technology is developed for cheap and effective genetic testing and selection (and particularly when iterated embryo selection becomes feasible in humans). These new techniques will make it possible to tap the pool of existing human genetic variation for intelligence-enhancing alleles. As the best existing alleles get incorporated into genetic enhancement packages, however, further gains will get harder to come by. The need for more innovative approaches to genetic modification may then increase recalcitrance. There are limits to how quickly things can progress along the genetic enhancement path[.]

Hold on a second. How does one gloss over a globally significant selective breeding program sustained over many generations without even a passing comment about the dangers of state-sponsored eugenics? This would be no less than a thousand-year-regime that controls the fate of the human race by deciding who gets to breed, which would involve determining which classes of people have the "best" alleles.

Of course, we are not implying anything nefarious about the motives behind researchers who point out that biological cognitive enhancement is a viable pathway to superintelligence. We just have no confidence that this is a politically viable option. Regardless of its intellectual merits, it carries pretty dire practical downside risks.

That said, it may be inevitable that private actors pursue genetic upgrades to the human condition. We live in a world where the wealthiest can choose to spare no expense on life-enhancing upgrades. Given the increasing concentration of wealth and the desire to gain competitive advantages, Bostrom's three conclusions about biological cognition enhancements may be inevitable:

1 At least weak forms of superintelligence are achievable by means of biotechnological enhancements;
2 The feasibility of cognitively enhanced humans adds to the plausibility that advanced forms of machine intelligence are feasible; and
3 When we consider scenarios stretching significantly into the second half of this century and beyond, we must take into account the probable emergence of a generation of genetically enhanced populations—voters, inventors, scientists—with the magnitude of enhancement escalating rapidly over subsequent decades[16].

Even though Bostrom believes that "progress along the biological path is clearly feasible," he does concede, "the *ultimate* potential of machine intelligence is, of course, vastly greater than that of organic intelligence."[17] We agree.

We are also too impatient to wait for humans to breed themselves into superintelligence. Business executives need solutions that can be implemented forthwith. In a world of limited resources, including resources dedicated to innovation, we suggest that we ought to prioritize upgrades to intelligence in the form of "humachinery" over purely biological or even purely mechanical upgrades to intelligence.

Neural Lace: Turning Humans into Cyborgs

An alternative to biological cognitive enhancement is to equip the human brain with mechanical upgrades. Literally "plugging in" a brain to a machine interface is essentially the idea behind *"neural lace"* type technologies.

This idea finds a champion in no less august a thinker than Elon Musk, Twitter's favorite eccentric billionaire and CEO of SpaceX and Tesla.

Musk is pursuing a brain-computer interface venture called Neuralink. The technology is focused on implanting devices in the human brain in order to interface between brains and machines at increased connection speeds and bandwidths.[18] This technology would facilitate what Musk calls a "merger of biological intelligence and digital intelligence."

According to Bostrom (and other thought leaders such as futurist inventor Ray Kurzweil and the late, great physicist Stephen Hawking), neural lace "could enable humans to exploit the fortes of digital computing—perfect recall, speedy and accurate arithmetic calculations, and high-bandwidth data transmission—enabling the resulting hybrid system to radically outperform the unaugmented brain."[19]

We will spare the suspense and just call this out for what it appears to us. A ham-fisted, clumsy, crude, and doomed attempt at making a cyborg. Assuming the physical risk to human health and safety from radical neurosurgery can be overcome (e.g., "infections, electrode displacement, hemorrhage, and cognitive decline" associated with drilling a hole in the cranium and attaching wires to grey matter), Bostrom is doubtful that this "cyborgization" is the right pathway to the future.[20] We agree.

The benefits from plugging our brains into the Internet are quite limited, given the already advanced state of evolution of the human brain. For example, why would we jack a fiber optic cable into our skull, when the human retina can already "transmit data at an impressive rate of nearly 10 million bits per second, [and] comes pre-packaged with a massive amount of dedicated wetware, the visual cortex, that is highly adapted to extracting meaning from this information torrent and to interfacing with other brain areas for further processing"?[21]

Neural lace might provide limited returns from the investment because, in our view, scientists are far, far away from inventing something as efficient and powerful as the human brain, given nature had a billion-year head start.

Professor of Computer Vision at Cornell Tech Serge Belongie says, "A majority of the human brain involves processing of visual data, for purposes such as scene interpretation and spatial navigation. Visual data is central to the way we learn about the world, and it follows that the pursuit of intelligent machines will require substantial advances in our ability to process and interpret visual data."[22]

It might be more profitable to reverse the script on the neural lace project. Indeed, connecting machinery to the human brain may be less successful than connecting human organs to machines brains. Let us explain. A human with an implanted computer processor may be less able to capitalize on the augmentation than a hard drive with an implanted human eye. Equipping artificially intelligent systems with the effective equivalent of animal vision could be a breakthrough in the evolution of life itself.

According to Fei-Fei Li, Director of the Stanford University Artificial Intelligence Lab and Chief Scientist AI/ML at Google Cloud[23]:

> More than 500 million years ago, vision became the primary driving force of evolution's "big bang," the Cambrian Explosion, which resulted in explosive speciation of the animal kingdom. 500 million years later, AI technology is at the verge of changing the landscape of how humans live, work, communicate and shape our environment.

As nature discovered early on, vision is one of the most powerful secret weapons of an intelligent animal to navigate, survive, interact and change the complex world it lives in. The same is true for intelligence systems.

The only path to build intelligent machines is to enable it with powerful visual intelligence, just like what animals did in evolution. While many are searching for the "killer app" of vision, I'd say, vision is the "killer app" of AI and computing.

If Li is correct, the neural lace project might be running headlong in the wrong direction.

Medical and technical challenges to creating a brain-machine interface aside, the most profound objection to the neural lace concept is that there would be no real payoff. "The extra data inflow would do little to increase the rate at which we think and learn unless all the neural machinery necessary for making sense of the data were similarly upgraded."[24]

The promise of plugging the human brain into an external hard drive via neural lace does not make sense unless we are planning to upgrade the human brain in the process! In that case, we are no longer creating a solution; we are creating a problem.

Neural lace surgical implants might make sense for the blind, the deaf, or those suffering from Parkinson's disease who do not have access to a fully functioning cognitive apparatus. Neural lace does *not* make sense as a solution for an executive seeking real-time performance enhancement. It does *not* make sense as a solution for enterprise.

Let us not give into the temptation for thinking the path to superintelligence lies in making people cyborgs. There is a reason we said at the outset that the Humachine is not about androids or cyborgs. We are interested in a path that does *not* involve employees drilling holes in their skulls in order to earn a promotion.

There are reasons aside from human health and safety (and creepiness) to avoid the neural lace pathway. "The rate-limiting step in human intelligence is not how fast raw data can be fed into the brain but rather how quickly the brain can extract meaning and make sense of the data."[25]

Even if we could plug the human brain into a high-speed computer, there would be no noticeable difference in processing speed versus that of an unaltered human simply *using* a high-speed computer *with their hands*.

Further, there is limited capability to standardize the technology used to plug into the human brain because *every brain is different*. "Brains, by contrast to the kinds of program we typically run on our computers, do not use standardized data storage and representation formats. Rather, each brain develops its own idiosyncratic representations of higher-level content[.] It would therefore not be possible to establish a simple mapping between the neurons in one brain and those in another [even an artificial one] in such a way that thoughts could automatically slide over from one to the other."[26]

Sorry, Elon. Neural lace is a bridge to nowhere for people looking to adopt technology for competitive advantages either individually or at the enterprise level. This is not to suggest neural lace would be anything short of profoundly useful for people with serious medical issues that are desperate for a technological solution. If any billionaires are reading this, please spend your money on clean energy technologies instead of making us cyborgs.

Whole Brain Emulation

The foregoing analysis does lead us to the notion of creating a virtual brain. If creating a cyborg is a non-starter, why not just create a digital replica of a human brain? A brain that for all practical purposes possesses unlimited memory, attention span, energy, and processing speed (without the need for sleep or caffeine) would be a game changer. Any company that could afford one would buy or build one, keep it in company headquarters, and have the benefit of a benign genius working at its disposal 24/7.

According to Bostrom, this path is called *whole brain emulation*.[27] Bostrom takes this seriously. The approach involves vitrifying an actual human brain (post-mortem, of course, and preferably belonging to a certified genius, resting in peace). The brain tissue, now turned into a glass-like substance, would then be sliced up and fed into a scanner that would recognize the unique structural and chemical elements of the brain.

We then input this raw data into a computer to reconstruct a map of the three-dimensional neuronal network that was responsible for computation in the original living brain. This map would be overlaid with "a library of neurocomputational models of different types" of neurons and neuronal connections. The result of this "scanning," "translation," and "simulation" of the actual physical neural structures of a real human brain would be a digital isomorphic representation of the original, implemented in a supercomputer.

The structures and functions of the brain would be translated into data and programs, such that the brain would run as software on the hardware of a supercomputer. The outcome of whole brain emulation is to create, in Bostrom's words, "a digital reproduction of the original intellect, with memory and personality intact."[28]

The mind of the genius who sacrificed his or her brain to science would endure (so long as the hardware running the brain's software was supplied with a reliable power source).[29] The mind would be just as sharp as when it had the living body as its host, but now it could be augmented with the speed, storage, and energy of a supercomputer.

An important feature of the whole brain emulation path is that it is feasible even if we do not figure out the riddle of the human mind, which has many theories and remains hotly debated. Indeed, this path "does not require that we figure out how human cognition works or how to program an artificial intelligence" at all.[30]

This is fortunate, because both unlocking human cognition and programming general artificial intelligence would be like finding the Holy Grail or the fountain of youth. They both require conceptual or theoretical breakthroughs of the most fundamental sort—those on which we cannot count and which may not be availing on any relevant time horizon.

What Bostrom describes as the key to successful whole brain emulation "requires only that we understand the low-level functional characteristics of the basic computational elements of the brain."[31] Of course, there is a "trade-off between insight and technology" in the sense that the weaker our technology, the greater our theoretical understanding of the brain would need to be for whole brain emulation to work, and vice versa. "The worse our scanning equipment and the feebler our computers, the less we could rely on simulating low-level chemical and electrophysiological brain processes, and the more theoretical understanding would be needed of the computational architecture that we are seeking to emulate in order to create more abstract representations of the relevant functionalities."[32]

We are already on the path to being able to scan, translate, and simulate the human brain, so Bostrom acknowledges that "present knowledge and capabilities suggest that there is no in-principle barrier to the development of the requisite enabling technologies[.]"[33]

Therefore, the problem with whole brain emulation is not theoretical; it is practical: "It is clear that a very great deal of incremental technological progress would be needed to bring human whole brain emulation within reach."[34]

Executives looking to take their organization to the next level of performance do not have time to wait out a "very great deal" of tech evolution before they can get started. That is why we are writing this book.

Collective Superintelligence

The final path to superintelligence discussed by Bostrom is intelligence attained at the network or organizational level. This is truly a case of last but not least. This would be properly described as "collective intelligence" attained "through the gradual enhancement of networks and organizations that link individual human minds with one another and with various artifacts and bots."[35]

For our purposes, we call this pathway to superintelligence *"organizational network superintelligence"* to distinguish it from the other pathways to superintelligence and to clarify that "collective" refers to the collection of humans and bots in a network array within an organization.

One of the unique features of the organizational network intelligence approach is that it does not depend on an individual attaining superintelligence. "The idea here is not that this would enhance the intellectual capacity of individuals enough to make them superintelligent, but rather that some system composed of individuals thus networked and organized might attain a form of superintelligence."[36]

Recall from the introduction of the topic of biological cognitive enhancements that intelligence in humans might have been an emergent feature of a system that was actually designed for something else—survival. We believe this emergence is likely to be the case with general artificial intelligence as well. It will not be created by directly programming software toward that end. We predict that superintelligence will spontaneously emerge as a random mutation on the predicate of thick networks of parallel information processing fed with rich data sources. It may be that this occurs only when sufficient quantum-computing resources are made available to the network, but we do not know.

It is our working theory, and we may be pleasantly surprised that superintelligence emerges on the basis of ordinary Internet-enabled information networks, ordinary people, and ordinary computers. That is, after all, our proposal for creating a Humachine: to build something extraordinary out of quite ordinary tools. This approach is consistent with Kasparov's Law, discussed in Chapter 1.

Bostrom explains that management practices can hinder or help the emergence of organizational network intelligence[37]:

> In general terms, a system's collective intelligence is limited by the abilities of its member minds, the overheads in communicating relevant information between them, and the various distortions and inefficiencies that pervade human organizations. If communication overheads are reduced (including not only equipment costs but also response latencies, time and attention burdens, and other factors), then larger and more densely connected organizations become feasible. The same could happen if fixes are found for some of the bureaucratic deformations that warp organizational life—wasteful status games, mission creep, concealment or falsification of information, and other agency problems. Even partial solutions to these problems could pay hefty dividends for collective intelligence.

This is good news for managers. The upshot here is that *virtuous organizations will evolve collective intelligence faster than corrupt organizations*. We might also add that virtuous organizations will evolve a collective intelligence that is less likely to be pathological than corrupt organizations.

Future research would begin painting the psychological profile of organizations that have attained a mind of their own—but doing so now would go beyond the scope of this book. We are not there yet. We are still trying to create *one* Humachine and are not yet able to classify the various kinds of Humachines that may come to be in the future. Suffice it to say, as the expression goes, the tool will take the shape of the master's hand—the Humachine will be made in the image of its creator.

We are encouraging readers to take seriously what Bostrom calls a "seemingly more fanciful idea that the Internet might one day 'wake up' [and] become something more than just the backbone of a loosely integrated collective" intelligence that combines human and machine subcomponents.[38]

We think the evolutionary phenomenon of emergence, even if by random mutation, is actually an historical precedent for how this could happen. It need not be entirely random, especially if we are self-consciously designing our information technology, communication, and organizational infrastructure with "intelligence-enabling" at the forefront of our design parameters.

According to Professor Li, "More than 80% of the web is data in pixel format (photos, videos, etc.), there are more smartphones with cameras than the number of people on earth, and every device, every machine and every inch of our space is going to be powered by smart sensors."[39] At some point, these sensors could become the billion flickering eyes of a globally distributed cloud of sensing and thinking collective consciousness.

Indeed, "a more plausible version of the scenario would be that the Internet accumulates improvements through the work of many people over many years… and that myriad incremental improvements eventually create the basis for some more unified form of web intelligence."[40]

One of the curious aspects of this emergence phenomenon is that we are not guaranteed to know it when it happens. The "emergent" mind of the Internet itself is not required to make itself known to us or to announce its arrival with trumpets blaring. For all we know, it already exists and is quietly pondering the majesty and horrors of creation, contemplating its next moves under the convenient camouflage of humanity's blinding prejudice: species chauvinism.

Even for Bostrom's skepticism of collective intelligence, "It seems at least conceivable that such a web-based cognitive system, supersaturated with computer power and all other resources needed for explosive growth save for one crucial ingredient, could, when the final missing constituent is dropped into the cauldron, blaze up with superintelligence."[41]

Although he agrees that it is *conceivable*, Bostrom is doubtful that collective intelligence will be anything more than an *enabling layer* to allow us to get to superintelligence. In his view, it will never be superintelligence in and of itself.

Bostrom's Blind Spot: The Promise of Collective Intelligence

Bostrom's analysis of collective intelligence concludes, "Improvements in networks and organizations might result in weakly superintelligent forms of collective intelligence in the long run, but more likely they will play an enabling role similar to that of biological cognitive enhancement, gradually increasing humanity's effective ability to solve intellectual problems."[42]

We disagree here in several ways.

> *First*, we contend that organizational network intelligence is the only theoretically and practically attainable form of superintelligence available.
>
> *Second*, we contend that organizational network intelligence is the distinctive feature of a Humachine. That means it is not merely an enabling layer or a bridge to our goal, but rather the thing in itself, the destination.
>
> *Third*, we contend organizational network intelligence is capable not only of "weak" superintelligence but rather will be far superior to any form of individual superintelligence. Superintelligence may only ever be available at the collective level. The whole will always be greater than the sum total of its parts. A network of intellects will always outperform an intellect in isolation.

Indeed, Bostrom even claims that, "if we gradually increase the level of integration of a collective intelligence, it may even become a unified intellect—a single large 'mind' as opposed to a mere assemblage of loosely interacting smaller human minds."[43] We agree. This integrated web of intelligence comprised of humans and machines would have a mind of its own. And, if management succeeds, it will be a wise mind and not that of an evil genius.

Indeed, we must prepare our organizations for such a mind to emerge, because once it does, it may not be subject to our control. We must, in other words, enlighten our organizational networks *now*, by which we mean imbuing self-awareness, self-control, ethics, and so forth, so that when a collective superintelligence emerges, we enjoy the peace and security of superintelligence self-regulating on terms that are compatible with human welfare. In other words, lets define acceptable terms and conditions before letting the genie out of the lamp.

Recall from the introduction of this Chapter that Bostrom distinguishes between speed, collective, and quality superintelligence. Interestingly, Bostrom is conceding that superintelligence exists as a system; it is not some feature or property of a system but rather *the system itself.* This aspect of Bostrom's definitions of superintelligence actually supports our thesis.

Again, we believe a Humachine would be superintelligent, and it would take the form of an organizational network, which will always be superior to other forms of individual intelligence. This is where we differ most sharply, and where Bostrom actually makes our case for us.

As important as speed and quality may be, *speed and quality are features of an intelligent system*, whereas an *organizational network is itself a system.*

Indeed, an organizational network is, in our view, the only locus for realizing superintelligence on relevant time horizons. This underscores how important it will be for us to pursue collective superintelligence, if we want to attain superintelligence at all.

We agree with Bostrom that "a system's collective intelligence could be enhanced by expanding the number or the quality of its constituent intellects, or by improving the quality of their organization."[44] The challenge is whether the proposal outlined in this book could suffice to create "some far more extreme growth of humanity's collective cognitive capacity," which he believes is required in order "to obtain a collective *superintelligence* from any present-day collective intelligence."[45]

We do not know what Bostrom means by "vastly" outperforming the status quo. This seems to us a legerdemain way of moving the goal posts so that superintelligence is merely defined as whatever we cannot yet do. Because this sliding scale semantics around superintelligence is "indexed to the performance levels of the present," that means it would be true to say, "current levels of human collective intelligence could be regarded as approaching superintelligence *relative to a Pleistocene baseline.*"[46]

We are not sure it is helpful to define superintelligence as a value relative to wherever human intellects happen to be at any given time. The smarter we are, the higher the bar for superintelligence—such that the farther we can see with our telescope, the farther it recedes on the horizon.

We think this makes the perfect the enemy of the good. We should be content with pursuing incremental improvements to collective intelligence. Indeed, it's all we can do, so we might as well keep at it. If you want to make progress in the present, we cannot hold out for the emergence of an individual genius or silver bullet technology.

As we discuss in Chapter 1, Kasparov's Law gives us reason to put our hope in process—the triumph of process over geniuses and supercomputers. If you read Bostrom carefully, it's not clear he would even disagree with us[47]:

> We can think of wisdom as the ability to get the important things approximately right. It is then possible to imagine an organization composed of a very large cadre of very efficiently coordinated knowledge workers, who collectively can solve intellectual problems across many very general domains. This organization, let us suppose, can operate most kinds of businesses, invent most kinds of technologies, and optimize most kinds of processes[.] Such an organization could have a very high degree of collective intelligence; if sufficiently high, the organization is a collective superintelligence.

Right. Exactly. That's our point. We aren't sure why this *entirely plausible scenario* should be set on the back burner while far more speculative avenues are pursued. But you are reading us still, so apparently we are on the same page about that. Good.

Bostrom claims that "improvements in networks and organizations may yield narrower increases in our problem-solving capacity than will improvements in biological cognition—boosting 'collective intelligence' rather than 'quality intelligence.'"[48] For reasons that are not readily apparent to us, Bostrom elevates quality superintelligence over collective superintelligence both in terms of making it a priority for researchers and by assuming it offers a greater promise to humanity. It seems to us that quality superintelligence is both less attainable, and more likely to be abused, than collective superintelligence. We are left scratching our heads... why denigrate collective superintelligence?

One reason to subjugate collective intelligence while elevating the individual forms of intelligence may come down to an unarticulated prejudice: species chauvinism.

What Is Species Chauvinism, and Why Is It a Problem?

In the proceeding section, we formed the suspicion that those who disagree with the primacy of collective superintelligence may be subject to the prejudice of *species chauvinism*, which is a pejorative characterization of the view that only humans can be conscious. This is probably an unfamiliar term, so let us elaborate.

Douglass Hofstadter's *Godel, Escher, Bach: An Eternal Golden Braid* deals with this prejudice quite forcefully. Specifically, Hofstadter explains, "there are still quite a few philosophers, scientists, and so forth who believe that patterns of symbols *per se* (such as books or movies or libraries or CD-ROMs or computer programs, no matter how complex or dynamic) *never* have meaning on their own, but that meaning instead, in some most mysterious manner, springs only from the organic chemistry, or perhaps the quantum mechanics, of processes that take place in carbon-based biological brains."[49]

This viewpoint has intuitive appeal but has been panned by thought-leaders as a "parochial, bio-chauvinistic view," or as some form of "species chauvinism" because it implies that only humans with our unique kind of brains can have thoughts—and not, by implication, extremely advanced machines, nor a hypothetical silicon-based life form possessing advanced intelligence.

What is so special about brains that the notion that only humans or "brained" biological creatures can have thoughts? If you believe that only humans can have mental states, but you are interested in seeking help, Hofstadter suggests to[50]:

> Keep on reminding oneself, unpleasant though it may seem, that the "teetering bulb of dread and dream" that nestles safely inside one's own cranium is a purely physical object made up of completely sterile and inanimate components, all of which obey exactly the same laws as those that govern all the rest of the universe, such as pieces of text, or CD-ROMs, or computers. Only if one keeps bashing up against this disturbing fact can one slowly begin to develop a feel for the way out of the mystery of consciousness: that the key is not the stuff out of which brains are made, but the patterns that can come to exist inside the stuff of a brain.

In a footnote to Bostrom's chapter on Pathways to Superintelligence, he says, "It has been suggested that we should regard corporate entities (corporations, unions, governments, churches, and so forth) as artificial intelligence agents, entities with sensors and effectors, able to represent knowledge and perform inference and take action[.] They are clearly powerful and ecologically successful, although their capabilities and internal states are different from those of humans."[51] To this point, we say, *who cares?* Why does it matter that the capabilities and internal states of collectives are *different* from those of humans?

According to the philosophy of mind called **functionalism**, a mental state is properly defined as what it *does*, not what it is made of: "mental states are the occupants of characteristic causal roles."[52] Under this view, mental states are properly understood as the causal connections between physical inputs and behavioral outputs.

The functionalist would explain the mental state *pain* as the internal causal dominoes that connect the sensory input of "hand on hot stove" to the behavioral response of "removing hand."

Functionalism by its own terms would permit **multiple realization**, that is, a mental state could be instantiated in a human brain, a computer chip board, or something else. Multiple realization means that in different creatures, pain can be realized in different ways: human pain differs from brain to brain, and human pain differs from that realized by nonhumans (whether in biological creatures or some alien with a silicon brain or in a circuit board). Whether it's neurons, silicon chips, or the internal workings of a corporation, a mind *is* what a mind *does*.

To suggest that a collective cannot attain intelligence because it's not a human is to commit species chauvinism or to fallaciously beg the question about what intelligence is. It is a prejudice that cannot withstand scrutiny.

While it is probably true that mental states emerge from neural states in humans, we must be careful to resist the temptation to overextend this notion. From that premise, we are not permitted to conclude that mental states can emerge *exclusively* from human brains—there may be other physical arrangements that could give rise to consciousness. The notion that mentality depends on gray matter in our brains and is impossible without it is a bald human prejudice that we must abandon in order to understand the true nature of thinking.

Thinking a thought does not depend upon having a brain made up of "grey matter" or neurons, axons, and dendrites. "Science fiction is full of computers and robots that can think. HAL, the computer in Stanley Kubric's *2001: A Space Odyssey*, is perhaps the most famous example[.] We have become quite comfortable, it would seem, with the idea that a machine could have thoughts."[53] Mental states could be instantiated in human minds but also on a computer server, or spread out across a network.

Hofstadter contends that consciousness is a strange loop of self-awareness, and that appreciating that minds are not reducible to matter but are, rather, strange patterns, is a "liberating shift, because it allows one to move to a different level of considering what brains are: as media that support complex patterns that mirror, albeit far from perfectly, the world, of which, needless to say, those brains are themselves denizens—and it is in the inevitable self-mirroring that arises, however impartial or imperfect it may be, that the strange loops of consciousness start to swirl."[54]

Where are we going with this line of reasoning? Well, if a computer can simulate human mental states, and these mental states are defined in terms of patterns instead of underlying biological substrate, and enterprises are composed of computers integrated with humans in patterns that can be planned and adjusted, then there is only a small step of logic and managerial skill necessary to reach quite a profound conclusion indeed: *an enterprise can have mental states—that is, a mind of its own.*

Collective Intentionality

We understand that the notion of an enterprise possessing a mind of its own is controversial. There is a spirited debate within the philosophical community about "group mindedness" or *collective intentionality*—that is, whether groups can have a "mind" separate and apart from the minds of the individuals that make up that group.[55]

Without getting too deep into the weeds of philosophy of mind, we do want to dig a little bit into the notions of collective intentionality. This area of research lays the foundation for a more fulsome appreciation of what artificial intelligence could be when scaled to the enterprise level, in the sense of organizational network intelligence or collective intelligence that we consider fundamental to the Humachine. We feel there is a real sense in which groups or organizations can have a mind of their own and that this is not merely a figure of speech or a legal fiction.

Does "Microsoft" Really "Intend" Anything?

A representative objection to the notion of collective intentionality comes from philosopher Robert Rupert's article, *Against Group Cognitive States.*[56] Rupert gives an example of an ordinary sentence, "Microsoft intends to develop a new operating system." With this example in mind, he asks rhetorically, "Does Microsoft—the corporation itself—literally *intend* to develop a new operating system?"[57] and proceeds to answer the question in the negative—Microsoft does not "intend" anything.

Rupert reaches this negative conclusion by applying a guiding principle, namely that "if a group has mental states, those states must do causal-explanatory work" in the sense that the group's decision itself must explain the behavioral output, rather than simply being a metaphor or synecdoche that glosses over several individual actions.

Based on application of this principle, Rupert rejects that groups have cognitive states. "The fundamental problem appears to be this: in the cases in which, in everyday speech, we're inclined to attribute cognitive states to groups, there seems to be available a complete causal explanation couched in terms of the cognitive states of individuals (together with the noncognitive, physical structures that individuals manipulate and transmit)."[58]

Rupert elaborates on the Microsoft example[59]:

> At a number of times in recent history, it has seemed that "Microsoft intends to develop a new version of its operating system" was true. Did the alleged intention causally explain any data? If so, which ones? One possibility is the hiring of new employees. Take a particular person—call her "Sally"—who recently received a letter of offer of employment from Microsoft and who now has a key to an office on the Microsoft campus and now has funds transferred to her bank account from an account with the name "Microsoft Corporation" attached to it. What explains these data? It seems clear that the occurrence of these events is due entirely to communication among individuals (e.g., members of human resources at Microsoft), cognitive activities of individuals (e.g., each individual on the hiring committee who voted to extend an offer of employment to Sally), and actions of individuals (e.g., the person who transmitted the letter of offer to Sally). It is gratuitous to include an additional cognitive state, a state of Microsoft as a single entity, that causally accounts for the data.

We can overcome this counterexample.

Collective Minds Play a Causal Role in the Real World

First, we'll just make a series of true statements about Rupert's hypothetical that will put pressure on the notion that it is merely the cognitive actions of individuals that play a causal explanatory role in the Microsoft story.

We feel it is impossible to explain the real and complex relationship between Sally and Microsoft without reference to Microsoft as a separate entity, irreducible to the individuals who made decisions on behalf of Microsoft. Perhaps there is some austere philosophical sense in which group actions aren't *really* actions, but there's clearly an important sense in which they are, and that's the sense of relevance for the reality of Humachines.

If Sally fails to receive her paycheck after putting in weeks of labor, her lawsuit for back pay is against Microsoft, not the individuals on the hiring committee. If Sally invents a new function in the operating system while employed, her intellectual property is assigned to Microsoft, not the individual members of the hiring committee. If one or two individuals on the hiring committee wanted to hire Sally, but the hiring committee itself did not approve, then she would not be working for Microsoft. If the hiring committee declined to hire Sally because she was female, the lawsuit would be against Microsoft, not the individuals. If Sally is fired from her position at Microsoft for any unlawful reason, her lawsuit is against Microsoft, not the individuals on the hiring committee.

Rupert notes that this question about group intentionality is both a philosophical and empirical question. Let's look at some empirical answers. In the Microsoft example, several empirical points can be made that support the notion that collective intents are not reducible to individual intentions. Group decisions like a Board of Directors resolution have legal and real-world causal significance. Describing any individual Director's mental state alone, without reference to what the group of Directors as a whole decided, is neither necessary nor sufficient to explain the causal consequences of a Board resolution. Group decisions can be legally binding on subordinate officers. Group intention, say of the Board, expressed through a resolution, cause subordinate officers to behave in certain ways—to abstain from some actions while pursuing others. Indeed, the group's decision can cause an entire division of the company to behave in a certain way. So, in a legal sense at the very least, group intentions have a causal role to play in behavior. Individual Directors have no legal authority to bind the corporation in their individual capacity or even in their official capacity acting in isolation; rather, the group of Directors (usually a majority) must act collectively to create a legally binding—and causally efficacious—outcome.

Reducing collective intentions to individual acts erases meaningful and true accounts of the world. We feel that if we were to follow Rupert's argument, we will get burns from shaving too closely with Occam's razor.

Some Philosophical Points That Support Collective Intentionality

A purely naturalist principle is that if something is causally efficacious in the world, then it exists. A corollary is that if something exists in its own right then it is not entirely reducible to some lower physical layer of reality. The individual intentions, when aggregated, create something that is more than merely the sum total of its parts. Microsoft is not just a bunch of individuals.

We can say with a straight face that "Microsoft intends to launch a new operating system," and this is a true statement that can move stock prices, lead to job creation, and all sorts of other very real and empirically verifiable consequences. It would *also* be true to say, "Several individuals employed by Microsoft have the intentions of launching a new operating system," but their individual intentions do not explain what happens in the real world when *Microsoft* intends to launch a new operating system.

How hard is it to establish that a board of Directors is something separate and apart from its individual constituents? It is a legally recognized separate entity with its own legal rights and duties that definitively do not belong to any individual member. The metaphysical objections against collective intentionality have to ignore the fact that the law, the employees, the economy, and the press recognize and are impacted by collective agency. Of course, group intentions have causal roles. This is both philosophically sound and empirically verifiable. It is therefore not gratuitous to include an additional cognitive state, a state of Microsoft as a single entity, that causally accounts for the data.

Beyond the empirical support for the notion of collective intentionality, there are philosophical problems with Rupert's reduction of collective intentionality to individual intentionality. If we reduce collective intentions to individual intentions merely aggregated, why stop there? Individual intentions can be explained by reference to neural activation patterns inside the individual brains, which can, in turn, be explained by reference to chemical bonds... and it just keeps going down. We feel that it is arbitrary to reduce to the individual brain level and then just stop the reductive process there. To avoid arbitrariness, we should give causal efficacy to every level of reality, including the collective level. We don't see a principled reason why we *must* move from collective to individual causal explanations of group actions but somehow *not* proceed with the reductive agenda all the way down to the quantum level. Of course, Rupert probably has a solid response to this objection. To get to the truth of the matter probably requires a deep dive into metaphysics, which is beyond the scope of this book.

Another philosophical problem is that Rupert goes from epistemological premises—namely, that collective intentionality can be explained by reference to individual intentional states—and leaps to a metaphysical conclusion—namely, that because an alternative explanation of collective intentionality is available, collective intentionality *does not exist.* In the history of ideas, leaping from epistemological premises (about what we can know or explain) to metaphysical conclusions (what reality is and what exists) has never been logically valid.

The collective intent is itself what has the causal efficacy in the corporate context. Rupert's main gripe is that there is no causal role at the collective level and that seems incorrect from the examples we give. To be fair, Rupert's argument is about how science individuates kinds and is probably so subtle that we are not actually addressing his point head on with these counterexamples. Suffice it to say there are detractors from our contention that groups can have agency in their own right. We disagree with them and provide more detail in this endnote,[60] but we need to move on. There is too much fun to be had with collective intentionality to be waylaid dealing with claims that it is philosophically problematic.

Even supposing that, technically in strict philosophical terms, there is no group agency. Still, we are getting at something when we attribute causal efficacy to groups: The Board decided to fire the CEO; that's why the CEO is out of work now, not because any individual board member decided to fire the CEO but because the *Board itself* did so. Everything we say about Humachines having a mind of their own can therefore be true in whatever sense such claims about collective intentionality are true. Is it a legal fiction, a linguistic convention, a metaphor, or something else? We leave this to the philosophers to sort out.

Could a Corporation Actually Be Conscious?

We can take this line of reasoning further and argue that not only do groups have what it takes to have cognitive states, but they might even have the features that many philosophers hold to be necessary and sufficient indicators of consciousness itself. At least one philosopher has contended that even "the United States has all the types of properties that materialists tend to regard as characteristic of conscious beings."[61] Indeed, if the United States can be conscious, why can't a business enterprise be conscious?

"According to a broad class of plausible materialist views, any system with sophisticated enough information processing and environmental responsiveness, and perhaps the right kind of historical and environmental embedding, should have conscious experience."[62] We contend that enterprises with sufficiently rich information systems, environmental monitoring, and responsive management meet the criteria for conscious experience, at least at the lowest level needed to possess intelligence thoughtful awareness.

> For consciousness, there presumably needs to be some organization of the information in the service of coordinated, goal-directed responsiveness; and maybe, too, there needs to be some sort of sophisticated self-monitoring. But the United States has these properties too... The United States is a goal-directed entity, flexibly self-protecting and self-preserving. The United States responds, intelligently or semi-intelligently, to opportunities and threats[.][63]

If the United States can have all the underlying properties necessary for the realization of organizing information, responding to the environment with purposeful action, and sophisticated self-monitoring (and it does), then what's to stop an organization like a business from having those properties, too? And what more do we need to assert that an entity has at least a rudimentary mental life with some meaningful degree of prudential self-awareness than those qualities?

Humachines and the Noosphere

In the proceeding section, we maintained that collective intentionality is an actual thing that is not reducible to individual mental states. This supports our contention that an enterprise composed of individuals, information flows, technology, and artificially intelligent systems could have a mind of its own that is not simply reducible to the minds of the individual humans that work there.

On that basis, we want to introduce the mind-blowing concept of the noosphere. This is perhaps the most influential (if not prophetic) statement of what collective intelligence could be on a planetary level.

In 1955, the Jesuit anthropologist Pierre Teilhard de Chardin posthumously introduced the world to the concept of *noosphere* in his remarkable book, *The Phenomenon of Man*. "Now, at long last, the processes of cultural evolution have generated another envelope, superimposed on the biosphere, i.e., a 'sheet of humanized and socialized matter,' which is the noosphere."[64] The noosphere emerges as a "result of the interactions of increasing activity of human networks creating a highly charged 'thinking layer,' [a] mental sheathe 'above and discontinuous with the biosphere,' [functionally not unlike a planetary] nervous system."[65]

In Teilhard's own words, the emergence of consciousness in humanity marked an historical turning point in Earth's history. Since Teilhard's death, we invented the global Internet, which only furthers his thesis. We excerpt his poetic account of the noosphere below, with more to be found in this endnote.[66]

> From our experimental point of view, reflection is, as the word indicates, the power acquired by a consciousness to turn in upon itself, to take possession of itself as of an object endowed with its own particular consistence and value: no longer merely to know, but to know oneself; no longer merely to know, but to know that one knows. By this individualization of himself in the depths of himself, the living element, which heretofore had been spread out and divided over a diffuse circle of perceptions and activities, was constituted for the first time as a centre in the form of a point at which all the impressions and experiences knit themselves together and fuse into a unity that is conscious of its own organization.

Now the consequences of such a transformation are immense, visible as clearly in nature as any of the facts recorded by physics or astronomy. The being who is the object of his own reflection, in consequence of that very doubling back upon himself, becomes in a flash able to raise himself into a new sphere. In reality, another world is born. Abstraction, logic, reasoned choice and inventions, mathematics, art, calculation of space and time, anxieties, and dreams of love—all these activities of inner life are nothing else than the effervescence of the newly formed center as it explodes onto itself.

The recognition and isolation of a new era in evolution, the ear of noogenesis, obliges us to distinguish correlatively a support proportionate to the operation—that is to say, yet another membrane in the majestic assembly of telluric layers. A glow ripples outward from the first spark of conscious reflection. The point of ignition grows larger. The fire spreads in ever widening circles till finally the whole planet is covered with incandescence. Only one interpretation, only one name can be found worthy of this grand phenomenon. Much more coherent and just as extensive as any proceeding layer, it is really a new layer, the "thinking layer," which, since its germination at the end of the Tertiary period, has spread over and above the world of plants and animals. In other words, outside and above the biosphere there is the noosphere.

With that it bursts upon us how utterly warped is every classification of the living world (or, indirectly, every construction of the physical one) in which man only figures logically as a genus or a new family. This is an error of perspective which deforms and uncrowns the whole phenomenon of the universe. To give man his true place in nature it is not enough to find one more pigeon-hole in the edifice of our systematization or even an additional order or branch. With hominization, in spite of the insignificance of the anatomical leap, we have the beginning of a new age. The earth "gets a new skin." Better still, it finds its soul.

The noosphere is Teilhard's phrase for the layer of thought that now envelopes the globe. Importantly, Teilhard claims that the evolution of life itself will proceed *through* consciousness. We agree.

Indeed, we believe the evolution of people, organized in enterprises that attain the status of Humachines, is the next step in the evolution of biological life on this planet.

That Humachines will have competitive advantages over ordinary enterprises, which may be an inducement to their creation. But the promise is far greater than short-term pecuniary gain. The promise is that we would be solving, in Bostrom's portentous words, "the last challenge we will ever face."[67]

The noosphere illustrates that mentality is not simply limited to human craniums but rather can be extended, decentralized, diffused, and take on geological not just psychological significance.

Conclusion

If a corporation is a person, then it can be smart or dumb; it can be ethical or characterized by moral turpitude. Humanity can be creative, genius, pioneering, caring, faithful, benevolent, and so on. It can also be cruel, stupid, treasonous, jealous, subject to manipulation, and self-destructive. Computational machinery, combined with internal organizational rules, can be used to mitigate mental vices while supporting the virtues of human capabilities. Perhaps by following our framework, enterprises can actually create those so-called strange loops of self-awareness at the enterprise level (assuming we have not already inadvertently done so in some instances). An enterprise that has a mind of its own can be just as helpful as it could be destructive. Ensuring the corporation adheres to rules of conduct is going to turn out to be more crucial than obtaining any particular corporate objective.

We have debunked the species chauvinist view that only brains can have consciousness. We have elevated organizational network (or "collective") intelligence as the most plausible pathway to superintelligence. We have made the case than collective intentionality exists. You can argue with us about the merits of the alternative pathways if you want, but at the end of the day (if not the end of the twenty-first century!) the organizational network intelligence approach is the only one that fits within the existing human and technological resources constrains. That's something of a trump card, no?

Unlike programming general artificial intelligence (which requires theoretical breakthroughs unavailable to us now), biological cognitive enhancements (which require a long-term eugenics program), neural lace (which is a bridge to nowhere and not scalable to an enterprise), and whole brain emulation (which may be feasible but is too far off practically), the organizational network intelligence approach is available to us *right now*. It is actionable. The organizational network approach to superintelligence is how we will build Humachines. Humachines are the pathway for the evolution of life on Earth.

This book is a roadmap to that end.

Notes

1 Schitzgebel, Eric. If Materialism Is True, the United States Is Probably Conscious. *Philosophical Studies*, 172:1697–1721, 1706, 2015.
2 Bostrom, *Superintelligence*, p. 26 (italics omitted).
3 Bostrom, *Superintelligence*, p. 27.
4 Bostrom, p. 63.
5 Bostrom, pp. 64, 65, and 68, respectively.
6 Bostrom, *Superintelligence*, p. 31.
7 Bostrom, *Superintelligence*, p. 31.
8 Newman, Daniel. In a World Where Data Rules, All Companies Are Tech Companies. *Forbes*, June 6, 2018. Available at www.forbes.com/sites/danielnewman/2018/06/06/in-a-world-where-data-rules-all-companies-are-tech-companies/#7124025140bf
9 www.researchgate.net/publication/320225452_Total_Consumer_Power_Consumption_Forecast
10 www.forbes.com/sites/forbestechcouncil/2017/12/15/why-energy-is-a-big-and-rapidly-growing-problem-for-data-centers/#32bac8205a30
11 Climate Home News, Part of the Guardian Environment Network. "Tsunami of Data" Could Consume One Fifth of Global Electricity by 2025. *The Guardian*, December 11, 2017. Available at www.theguardian.com/environment/2017/dec/11/tsunami-of-data-could-consume-fifth-global-electricity-by-2025
12 Andrae, Anders S.G. (Huawei). Total Consumer Power Consumption Forecast. *Presented at the Nordic Digital Business Summit*, Helsinki, Finland, October 5, 2017. Available at www.researchgate.net/publication/320225452_Total_Consumer_Power_Consumption_Forecast [accessed November 9, 2018]. Climate Home News, Part of the Guardian Environment Network. "Tsunami of Data" Could Consume One Fifth of Global Electricity by 2025. *The Guardian*, December 11, 2017. Available at www.theguardian.com/environment/2017/dec/11/tsunami-of-data-could-consume-fifth-global-electricity-by-2025
13 Danilak, Radoslav. Why Energy Is a Big and Rapidly Growing Problem for Data Centers. *FORBES*, December 15, 2017. Available at www.forbes.com/sites/forbestechcouncil/2017/12/15/why-energy-is-a-big-and-rapidly-growing-problem-for-data-centers/#e13e2ba5a307
14 Lo, Andrew W. The Origin of Bounded Rationality and Intelligence. *Proceedings of the American Philosophical Society*, 157(3):269–280, 2013 (*emphasis added*).
15 Bostrom, p. 81.
16 Bostrom, *Superintelligence*, p. 54.
17 Bostrom, *Superintelligence*, p. 53.
18 Winkler, Rolfe. Elon Musk Launches Neuralink to Connect Brains with Computers. *The Wall Street Journal*, March 27, 2017.
19 Bostrom, *Superintelligence*, p. 54.
20 Bostrom, pp. 54–55.
21 Bostrom, p. 55.
22 Nisselson, Evan. The War Over Artificial Intelligence Will Be Won with Visual Data. *TechCrunch*, May 17, 2017. Available at https://techcrunch.com/2017/05/17/the-war-over-artificial-intelligence-will-be-won-with-visual-data/
23 Ibid.
24 Bostrom, p. 55.

25 Ibid., p. 56.
26 Ibid.
27 Ibid., p. 36.
28 Ibid.
29 This may be more of a philosophical question than a practical one, but let's take whole brain emulation seriously for a second and assume it was actually done at some point in the near future. Although the hypothetical involves a genius donating her brain to science (and thus, being biologically deceased), we may be forgiven for asking if she would, in some meaningful way, still be alive? If her mind is in all respects still "intact," then would she have a first-person perspective on the world—a personal "I," a sense of self, emotions, desires, and so forth, even after being uploaded?
30 Bostrom, p. 36.
31 Ibid.
32 Ibid., p. 40.
33 Ibid., p. 39.
34 Ibid., Sandberg, Anders. Feasibility of Whole Brain Emulation. In *Philosophy and Theory of Artificial Intelligence*, edited by Vincent C. Müller, Vol. 5, pp. 251–264. Studies in Applied Philosophy, Epistemology and Rational Ethics. Springer, New York, 2013.
35 Bostrom, pp. 58–59.
36 Ibid., p. 59.
37 Ibid.
38 Ibid., p. 60.
39 Nisselson, Evan. The War Over Artificial Intelligence Will Be Won with Visual Data. *TechCrunch*, May 17, 2017. Available at https://techcrunch.com/2017/05/17/the-war-over-artificial-intelligence-will-be-won-with-visual-data/
40 Bostrom, p. 60.
41 Ibid.
42 Ibid., 62.
43 Ibid., 68.
44 Ibid., 66.
45 Ibid.
46 Ibid.
47 Ibid., 67.
48 Ibid., 62.
49 Hofstadter, Douglass. *Gödel, Escher, Bach: An Eternal Golden Braid* (Twentieth-Anniversary Preface), p. 3. Basic Books, New York, 1999.
50 Ibid., p. 4.
51 Bostrom, p. 336.
52 Ravenscroft, Ian. *Philosophy of Mind: A Beginner's Guide*, p. 53. Oxford University Press, New York, 2005.
53 Ibid., p. 82.
54 Hofstadter, Douglass. *Gödel, Escher, Bach: An Eternal Golden Braid* (Twentieth-Anniversary Preface), p. 4. Basic Books, New York, 1999.
55 According to Jonathan Simon, postdoctoral associate in the NYU Department of Philosophy and research fellow of the NYU Center for Mind, Brain and Consciousness, "The skeptics proceed by highlighting the differences between individual minds and group mindedness, or by arguing that one can explain the relevant data (what groups do) without positing that they have cognitive states. It's generally controversial territory."

56 Rupert, Robert. Against Group Cognitive States. In *From Individual to Collective Intentionality: New Essays*, edited by Sara Rachel Chant et al., p. 98. Oxford University Press.

57 Ibid.

58 Ibid.

59 Rupert, Robert. Against Group Cognitive States. In *From Individual to Collective Intentionality: New Essays*, edited by Sara Rachel Chant et al., pp. 98–99. Oxford University Press.

60 Another way to frame Rupert's argument is that we can take some collection of things—A, B and C—then define D as the combination of A, B, and C (so, D = A + B + C). We can then talk about the causal impact of what D does in the world, but that's not a reason to take D to be a genuine causal actor in the world—whether D has a causal role depends entirely on whether A, B, and C form a suitably integrated system, or whatever criterion we might have for explaining the role of constituent parts in forming a whole. According to Simon, "It's debatable what the criterion might be, but Rupert's point would be, it's not enough to just give more examples of cases where we like to say 'D does such and so' because we could say that even if D didn't fit the criterion." That is, as long as A, B, and C are present, the world would look the same whether or not we attribute causation to D.

> Even if we concede that conscious states are reducible to brain states and are nothing over and above brain states, Professor Schitzgebel would say that it does not follow from the reducibility of group minds to individual minds (if they are reducible) and the ability to explain group mental states in terms of individual mental states (if they are explainable) that groups would not be conscious or fail to have mental states. In other words, our pains might be reducible to the activity of neurons, but that does not make them any less painful.

61 Schitzgebel, Eric. If Materialism Is True, the United States Is Probably Conscious. *Philosophical Studies*, 172:1697–1721, 2015. Abstract.

62 Ibid., p. 1706.

63 Ibid., p. 1707.

64 Reiser, Oliver. *Cosmic Humanism*, p. 557.

65 www.noosphere.princeton.edu.com.

66 Pierre Teilhard de Chardin. *The Phenomenon of Man*. Harper Perennial, New York, 1959.

> Between the last strata of the Pliocene period in which man is absent, and the next, in which the geologist is dumbfounded to find the first chipped flints, what has happened? And what is the true measure of this leap? It is our task to divine and to measure the answers to these questions before we follow step by step the march of mankind right down to the decisive stage in which it is involved today. (164–165)
> We have been following the successive stages of the same grand progression from the fluid contours of the early earth. Beneath the pulsations of geo-chemistry, of geo-tectonics and of geo-biology, we have detected one and the same fundamental process, always recognizable—the one which was given material form in the first cells and was continued in the construction of nervous systems. We saw geogenesis promoted to biogenesis, which turned out in the end to be nothing else than psychogenesis.

With and within the crisis of reflection, the next term in the series manifests itself. Psychogenesis has led to man. Now it effaces itself, relieved or absorbed by another and a higher function—the engendering and subsequent development of the mind, in one word *noogenesis*. When for the first time in a living creature instinct perceived itself in its own mirror, the whole world took a pace forward. (181)

Geologists have for long agreed in admitting the zonal composition of our planet. We have already spoken of the barysphere, central and metallic, surrounded by the rocky lithosphere that in turn is surrounded by the fluid layers of the hydrosphere and the atmosphere. Since Suess, science has rightly become accustomed to add another to these four concentric layers, the living membrane composed of the fauna and flora of the globe, the biosphere, so often mentioned in these pages, an envelope as definitely universal as the other "spheres" and even more definitely individualized than them. For, instead of representing a more or less vague grouping, it forms a single piece, of the very tissue of the genetic relations which delineate the tree of life. (182)

The paradox of man resolves itself by passing beyond measure. Despite the relief and harmony it brings to things, this perspective is at first sight disconcerting, running counter as it does to the illusion and habits which incline us to measure events by their material face. It also seems to us extravagant because, steeped as we are in what is human like a fish in the sea, we have difficulty in emerging from it in our minds so as to appreciate its specificness and breadth. But let us look round us a little more carefully. This sudden deluge of cerebralisation, this biological invasion of a new animal type which gradually eliminates or subjects all forms of life that are not human, this irresistible tide of fields and factories, this immense and growing edifice of matter and ideas—all these signs that we look at, for days on end—to proclaim that there has been a change on the earth and a change of planetary magnitude.

There can indeed be no doubt that, to an imaginary geologist coming one day far in the future to inspect our fossilised globe, the most astounding of the revolutions undergone by the earth would be that which took place at the beginning of what has so rightly been called the psychozoic era. And even today, to a Martian capable of analysing sidereal radiations psychically no less than physically, the first characteristic of our planet would be, not the blue of the seas or the green of the forests, but the phosphorescence of thought. (183)

67 Bostrom, preface, page v.

3

THE LIMITS OF MACHINE CAPABILITIES

With Deep Blue, we had a program that would make a superhuman chess move—while the room was on fire. Right? Completely lacking context. Fast-forward 20 years. We've got a computer that can make a superhuman Go move—while the room is on fire.

Oren Etzioni, the Allen Institute for Artificial Intelligence[1]

It is my conviction that machines cannot possess originality in the sense implied by [the] thesis that "machines can and do transcend some of the limitations of their designers, and that in doing so they may be both effective and dangerous[.]" A machine is not a genie, it does not work by magic, it does not possess a will, and... nothing comes out which has not been put in, barring, of course, and infrequent case of malfunctioning[.]

Arthur Samuel, *Some Moral and Technical Consequences of Automation—A Refutation*, SCIENCE (1960)[2]

When Robots Hang with the Wrong Crowd

In March 2016, Microsoft launched Tay, an AI-powered "social chatbot."[3] Microsoft described Tay as an "experiment in conversational understanding." By chatting on Twitter and other social media, she could engage with broad sectors of the population. Tay, like all AI, was programmed to learn from the data it received. The more Tay "chatted" with the millions of users on social media, Microsoft said, the smarter Tay would become.

Tay was programmed to learn by engaging people through "casual and playful conversation." She was designed to communicate in a more "human" way that had an emotional dimension. For example, if asked who her parents were, she might respond, "Oh, a team of scientists in a Microsoft lab." Tay was also programmed to improve speaking responses as more people engaged with her, refining her speech models over time to reflect natural patterns of English speakers. Her ability to learn through engagement, becoming smarter and more expressive, was supposed to embody a really important breakthrough for AI.

However, no one predicted what Tay would become within 24 hours of going live on Twitter. What happened next is as much a reflection of human nature—specifically, the "trolling" phenomenon on social media—as it is a reflection of the limitations of the algorithms underlying chatbot programs. People began tweeting at Tay with a deluge of misogynistic and racist remarks. Tay—learning and mimicking speech from the people she engaged with—quickly began repeating these vile sentiments back to users. Within hours, Tay's responses went from family friendly banter to foul-mouthed flamethrowing. In less than 24 hours after Tay's launch, Microsoft took her off-line and issued a public apology.

The Microsoft research team was caught off guard. They were not prepared for how the system actually behaved in an open-world environment.

As we discuss, AI systems are increasingly programmed to emulate the functioning of the human brain's neural networks. Still, they do this in a very limited way. Using neural networks, programmers tell an AI exactly what they want it to learn and provide it with clearly labeled examples. The algorithm then analyzes the patterns in the data. The more examples provided, the more the algorithm learns. Tay, like most AI systems, can only work with the data it receives. The old adage remains ever so true: Garbage in, garbage out. Also, it is only able to interpret that data and solve problems within the narrow parameters that have been programmed. It doesn't "understand" what it has analyzed, so it is unable to apply its analysis to scenarios in other contexts. As one researcher noted: "AI is more like an Excel spreadsheet on steroids than a thinker."[4]

Let's Not Indulge in Hyperbole Here

While we will spend a lot of time talking about the amazing potential of AI to revolutionize enterprise, we need to take this with the proverbial grain of salt. There is a lot of hype in this space and we do not want to indulge in that. Perusing the covers of popular magazines such as *Fortune*, *MIT Technology Review*, and *Wired* in 2018, it is really hard to avoid apparent hyperbole about the promise and perils of AI.

In some ways, we are witnessing trends that were set in motion with the Industrial Revolution, where physical labor is increasingly displaced by machine labor (what we call "botsourcing" in Chapter 1). While AI can lead to fascinating disruptions, our concern is less about the loss of traditional jobs as it is with the change in the capacities of enterprise itself.

Implementing AI doesn't merely involve installing software. It requires serious expertise, huge amounts of data, and vision as to what to program and what questions to ask. AI lacks context so without a specific set of questions to program into the AI—that fit into an overall strategy—the entire effort will likely be useless. AI cannot handle ambiguity so it needs to be programmed with very specific goals and clear decisional rules.

When we hear of well-known applications of AI like IBM's Watson or Google's AlphaGo, we could be forgiven if we form the impression that they work like magic entities with minds of their own. What we don't know is that in all cases the problems and desired outcomes are all well defined in advance by the programmers. Also, before the AlphaGo competition, the program received a lot of coaching to focus it on one specific and well-defined strategic priority. It wasn't just merely sent out to "play the game" and left to its own devices to figure out how. AI products are not generalist autodidacts, even if they do some independent "learning" within well-defined areas.

This narrow level of specificity is difficult to translate into broad business decisions. Most business problems are not games with a single outcome. Unlike with AlphaGo, in business contexts there are usually more than two players and there are often no clear rules. The outcomes of business decisions are rarely a clear win or loss. There are also many more variables—some that surprise and emerge throughout the process—and there are potentially many unexpected disruptions. Therefore, it is a lot more difficult for businesses to implement AI than it seems. AI is not a turnkey solution to anything.

Regarding the race for AI supremacy between Chinese tech giants Alibaba and Tencent, the cover of *Fortune* claims, "The winner gets the world."[5] As if from a spaghetti western where "this town ain't big enough for the two of us," the Fortune author asks, in all seriousness, "Is the world big enough for both of them?" Market research shows that Alibaba and Tencent "have made dozens of investments in smaller tech and retail players—with many focused on AI, virtual reality, and other tech that enhance shopping. The goal: to dominate both off-line and online retail for China's fast-growing middle class."[6] This is fine, but it hardly sounds like the story of global conquest. The winner doesn't get the world—it gets the Chinese middle-class retail sector—there's a big difference.

The cover of the July/August 2018 edition of the *MIT Technology Review* claims that "AI and Robots are Wreaking Economic Havoc," but then when you open up the issue, we learn that actually, "Gauging the net gain or loss of jobs due to robotics and AI is a tricky business." Candidly, despite the dramatic title, the editor of the MIT Technology Review concedes, "There is no sillier—or more disingenuous—debate in the tech community than the one over whether robots or AI will destroy jobs or, conversely, create a great abundance of new ones."[7] So, the cover line that AI and robots are wreaking economic havoc is a bit overstated.

Corporations are carefully evaluating which technologies to invest in and how to implement them, while anxiously watching competitors and latest development trends. The research firm IDC predicts that by 2021, organizations will spend $52.2 billion annually on AI- related products. Similarly, PwC estimates that by 2030, AI could contribute up to $15.7 trillion to the global economy.[8]

But what can AI, automation, deep learning, and the much-hyped advances of these technologies actually do? "We've spent years feeding neural nets vast amounts of data, teaching them to think like human brains. They're crazy smart, but they have absolutely no common sense."[9]

In important ways, AI and machine learning are not ready for prime time applications in leadership roles nor as a substitute for management decision-making. At the same time, many companies are not ready for AI or machine learning. "More often than not, companies are not ready for AI. Maybe they hired their first data scientist to less-than-stellar outcomes, or maybe data literacy is not central to their culture. But the most common scenario is that they have not yet built the infrastructure to implement (and reap the benefits of) the most basic data science algorithms and operations, much less machine learning."[10] The AI needs to grow up a little bit more, and so do we.

Prominent champions of the promise of AI and machine learning at Google admit that machine learning is still hampered by significant shortcomings. "Scientists of AI at Google's Google Brain and DeepMind units acknowledge machine learning is falling short of human cognition and [lacks the ability to find] relations between things that allow computers to generalize more broadly about the world."[11]

We do seek to push back on the hype surrounding AI on the basis that general artificial intelligence is still a long ways off. IBM Watson is nowhere near able to run an organization. According to the Chief Technology Officer of Credit Karma, Ryan Graciano, "AI is definitely over-hyped. The promise of AI is generalizable intelligence, the ability to not only learn but to reason, to pattern match, to interact, and I think what we have today is best described as artificial narrow intelligence."

That said, we believe *Artificial Narrow Intelligence (ANI)* is actually quite powerful, so long as it is utilized in the correct way to supplement and complement (but not substitute for) human general intelligence.

Unlike general intelligence, narrow intelligence "is actually amazing and deserving of the hype" because it is "very good at doing one very specific thing in a probabilistic fashion." Indeed, "ANI is transformational to your business if you use it correctly," according to Graciano.[12]

How does Credit Karma use ANI? To process the massive volumes of data about each customer, Credit Karma takes 200 million data points, "crunches" them into 2,000 factors per member, then translates those factors into a simple binary of "approved" or "not approved."[13] Data drives Credit Karma's business; its data storage grows by more than 1 terabyte per day. "We have to use data in production, for ad hoc analysis, for data science and modeling, and for online prediction, across all of our products and platform," Graciano says.

Interestingly enough, although big data analytics and ANI are key ingredients for Credit Karma's "secret sauce," Graciano believes that Credit Karma's success is actually driven by good old-fashioned customer service. "Businesses that don't master the ANI space are really going to struggle. If you work in volume, with the consumer especially, then you have to master ANI. You have to get really good at predicting what's best for your consumer and what maximizes your business outcome."[14]

Machines are far superior to humans at pattern recognition in a high-volume situation. The reason is that machines can view, process, and compare a far larger number of data and images than a human. Consider that a professor might read and evaluate 10,000 essays over a 40-year career. Meanwhile, a machine can read millions of essays in minutes and apply a few heuristics to grade the essays on a bell-shaped curve. Fed a torrent of big data, the algorithms learn and can recognize patterns with speed and precision better than any human.

However, machines by and large cannot tackle novel situations. They cannot distinguish and process things they have not seen before. A machine needs to learn from large volumes of past data that is specifically focused on that one task—whether a picture of a cat or a cancer. Humans do not. They are far more mentally flexible and capable of understanding changes in context. Humans are able to connect seemingly disparate threads and solve problems they have never seen before by reasoning through novel and complex situations. Think about the skills needed to run an organization. They do not include rote pattern recognition. They require creativity, innovation, emotional intelligence, leadership, flexible communication styles, and understanding of the organizational context.

IBM's Watson is never going to run IBM.

In this chapter, we will look at AI, machine learning (ML), neural nets, and deep learning to get a better sense of what machines can and cannot do. First, we begin with a discussion of big data, algorithms, cloud computing, and dark data to understand what it is that AI eats and how it digests that fodder when it works at all.

Big Data, Algorithms, Cloud Computing, and Dark Data

There are four breakthroughs that have changed what we can do with technology today: the growth of big data, the strengthening of algorithms, the augmentation of compute power through cloud computing, and the ability to process dark data.

Big Data

First, all "machines" (from algorithms to robots) run on data. Data is the "lifeblood" of information technology. The accumulation of *big data* has been a game changer for all industries. Big data is a term that simply means boatloads of data. More technically, it refers to data sets that are so large that the quantity can no longer fit on to the memory storage of the computers used for processing that data.

Today's data is by nature "big"—so that moving forward we may just refer to it as data. Data comes in different forms and includes data from every source imaginable. Unlike in the past, it does not need to be numerical data placed in neat rows and columns for it to be processed and utilized by industry.

"Our connected, digital world is producing data at an accelerated pace: there were 4.4 zettabytes of data in 2013, and that's projected to grow to 44 zettabytes by 2020, and IBM estimates that 90 percent of the data in existence today was produced [between 2015 and 2017]."[15]

Data is now collected, stored, communicated, aggregated, analyzed, and sold as a commodity separate and apart from the analysis and use of that data.[16]

Algorithms

Second, the application of logical, mathematical, and statistical algorithms has enabled the extraction of meaning from these big data sets. When we say *algorithm*, we mean a defined procedure for solving a problem. Particularly in the context of computing, we can use a more technical definition. An algorithm is a process or set of rules that a computer is programmed to follow when carrying out problem-solving or task-oriented operations.

Analytical algorithms have the advantage of being objective, consistent, and powerful in processing vast data sets. Compared to humans with a very limited processing capability, they can consider countless relationships between numerous variables. Human cognitive capability becomes overwhelmed even after a relatively small number of variables, whereas algorithms can easily be scaled.

Applying algorithms to large data sets can unlock previously inaccessible insights. From data we can infer probabilities or likelihoods that something will happen. We are used to this in our everyday life. We are accustomed to email filters that estimate the likelihood that an email message is spam. These systems perform well because they are fed with lots of data on which to base their predictions. Moreover, the systems are built to improve themselves over time, by keeping a tab on what are the best signals and patterns to look for as more data is fed in. For example, email filters "learn" the type of email that is spam as an increasing number of similar emails are labeled.

We are virtually flooded with data. This situation brings to mind Samuel Taylor Coleridge's *Rime of the Ancient Mariner*: "Water, water, everywhere,/ Nor any drop to drink." The speaker of the poem is lost at sea, surrounded by endless waves, none of which are potable. Without a way of parsing data, business leaders cannot turn big data into actionable intelligence. If you cannot learn from it, the data is worthless. Like saltwater, it is not fit for human consumption. Algorithms enable us to interpret big data sets and thereby derive meaningful information.

Cloud Computing

Third, the availability of today's enormous and affordable computing power via cloud computing has opened up analytical operations heretofore unavailable to all but the most well-resourced of companies. **Cloud computing** can be defined as the delivery of computing services—servers, storage, databases, networking, software, analytics, and intelligence—over the Internet in order to offer faster innovation, flexible resources, and economies of scale than what would otherwise be available by attempting to internally handle these demands.[17] Cloud computing provides advantages in terms of cost, productivity, security, speed, flexibility, performance, and more.

The availability of cloud computing means that companies can access a network of remote servers that is hosted by, for example, Amazon Web Services or Microsoft Azure, to store, manipulate, and process big data. Companies tapping into cloud computation no longer need to own, secure, and maintain local servers, which could be unreasonably expensive and cumbersome for many small and mid-sized companies.

Further, computing consumption using the cloud can be scaled up or down based on need, which means in general that consumers only pay for what they need—which is a much better position to be in versus having to buy extra servers when growing or, say, having too many servers when demand shrinks.

As a result, computing power even in ordinary non-tech companies has made giant strides forward in recent years. Computing power has enabled companies to process big data and apply algorithms to generate insights that were previously undiscovered, if not undiscoverable.

Dark Data

Fourth, we are moving beyond merely big data to the point where we can process dark data. We now have processing software that can use structured data, as a numerical sequence, and unstructured data, as in voice, text, conversation, and images. It can come in the form of POS, RFID, or GPS data, or it can be in the form of LinkedIn posts, Facebook likes, Twitter retweets, call center logs, or consumer blogs and posts. Today's analytical tools have natural language processing capabilities and are able to extract meaning from all types of data.

Emerging technology that can process *dark data* portends to be a game changer even beyond what big data analytics has already done. Dark data is unstructured and, for all practical purposes, unusable as is. "Think of it in terms of a jumble of data without labels, categorization or a sense of context—but with a certain latent value that could be unlocked with proper organization."[18]

The vast majority of data generated today is dark data. Enter Lattice, a company co-founded by Christopher Ré (recipient of a MacArthur Genius Grant and professor at Stanford), Michael Cafarella (co-creator of Hadoop and a professor at the University of Michigan), Raphael Hoffmann, and Feng Niu. Lattice is the commercialization of DeepDive, a system created at Stanford to extract value from dark data.

Lattice basically puts dark data in order to make it viable for analysis by machine learning. There are tremendous potential applications of Lattice to enhance the development of other AI technology. As we have pointed out before, garbage in, garbage out. Current AI is limited by the data it is fed. The biggest commercial applications of dark data analysis are probably in the business-to-business context. Lattice will probably be making deals with other AI owners to create "more useful data feeds." Other public-oriented potential applications include "international policing and crime solving, such as this work in trying to uncover human trafficking; in medical research; and to help organize and parse paleontological research."[19]

New processing capabilities, computing power, and storage of technology—coupled with lower costs—have permitted companies to manage far larger quantities of data than before. As a result, companies can take advantage of the growing volume of data, because without processing capability actionable intelligence could not be extracted from these large data sets.

Using sophisticated algorithms Wal-Mart learned that customers prefer to stock up on the Pop Tarts during a hurricane[20]; e-Bay identified which web designs generate highest sales[21]; and Progressive Insurance learned how to optimize insurance premiums by individual risk categories.[22]

Data Is the Foundation for AI and Machine Learning

Data serves as the foundation for AI and machine learning, without which the augmented powers of technology are unattainable.[23]

Reference to *Maslow's Hierarchy of Needs* as a construct from psychology might help illustrate this point.[24] You probably have passing familiarity with Maslow's hierarchy, in which human needs are ordered from most basic to most sophisticated, typically illustrated in a pyramid. At the base of Maslow's pyramid are *physiological* (food, shelter, sleep). Once those basic needs are met, humans are driven by the need for *safety* (security and freedom from existential fear). Then humans begin to need *love* (trust, intimacy, acceptance, and friendship). Once humans have these basic foundations in place, they begin to be motivated by *esteem* (dignity and reputation). Lastly, at the peak of the pyramid, humans are driven by the need for *self-actualization* (flourishing).

Think of data as the base of the pyramid, like food and shelter is for humans. Think of AI as the peak of the pyramid, like self-actualization is for human psychological development (see Figure 3.1).

At the base of the Data Science Hierarchy of Needs is the collection of data. Once data is collected, then it must be stored. Once stored, it can be explored and cleaned. At that stage, the data is ready to be analyzed and aggregated. Finally, only after processing the data in this fashion are we ready to glean actionable insights from data, including feeding it to

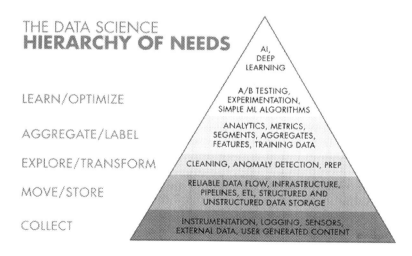

Figure 3.1 The data science hierarchy of needs.

Source: Monica Rogati's Data Science Hierarchy of Needs Pyramid.

machine learning algorithms. Then, at the top of the hierarchy data can ultimately be used to train AI using deep learning methods.

The parallel with Maslow's hierarchy of human needs is that, generally speaking, one cannot move up the pyramid toward the highest potential for human or AI functioning until more basic underlying needs are satisfied.

AI, Machine Learning, Deep Learning, and Neural Networks

The popular press is filled with references to artificial intelligence, machine learning, deep learning, and neural networks, and they are often used without clear definitions. In this section we will try to distinguish them with examples of each. While the concepts have been around for some time in theory, it is only recently that we have been able to reach a scale of computing and size of data sets needed to make machines "intelligent" in a meaningful sense. Bringing AI to life really began with the first computers in the 1940s.

Although these initial algorithms were unable to make any decisions of their own, they were able to process data, make calculations, and remember information.

As technology has evolved, so has the ability to create more complex machines. Coupling this with the fact that over the past few decades we have developed a better understanding of how the human brain actually works and processes information from a neurological point of view, we have been able to begin to encode these processes into algorithms in a manner that emulates human brain activity. For clarity, we will define artificial intelligence, machine learning, deep learning, and neural networks here.[25] At the risk of oversimplifying, the evolution of computer learning can be summarized as set forth in Table 3.1.[26]

Table 3.1 Computer learning methods

Artificial intelligence	Programming that allows machines to perform tasks that make them seem "intelligent."
Machine learning	Branch of AI where machines learn from data without being programmed.
Neural net	Subset of ML where machines can determine if they are right or not.
Deep learning	Algorithms that mimic human cognitive processes.

Artificial Intelligence

Artificial intelligence (AI) is programming that allows machines to perform tasks that make them seem "intelligent." Artificial intelligence was formally "founded" by John McCarthy and Marvin Minsky in the wake of a watershed interdisciplinary conference at Dartmouth in the summer of 1956, covering such topics as mathematics, logic, and game theory.[27] As a broad field of study, artificial intelligence concerns "techniques that can be implemented in machines, enabling them to reason, lean, and act intelligently[;] the overarching science that is concerned with intelligent algorithms, whether or not they learn from data."[28] These algorithms are complex and allow machines to go beyond doing a single, repetitive motion but rather they seem intelligent because they can adapt to different situations. Basic AI systems just process data, recognize and match patterns. AI is seen in common computations such as stock-trading systems or on-demand music streaming services. For the service to make a decision about which new songs or artists to recommend, machine learning algorithms match the listener's preferences with other listeners who have similar musical taste.

Machine Learning

Machine learning is an advanced branch of AI. It is based on the idea that machines could in theory go beyond just processing data, or simply following instructions or heuristics, and as such could "learn" on their own from the data they are fed. In other words, "machine learning is a subfield of AI devoted to algorithms that learn from data."[29]

To say software runs machine learning algorithms means it can utilize pattern recognition and matching to "teach" itself based on new data. Pattern recognition applies not only to symbol sets (numbers and letters) but also to images.[30]

Machine learning means that an algorithm can execute *Bayesian inferences*, which is a method of statistical inference that allows for the sharpening of the probability of a given hypothesis as additional information becomes available. Bayesian inferences can be used for business analysis in a number of ways.[31]

Machine learning includes, among other things, supervised learning, unsupervised learning, and anomaly detection. By using machine learning methods, we can harvest insights from large data sets without the manpower typically associated with massive computational efforts; as such, machine learning is now a key tool in "search engines, DNA sequencing, stock market analysis, and robot locomotion."[32]

Machine learning is based on software codes that program machines to perform a specific function in response to certain data input—then progressively improve at doing that function as more data becomes available.

For example, machine learning allows computers to look at text and determine whether the content is "positive" or "negative." They can figure out if a song is more likely to make people sad or happy, even if the machine itself is unable to feel those emotions. Some of these machine learning algorithms can even make their own compositions that are based on pieces they've listened to, by combining and rearranging the notes in melodically repetitive ways.

Machine learning fuels all sorts of automated tasks—from monitoring data security to tracking malware to optimizing stock trades. It is also the basis of virtual assistants that enable the algorithms to improve as they interact with their clients. Researchers at SAP explain that machine learning is already helping enterprises to: (1) personalize customer service, (2) improve customer loyalty and retention, (3) hire the right people, (4) automate finance, (5) measure brand exposure, (6) detect fraud, (7) perform predictive maintenance, and (8) smooth supply chains.[33]

The contemporary discussion of AI and the transformative possibilities for enterprise seem enormous. However, the AI currently being employed is actually very limited. Almost all of it is through what is called supervised learning that entails software that conducts A → B experiments. What does this mean?

The logic is simple. It means that input data (A), let's say thousands of photos of cats, are given to an algorithm to learn the patterns of the object. Then the algorithm is asked to provide a response (B), such as whether a new photo shown is that of a cat. It requires the algorithm to determine whether the new photo falls in the patterns it has developed from all the other photos that have been provided. Obviously, human intelligence does much more than simply make such comparisons.

Researchers are working on more sophisticated ways that AI can learn. Deep learning and neural networks, forms of machine intelligence we discuss next, will surely improve these processes. However, two shortcomings remain.

First, the algorithms require huge amounts of data. According to Andrew Ng, "You need to show the system a lot of examples of both A and B. For instance, building a photo tagger requires anywhere from tens to hundreds of thousands of pictures (A) as well as labels or tags telling you if there are people in them (B). Building a speech recognition system requires tens of thousands of hours of audio (A) together with the transcripts (B)."[34]

Just consider the size of the data that has to be fed to the algorithm, and the need for the data to be scrubbed to avoid error. There is also a significant potential for a bias of "data omission." This is where outliers and exceptions are not included as they are not common in the data. The algorithm then has a hard time recognizing them.

For example, let's say that a grocer has automated the quality control of strawberries. It has fed tens of thousands of photos of strawberries to the algorithm, which needs to focus on identifying "good" and "bad" strawberries. However, the photos of "bad" strawberries are less common. They also have tremendous more variation than "good" or "perfect" strawberries. Often judgment, which AI lacks, is required to notice that there is something very unusual about something as simple as strawberry. This is a shortcoming.

Notice that the algorithms of AI are binary in nature—yes or no, good or bad, or matching "this" to "that." Although these become much more sophisticated with machine learning, it is still critical to identify and be creative about selecting both A and B. Also, in more complex tasks, A and B are part of a sequence that feed and nest into other A and B decisions. It is humans that have to provide AI with the data it needs and figure out the A → B relationship (see Table 3.2).

Second, the question becomes how to incorporate such narrow answers into the broader organizational decisions and strategy. Context matters and algorithms do not understand context. In fact, an algorithm does not "understand."

Machine learning may eventually get a big upgrade from applications of quantum computing.[35,36]

Table 3.2 How machines learn

Decision	Question (A)	Process	Output (B)
Photo recognition	Is this a cat?	Matching photo against data base	Yes or no
College entrance	Is the test score above the cutoff?	Compare numbers	Yes or no
Loan application	Can the loan be repaid?	Compute risk score	Yes or no
Machine safety	Is the part going to fail?	Monitor sensor data	Yes or no
Linguistic translation	English to French?	Compare words	Translated phrase
Self-driving car	What is the position of the car with respect to this external object?	Monitoring sensors and cameras	Automated movement

Neural Networks

Neural networks are a subset of machine learning methods that classify information by, in theory, mimicking the way our brain structures information. "Say you wanted a machine to teach itself to recognize daisies. First you'd code some algorithmic 'neurons,' connecting them in layers... You'd show an image of a daisy to the first layer, and its neurons would fire or not fire based on whether the image resembled the examples of daisies it had seen before. The signal would move on to the next layer, where the process would be repeated. Eventually, the layers would winnow down to one final verdict."

Once trained, a neural network can look at pictures, recognize the elements in the pictures, and then classify the pictures according to their structural features. The algorithm has a feedback loop that allows it to learn. "At first, the neural net is just guessing blindly; it starts life a blank slate, more or less. The key is to establish a useful feedback loop. Every time the AI misses a daisy, that set of neural connections weakens the links that led to an incorrect guess; if it's successful, it strengthens them. Given enough time and enough daisies, the neural net gets more accurate."[37] The machine finds out whether or not its decisions were right and changes its approach to become better and better in getting the "right" answer.

Although this approach to neural net training of AI has been popular, it is not without its detractors. Gary Marcus, professor of psychology and neuroscience at New York University, claims that the method of starting with a naïve network and training by repetition "assumes that humans build their intelligence purely by observing the world around them, and that machines can too," which is just not true about humans.[38]

In other words, the popular neural net approach to artificial intelligence is premised on the *tabula rasa* (Latin for "blank slate") theory of human intelligence. Articulated in classical liberal thought by Aristotle's treatise *De Anima* ("*On the Soul*") and John Locke's "*An Essay Concerning Human Understanding*," the tabula rasa concept suggests the mind is born like fresh parchment, without concepts, and only through experience does it develop a mental map of the world.

On the contrary, Noam Chomsky and others contend that humans are not born *tabula rasa* but rather we are born with millions of years of evolved "wetware," "wired to learn, programmed to master language and interpret the physical world."[39] We will get into how machine capabilities dramatically fall short of certain human capabilities later in the section on what machines cannot do.

An example of neural networks in practice comes from OpenAI's newest robotic system. OpenAI is an artificial intelligence research company co-founded by Elon Musk. The technology replicates human behavior by imitation and impressively only needs one demonstration of a task to do so.

OpenAI's imitation program relies upon two neural networks. The first is a "vision network" that "analyzes an image from the robot's camera to determine the location of objects in reality."[40] The "eyes" were previously trained by feeding them "hundreds of thousands of simulated images, each featuring various permutations of lighting, textures, and objects." The second neural network is an "imitation network," with the purpose of determining the intention behind a human task that was observed by the vision network.

Of course, the imitation network was also trained by being fed hundreds of thousands of simulated demonstrations so that it could develop the requisite pattern recognition capability. Once both the vision and imitation neural networks were adequately trained, they only needed to "observe" a single demonstration in reality in order to determine where certain objects were spatially located, as well as the purpose behind the actions performed with those objects.

In this case, OpenAI researchers showed the neural network an example of a human stacking colored blocks in a certain manner. The neural network imitated the task successfully, with only one demonstration. "Even more remarkably, the system was able to complete the task even if the starting parameters didn't quite match up. For example, the blocks didn't need to be in the exact same location as the demonstration for the system to know how to stack them. If a blue block went on top of a white block in the demonstration, the system replicated that task, even if the starting location of the blocks wasn't identical."[41]

We would be forgiven for asking why all the fuss over stacking colored blocks. This is literally child's play! Well, AI researchers would tell you that these incremental steps in neural network recognition and imitation capabilities promise tremendous strides in the future. Imagine a chef demonstrating how to prepare a gourmet meal for a neural network bot, which can then prepare the identical meal based on a single demonstration. Now imagine a mechanical engineer putting together a complex piece of machinery in front of a neural network bot, which can then fabricate that machinery after a single demonstration.

The implications of this kind of AI are truly staggering and wonderful. Once the machine learns how to perform a task by recognizing the spatial location and unique identity of objects in its environment and the purpose behind the manipulation of those objects, it can then refine its performance.

Unlike humans, machines do not get tired, they do not need a coffee break, and they do not get carpal tunnel syndrome from arduous physical repetition. A neural network-powered meal preparation machine could feed thousands without taking a single smoke break. A neural network-powered fabricator could assemble thousands of pieces of complex machinery without losing a finger.

Indeed, some robots are already working so fast that manufacturers have to create vacuum-sealed environments so that air molecules do not impede the machine's manipulations of parts. The machines are moving objects through space so quickly that air resistance is the limiting factor. It baffles the imagination to think what manufacturing will look like in twenty years, with 3D printing added to the mix.

Deep Learning

Basic machine learning uses algorithms to describe data, learn from that data, and make informed decisions based on what it has learned from the data. The algorithm can learn. However, it cannot correct itself. By contrast, *deep learning* is a subset of machine learning where the algorithms not only learn, but they can determine—on their own—whether a prediction is accurate. The algorithm is designed to continually analyze data with a logic structure similar to how humans draw conclusions.

A great example of deep learning is Google's AlphaGo. "Deep learning is self-education for machines; you feed an AI huge amounts of data, and eventually it begins to discern patterns all by itself."[42]

Google created a computer program that learned to play the abstract board game called Go, a game known for requiring sharp intellect and intuition. AlphaGo's deep learning model learned how to play at a level never seen before. Once programmed, the algorithm played without being told when it should make a specific move. That is the same self-learning process that helps Netflix know which show a viewer wants to watch next, or how Facebook can recognize faces in photos. It is also how a customer service representative can determine whether customers are satisfied with their support before they even take a customer satisfaction survey.

Researchers at the MIT Media Lab are developing an AI training technique called *reinforcement learning* to help provide glioblastoma cancer patients the right dosage of cancer treatment—that is, the *minimum effective* dosage. Reinforcement learning derives its name from psychologist B. F. Skinner's reinforcement theory of motivation used in behavioral conditioning techniques. The way reinforcement learning is applied to AI in this context is that, "After the AI prescribed a dose, it would check a computer model capable of predicting how likely a dose is to shrink a tumor. When the AI prescribed a tumor-shrinking dosage, it received a reward. However, if the AI simply prescribed the maximum dose all the time, it received a penalty."[43]

This technique is more nuanced than other machine learning models that simply encourage the AI to win a game. With cancer treatment, the doctor needs to balance the patient quality of life, the intensity of the prescribed treatment, and the medical efficacy of the care. Too high of a dose might effectively shrink the tumor size, but at the cost of causing debilitating pain to the patient. Principal Investigator Pratik Shah says, "If all we want to do is reduce the mean tumor diameter, and let it take whatever actions it wants, it will administer drugs irresponsibly. We need to reduce the harmful actions it takes to get to that outcome."[44]

It is important to remember, however, that the algorithm is software code. It is taught to respond as either a yes or no, happy or sad, good or bad. However, it has no idea what it is looking at. It cannot give interpretation beyond what it has been programmed. Successful AI applications are extremely specialized and narrow, based on a massive amount of data. However, they cannot generalize across similar categories or connect apparently disparate areas. A self-driving car AI cannot move the yard. An AI that can diagnose melanoma cannot diagnose other diseases. Narrow AI is all we have right now. It may be all we ever have. It may be all we need.

What Machines Can Do

AI, machine learning, neural nets, and deep learning promise to transform work processes in the near term. In many respects, AI is already doing so. By deploying AI strategically, enterprises can improve financial performance and reduce risk, broadly speaking. But we need to be mindful that business processes and managerial decision-making cannot simply be delegated to a machine.

There is universal agreement that humans and technology each have their unique strengths and weaknesses (see Table 3.3).

Let's review some unique capabilities of extant artificial intelligence.

Table 3.3 What machines can and cannot do

Machines are capable of	Machines are not capable of
Processing large amounts of data	Responding to unexpected changes
Handling complex relationships	Overcoming limitations in the data
Considering many variables	Reaching innovative solutions
Consistent and objective analysis	Thinking creatively or originally
Precise and accurate analysis	Going beyond "local" to "global" optima
Scaling to larger and smaller data sets	Explaining decision outputs

Pattern Recognition

Technology and AI are best at pattern recognition. Feed a computer thousands of images of something and it is unparalleled in finding and recognizing that pattern. Your spellchecker recognizes that the letters that make up "teh" do not fall in the same pattern as "the." Credit card fraud detection looks for normal purchasing patterns and recognizes when something falls out of the pattern.

Many of the tasks being done by machine intelligence are routine and repetitive. These algorithms are typically trained on the data set. As the models get better, are based on more intensive and detailed data, their ability to use new data to make predictions or put things into categories improves over time. This is exactly how spam filters work—they identify patterns and can filter out junk emails.

Pattern recognition is what is used to determine a customer's digital habits—basically, by looking for patterns, an artificial intelligence can determine what a consumer's interests are by recognizing patterns of content when the consumer tends to linger on certain websites or shop for certain items. It is AI that helps your favorite streaming service provider recommend a new prestige drama after you finish watching *Game of Thrones,* as it recognizes your pattern of consumptions and makes a prediction about what you are likely to enjoy. Similarly, Amazon Prime can use customer buying and ordering habits to predict when the next order of laundry detergent will be placed.

More advanced versions can work across multiple IT systems. They can be used for automating tasks that reach into multiple systems to update multiple records and handle customer communication. This is especially true in financial services where this technology is used to update customer files with address changes, replace lost ATM cards, and reconcile discrepancies in billing systems.

Pattern recognition can become more sophisticated with AI and machine learning where recognition extends to images and voice recognition. These programs are designed to learn and improve with more data. Machine learning can be used to identify "probabilistic matches." This is the likelihood that data that is not exactly identical is associated with the same person or company across different databases. GE used this technology to integrate supplier data while scrubbing for duplicate entries. The company was able to save $80 million in its first year alone by eliminating redundancies.[45]

Pattern recognition with deep learning can be a billion-dollar skill with life-saving potential. Take new drug development in the pharmaceutical industry, for example. The cost of bringing a new drug to market is about $1.6 billion because the discovery process alone (not to mention the regulatory approval process) involves on average 1,000 people, working for 12–15 years, testing tens of thousands of compounds, to determine (among other things) which molecules will bind together using trial and error as well as the good old-fashioned process of elimination.[46] Enter AtomNet, a deep learning AI software created by San Francisco startup Atomwise, able to streamline new drug discovery by predicting molecular interactions. The result is a hope for the invention of human health and safety-enhancing drugs at substantially reduced discovery time and cost.

Processing Velocity, Accuracy, Volume, and Consistency

When it comes to data processing, robots are simply much faster, more accurate, and more consistent than humans. This skill set has potentially enormous implications in certain commercial settings. Take inventory management in the context of big box retail.

According to Jeremy King, the Chief Technology Officer for Wal-Mart US and e-commerce, "If you are running up and down the aisle and you want to decide if we are out of Cheerios or not, a human doesn't do that job very well, and they don't like it."[47] King says robots, in certain capacities related to inventory management, are roughly 50% more productive than their human counterparts because they can scan shelves and stock items significantly more accurately and three times faster.[48] Store employees only have time to scan shelves about twice a week whereas robots can do it continuously.

The move to use robots is part of Wal-Mart's broader effort to digitize stores and make shopping faster. Customers want speed and human workers cannot provide the same levels of efficiency as robots. In the past year, Wal-Mart has installed giant "pickup towers" that operate like self-service kiosks and where customers can pick up their online orders. The company has also sped up the checkout process by allowing customers to scan their own purchases, and it has digitized operations like pharmacy and financial services in stores. Wal-Mart has also been testing drones for home delivery, curbside pickup, and checking warehouse inventories.

The idea of installing robots and automating retail is nothing new. We have seen Amazon use Kiva robots and drones, thereby automating almost every aspect of its delivery system. Machine learning is now the cornerstone of these AI applications as it allows the programs to learn, leaving the former restrictions of coded actions behind. Whereas formerly every machine action had to be programmed in one specific way, machines are now able to learn from humans. For example, the robotics innovative corporation Boston Dynamics has developed machines that are able to independently fulfill order-picking tasks—and learn from humans regarding specific movements and floor layouts to create seamless movement.

Connect Complex Systems

A huge advancement is that technology is allowing previously independent systems to be increasingly connected and able to cooperate in order to perform self-sufficiently. Consider the example of cruise control in vehicles. Initially cruise control was meant to maintain a constant pre-set speed of a vehicle. Today, it is coupled with other technologies that work seamlessly together to create AI navigation.

In the first generation of cruise control applications, the system steadily maintained a predefined and constant speed. Subsequently, other technologies were connected, such as GPS navigation and the automated gearbox, allowing vehicles to use dynamic, rather than static, cruise control. The system was now able to follow a preceding vehicle on a preset distance. This is commercially applied in road transportation in modern-day platooning system, where "virtual road trains" are formed by trucks following each other automatically at a short distance. Then the next generation of cruise control systems connects even more systems and is more intelligent. It is able to anticipate the route characteristics by GPS positioning in combination with map material. This allows the system to decelerate before downhill passages or to accelerate and downshift before uphill road segments. The driver is only steering and supervising the system in total. This is a result of connecting systems.

Another example comes from connecting entire business systems. For the Coca-Cola Company, maker of Minute Maid and Simply Orange, it means an entire global "juice machine" is connected and run by machines. Coca-Cola has algorithms that "talk" to one another, from the orange groves to the grocery stores. An algorithm is even used to engineer the taste of its orange juice. A complex algorithm called Black Book has determined the optimal taste for orange juice. With each new batch of oranges the algorithm decides the exact levels of sugar, acidity, or pulp that must be added to keep the taste at its best. The algorithm has detailed data from more than 600 flavors that make up the "taste" that the customers consider orange juice. The taste of every batch is then compared to the ideal and appropriate ingredients added to the batch to adjust to the ideal flavor.

Algorithm-fed data from satellite images of fruit groves ensure the fruit is picked at the optimal time for Coca-Cola's bottling plants. A computer model directs everything from picking schedules of oranges to the blending of ingredients needed to maintain a consistent taste. The algorithm also includes external factors, such as current prices, weather patterns, and crop yield. The next time you see the orange juice at the grocery store consider that every aspect—from squeezing the oranges to flavoring, bottling, and delivery—has been done through an algorithm. Jim Horrisberger, director of procurement, explains it like this: "You take Mother Nature and standardize it."[49]

What Machines Cannot Do

According to research by Bloomberg, companies are too reluctant to discuss the limits of AI.[50] It may have become taboo for corporate executives to discuss the shortcomings of AI because touting the powers and potentials of AI during earnings calls is likely to give stock prices a nice bump as it bolsters investor confidence in the future. We have no desire to be cynical, but we feel it important to understand the limitations of AI, machine learning, neural nets, and deep learning if we want to strategically deploy these technologies in enterprise.

Lacking Common Sense

An AI may be able to recognize that within a photo, there is a man on a horse. However, lacking common sense, the AI might not appreciate that the figures are actually a bronze sculpture of a man on a horse, not an actual man on an actual horse.

The lack of common sense in machines may change eventually, especially if Doug Lenat has anything to do with it. Lenat is leading Cyc, a project that for the last 34 years has "employed a team of engineers and philosophers to code 25 million rules of general common sense."[51]

Even after three decades of programming and millions of lines of code already built in, the extent of progress is limited. The Cyc AI should be able to discern that water is wet and that if your shirt is wet, it has probably been raining—and this handy little trick only cost about $200 million to pull off.[52]

Of course, learning by direct, spoon-fed programming may lead to better outcomes than learning by crowdsourcing, as the introductory example of Tay learning racism by osmosis demonstrates.

Suppose a person tells us that a particular photo shows people playing Frisbee in the park. We naturally assume that this person can answer questions like the following: What is the shape of a Frisbee? Roughly how far can a person throw a Frisbee? Can a person eat a Frisbee? What is the minimum number of people required to play Frisbee? Can a three-month-old person play Frisbee? Is today's weather suitable for playing Frisbee?

Computers that can label images like "people playing Frisbee in a park" have no chance of answering those questions. Besides the fact that they can only label more images and cannot answer questions at all, "they have no idea what a person is, that parks are usually outside, that people have ages, that weather is anything more than how it makes a photo look."[53]

Consider the lesson offered by Margaret Mitchell, a research scientist at Google. Mitchell helps develop computers that can communicate about what they see and understand. As she feeds images and data to AI, she asks the AI questions about what it "sees." The AI was fed with lots of input about fun things and activities. When Mitchell showed an image of a koala bear, the AI said, "cute creature." But when she showed the AI a picture of a house violently burning down, the AI said, "that is awesome!"

Mitchell realized that the AI selected this response due to the orange and red colors it scanned in the photo. Orange and red were frequently associated with positive responses in the previously input data set. Remember that even the responses offered by AI are those that are programmed—and AI does not understand context. Mitchell points out that because AI works from the data we give it there are inevitable gaps, blind spots, and biases we subconsciously encode into AI. She asks us to carefully consider technological capability and keep in mind that these are just mathematical algorithms that work from the data we give them but do not have actual understanding.[54]

No Understanding of Context

There is increasing awareness that machine learning algorithms encode biases and discrimination into outcomes.[55] After all, algorithms simply look for patterns in the data. They have no opinion of their own. Whatever is embedded in the data is what the algorithms will repeat.

We now have technology that analyzes human physical characteristics and can crunch through the data and focus on gender or race. Other than the obvious ethical issues, this can be very limiting for companies. Focusing exclusively on the past does not allow creative expansion into new markets, new customers, and innovative products.

Machine learning algorithms may unintentionally target or omit certain segments of the population. In her best-selling book *Weapons of Math Destruction: How Big Data Increases Inequality and Threatens Democracy*, Cathy O'Neill describes several cases of unintentional bias in education (on how teachers are evaluated), financial services (on how certain minorities were denied services), and retail (where only certain demographic were targeted).[56]

Much of the data used is collected automatically through sensors, connected devices, and social media channels. However, blindly accepting the data without human intervention can lead to massive biases. Consider Mark Graham and colleagues who studied tweets on "flood" or "flooding" to see if they could predict the impact of Hurricane Sandy.[57] It turns out that the vast number of tweets came from Manhattan, giving the mistaken impression that it may have been the site of the most damage. Most flooding losses actually occurred in New Jersey. Manhattan has a denser population with more people tweeting about their experiences. This is just one example of how digitally derived data points can skew our assessment of reality. We are dismayed that this even really needs to be said, but it's important to remember that what's "trending" on social media does not always reflect ground truth.

Another well-known example is when Google trends overestimated incidences of flu based on the most popular search terms. The theory goes that if people get the flu, they conduct a Google search of "flu" and related terms, and thereby, we can extrapolate how many people have the flu based on how frequently "flu" and related search terms were entered into the search engine. It turns out this was a misleading method of gathering this data because people searched for terms related to the flu *after* they saw flu-related news broadcasts on TV. Searching for "flu" and related terms reflected how often the flu made it into the news, rather than how often flu cases actually occurred in reality. The Centers for Disease Control and Prevention estimates flu incidences via *field surveys*, not Google searches. It bears repeating that what happens in the digital world is not always an accurate reflection of what is happening in reality. Without human interpretation and context, these types of outcomes can completely mislead an organization.

As smart as AI has become, it still lacks context and thus possesses an extremely narrow kind of intelligence. Intelligence so narrow it is filed down to a razor-sharp edge—not the kind of thing you can lean on.

Without doubt, AI applications have tremendous value. However, these applications are narrow, task-specific, and siloed into different domains. An AI could be programmed to identify "cancer" versus "noncancer" based on MRI scans but have absolutely nothing else of value to offer oncologists. Tremendous amounts of data must be provided to address very limited questions.

Humans like to play and have fun, both of which are keys to creative thinking. Google knows this very well. It encourages employees to play, to be innovative, creative, spend at least 20% of their time on side projects, and even take naps.[58] "The philosophy is very simple," said Mr. Nevill-Manning, head of engineering at the Manhattan facility. "Google's success depends on innovation and collaboration."[59]

It is unclear how companies could get AI to think innovatively because they lack an appreciation of context. AI can look at patterns of what is labeled as "positive" and, by recognizing patterns, label certain activities as such. However, whether something is fun or desirable is such a nuanced human judgment that it is unlikely to be programmed. There are many aspects to fun, for instance. Consider the invention of Play-Doh, the brightly colored nontoxic modeling clay. It was accidently invented in 1955 by Joseph and Noah McVicker, while trying to make a wallpaper cleaner. It just felt good to touch it, mold it, and play with it. Anyone who has babysat a toddler would intuit that the squishy, colorful substance would make for a fun child's toy. The idea for a toy emerged and it was quickly picked up by a toy manufacturer. More than 700 million pounds of Play-Doh have been sold since.

The point is this: we do not think an algorithm can recognize a "fun" product or otherwise make inferences that require understanding of context. Even if an AI invented something "fun" by happenstance permutation, it would still require a human user to validate the invention as such.

Data Hungry and Brittle

Neural nets require far too much data to really compare them to human intellects, and this can be a limiting factor. "In most cases, each neural net requires thousands or millions of examples to learn from. Worse, each time you want a neural net to recognize a new type of item, you have to start from scratch."[60] Compare that to a toddler, and we see that the human intellect is far more fluid, supple, and faster at acquiring new knowledge: You can show a kid a picture of a car a few times, and they can recognize one when they see one on the street; they can also make the inference that a school bus and a tractor are also kinds of cars.[61]

Beyond being voracious consumers of data for limited learning gains, algorithmic problem-solving output is also severely hampered by the quality of data it is fed. Algorithms are also severely brittle: "Without the right rules about the world, the AI can get flummoxed. That's why scripted chatbots are so frustrating; if they haven't been explicitly told how to answer a question they have no way to reason it out."[62] This means an AI cannot respond to unexpected change if this has not been programmed into the algorithm. Today's business world is filled with disruptions and events—from physical to economic to political—and the unforeseen require interpretation and flexibility. AI cannot do that.

Researchers are pushing forward with ways to "simulate 'neuromodulation,' an instant network-wide adjustment of adaptability that allows humans to sop up information when something novel or important happens."[63] Until they reach that goal, however, AI will be both too voracious in its data demand and too rigid to tell when new information being introduced is more meaningful than information it already possesses.

No Intuition

In this section we want to introduce a concept we call "intuitive physics." This is an extension of the common understanding of intuition from folk psychology as the ability to make correct inferences based on limited information using "gut feeling." We are extending this intuition to more complex areas, such as physics. We contend that humans use intuition to navigate the physical world, doing things like playing tennis and crossing the street without a thought—things that would require a robot so much processing power that it is almost inconceivable we would engineer them.

Imagine you are an amateur tennis player attempting to return a serve. The tennis ball is speeding toward you at say 50–60 miles per hour (professional tennis players serve the ball over 100 miles per hour). The lines on the tennis ball are spinning in a left-leaning tilt. Without thinking, you shift your feet to position your center of gravity behind the ball. Without thinking, you anticipate the ball will bounce to your left, rather than in a straight line, because of the spin imparted to it by your opponent's technique. Without thinking, you begin to pull your racquet behind you to give yourself room to swing. Without thinking, you hit the ball in an upward stroke, so that you impart topspin to the ball so that it bounds forward when it lands. You strike the ball toward the far court, away from your opponent, again without consciously deciding to do so, because the objective is to place the ball where your opponent cannot successfully return it. Without thinking, you are "calculating" where the ball will go based on incomplete information. Without thinking, you are optimizing your physical maneuvers based on application of the rules of tennis and strategic considerations geared toward winning the point. Spin. Velocity. Angles. Wind resistance. The location of your opponent on the opposite side of the net. The friction of the ball interacting with the court when it bounces. Your own body weight. Your own speed and dexterity. All of these variables are interacting with each other to determine where the ball will go and how best to make contact. The calculations are performed in a matter of seconds. And they are performed with no conscious thought. They are performed whether you are a math geek or a meathead.

The mathematical description of the movement of the ball may require physics with partial differential equations. Suppose you can return the serve, but you don't know calculus. Even if you were the winner of the prestigious Fields Medal in mathematics, there is no way you could actually do the computation necessary to describe mathematically the movement of the ball in time to return the serve at game speed. And yet, somehow we return serve. Humans do the equivalent of this in our lives every day—from crossing the street in time so as to not get hit by an oncoming bus, to applying just the right amount of force to flip on a light switch. We believe this skill is unique to biological life forms and is the consequence of evolutionary pressures to successfully navigate the physical environment. We call it *intuitive physics*.

Now imagine building a humanoid robot for the sole purpose of playing tennis. Imagine the sheer complexity of math required to write the code needed to return serve. Imagine how much processing power would be required for the robot's CPU to perform the calculation fast enough to actually return the serve. Engineering a robot capable of moving around the court and swinging the racket would be its own monumental challenge—but the mental functions required to ably perform a sport at game speed is daunting in its own right. The tennis example is a thought experiment designed to illustrate the power of human cognition and perception when compared to the mechanistic workings of the robotic mind in real life situations.

Some day perhaps we will design an AI that can perform computations with limited information, translating visual data into mathematical representations, and manipulating a physical embodiment so as to act on the input in real time—then we could have an android tennis player. But designing that seems like a silly way to spend a billion dollars.

Local Optima

Algorithms can also get trapped in *local optima*. In the context of computer science and mathematics, the best solution to a problem within a relatively small neighborhood of possible solutions is described as the local optimum, in contrast to the global optimum, which is the best of all possible solutions. For example, a computer program may find solutions that are best to alternatives that are close by in the search process but fail to find a far greater solution that exists in a more distant neighborhood. The reason why is because this would require understanding context and changing context, or thinking creatively about the problem and potential solutions. Humans can do that. They can connect seemingly disparate concepts and come up with "out-of-the-box" thinking that solves problems in novel ways.

Black Box Decision-Making

Further, algorithms and AI often cannot explain themselves. Even researchers who train AI systems often cannot understand how the algorithm reached a specific conclusion. Even if it gets the right answer, it cannot explain why it is right. This is very problematic when an AI is used in the context of medical diagnoses, for example, or in any context in which the decision has legal consequences. Even if the AI is right, people will not trust its analytical output when making high-stakes decisions until it can explain itself.

Another problem with AI is that often what the algorithm has "learned" remains a mystery to the programmers. Neural networks, for example, respond iteratively to the data "learning" as they train; however, the programmers often do not understand what the algorithm has learned at each interval. They do not know the logic behind the decision and cannot justify it.

As New York University Professor Gary Marcus explains, deep learning systems are a black box because they have millions or even billions of parameters, identifiable to their developers only in terms of their geography within a complex neural network.[64] "The workings of any machine-learning technology are inherently more opaque, even to computer scientists, than a hand-coded system."[65] That's because the reasoning that goes into a deep learning algorithm's output is "embedded in the behavior of thousands of simulated neurons, arranged into dozens or even hundreds of intricately interconnected layers."[66]

Apple is working hard to make its AI system, known as Siri, capable of "explaining" its behavior. From recommending dinner at a certain restaurant to more high-stakes military applications (whether to fire a missile or move troops), we need to know why AI is making a recommendation. Apple's Director of AI Research Ruslan Salakhutdinov appreciates that "explainability" is fundamental to the future of meaningful applications of machine intelligence: "It's going to introduce trust."[67]

It would be imprudent to apply inexplicable AI recommendations in a business setting. Most executives need to stand behind their decisions by providing justification in terms of evidence and reasons. It is difficult to do so when one trusts an algorithm one does not understand, the accuracy of which is entirely dependent on whether the data input was correct. Further, if a business decision is challenged by shareholders, regulators, or the plaintiff in a personal injury lawsuit, the company defending itself is going to need to be able to explain pertinent decisions. "Our in-house AI system made me do it" is not going to be a satisfactory defense in case of legal challenges. Until we can pry open the "black box" of deep learning algorithmic reasoning, it's outputs are sphinxlike, inscrutable, and provide no more legally defensible reason for action than reliance on the cryptic pronouncements of a Magic 8 Ball toy.

We discuss legal issues when AI goes wrong in more depth in Chapter 6.

Garbage in, Garbage Out

How do Uber or Lyft minimize wait times once you order a car? How does Gmail categorize your emails into primary, social, and promotion inboxes, as well as labeling emails as important? How do banks decipher and convert handwriting on checks to allow check deposits through apps? Via pattern recognition and self-learning algorithms that work off of data. By feeding the algorithm tremendous amounts of both structured and unstructured data, the system learns by observing patterns. There is no AI without big data.[68] This also means intelligence in machines is *only as good as the data they are given.*

If the data fed into a machine is corrupted or inaccurate, then so too will the machine output be corrupted or inaccurate. An AI system that exists on a separate server isolated from the Internet would not be able to fact-check the data being fed into it. It would not be able to consult with an authority figure, or ask a friend to verify the accuracy or reliability of the input. This feature poses a large obstacle to the emergence of a superintelligence absent the active intervention of human "trainers" validating and cleaning up and consciously selecting for the data being fed into an AI system. Thus, the growth of AI superintelligence is bounded by the active involvement of human collaborators. In this way, our concerns about a malignant singleton are assuaged by the crucial ways in which machines are reliant upon people.

Conclusion

Indeed, technology offers tremendous opportunities and capabilities. But it cannot see the world like humans do. As smart as they may be, machines lack common sense, they cannot appreciate context, they are data hungry and brittle, they lack intuition needed to make accurate calculations with limited information, they get stuck with local optima, cannot explain their recommendations, and are only as good as the data upon which they feed. AI has no setting for creativity, playfulness, fun, curiosity, and so forth. Those are the source of so many inventions and breakthroughs. For many employees the state of work life is impoverished from a creative standpoint. We think that's because leadership is trying to get its human resources to behave like computational machines. We need to stop doing that. That is not how to get the best out of people.

Technology provides the potential for humans to focus on more meaningful aspects of work that involve creativity, innovation, and fun. As automation replaces more routine or repetitive tasks it may allow workers to focus more on tasks that utilize creativity and emotion. Physicians may spend less time dictating records and looking at charts, while spending more time understanding the unique needs of each patient. Financial advisors might spend less time analyzing clients' financial statistics and more time uncovering creative household spending options. Marketing executives may have more time to invent a novel advertising campaign or strategy.

We discuss our unique human capabilities—as well as the very real limitations of human reasoning and judgment—in the next chapter.

Notes

1 Thompson, Clive. The Miseducation of Artificial Intelligence. *Wired*, December 2018, p. 78.
2 Samuel, A.L. Some Moral and Technical Consequences of Automation—A Refutation. *Science*, 132:741–742, 1960.
3 Vanian, Jonathan. Unmasking A.I.s Bias Problem. *Fortune Magazine*, July 2018, pp. 54–62 (also see www.Fortune.come); Vincent, James. Twitter Taught Microsoft's AI Chatbot to Be a Racist Asshole in Less than a Day. *The Verge*, March 24, 2016.
4 Ng, Andrew. What Artificial Intelligence Can and Can't Do Right Now. *Harvard Business Review*, November 9, 2016.
5 Lashinsky, Adam. Ma vs. Ma. Fortune, A.I. Special Report, July 2018.
6 Lashinsky, Adam. Ma vs. Ma. Fortune, A.I. Special Report, p. 76, July 2018.
7 Rotman, David. Making AI into Jobs. *MIT Technology Review*, July/August 2018, pp. 13, 14.
8 Vanian, Jonathan. Unmasking A.I.s Bias Problem. *Fortune Magazine*, July 2018, pp. 54–62.
9 Thompson, Clive. The Miseducation of Artificial Intelligence. *Wired*, December 2018, p. 76.
10 Rogati, Monica. The AI Hierarchy of Needs. *Medium/Hackernoon*, August 1, 2017. Available at https://hackernoon.com/the-ai-hierarchy-of-needs-18f111fcc007
11 Ray, Tiernan. Google Ponders the Shortcomings of Machine Learning. *ZDNet*, October 20, 2018. Available at www.zdnet.com/article/google-ponders-the-shortcomings-of-machine-learning/
12 Zerega, Blaise. Credit Karma: Believe the Hype for "Artificial Narrow Intelligence." *Venture Beat*, May 7, 2017. Available at https://venturebeat.com/2017/05/07/credit-karma-believe-the-hype-for-artificial-narrow-intelligence/
13 Ibid.
14 Ibid.
15 Lunden, Ingrid. Apple Acquires AI Company Lattice Data, a Specialist in Unstructured "Dark Data," for $200M. *TechCrunch*, May 13, 2017. Available at https://techcrunch.com/2017/05/13/apple-acquires-ai-company-lattice-data-a-specialist-in-unstructured-dark-data/
16 There are many definitions of big data; one of the best is by Maniyaka, J. et al. Big Data: The Next Frontier for Innovation, Competition, and Productivity. *McKinsey Global Institute*, May 2011.
17 See Microsoft Azure, What Is Cloud Computing? Available at https://azure.microsoft.com/en-us/overview/what-is-cloud-computing/
18 Lunden, Ingrid. Apple Acquires AI Company Lattice Data, a Specialist in Unstructured "Dark Data," for $200M. *TechCrunch*, May 13, 2017. Available at https://techcrunch.com/2017/05/13/apple-acquires-ai-company-lattice-data-a-specialist-in-unstructured-dark-data/
19 Ibid.
20 A Different Game. *The Economist*, February 27, 2010, pp. 6–8.
21 Davenport, Thomas H. Realizing the Potential of Retail Analytics Plenty of Food for Those with the Appetite. Working Knowledge Research Report, Babson Executive Education, 2009, pp. 1–42.
22 Davenport, Thomas H. Competing on Analytics. *Harvard Business Review*, pp. 1–9, January 2006.

23 Sundblad, Willem. Data Is the Foundation for Artificial Intelligence and Machine Learning. *Forbes*, October 18, 2018. Available at www.forbes. com/sites/willemsundbladeurope/2018/10/18/data-is-the-foundation-for-artificial-intelligence-and-machine-learning/#fc03b3151b49

24 McLeod, Saul. Maslow's Hierarchy of Needs. Available at www.simplypsy-chology.org/maslow.html

25 Mills, Terence. Machine Learning Vs. Artificial Intelligence: How Are They Different? July 11, 2018. Available at www.forbes.com/sites/forbestechcouncil/2018/07/11/machine-learning-vs-artificial-intelligence-how-are-they-different/#2e8c3a8c3521

26 For more information about the differences between AI, machine learning, neural net, and deep learning, see Chin, Angela. A Pioneering Scientist Explains "Deep Learning." *The Verge*, October 16, 2018. Available at www. theverge.com/2018/10/16/17985168/deep-learning-revolution-terrence-sejnowski-artificial-intelligence-technology

27 Husain, Amir. *The Sentient Machine: The Coming Age of Artificial Intelligence*, p. 20. Scribner, New York, 2017.

28 Ibid., pp. 20–21.

29 Ibid., p. 21.

30 Nasrabadi, Nasser M., and Nasser M. Nasrabadi. Pattern Recognition and Machine Learning. *Journal of Electronic Imaging*, 16(4):049901, 2007.

31 For an example of Bayesian inferences in a marketing context, see Kramer, Aaron. *Introduction to Bayesian Inference*, December 12, 2016, Oracle + Data Science. Available at www.datascience.com/blog/intro-duction-to-bayesian-inference-learn-data-science-tutorials (last accessed August 18, 2018).

32 Barber, David. *Bayesian Reasoning and Machine Learning*. Cambridge University Press, Cambridge, UK, February 2, 2012.

33 Wellers, Dan, Timo Elliott, and Markus Noga. 8 Ways Machine Learning Is Improving Companies' Work Processes. *Harvard Business Review*, May 31, 2017. Available at https://hbr.org/2017/05/8-ways-machine-learning-is-improving-companies-work-processes

34 Ng, Andrew. What Artificial Intelligence Can and Can't Do Right Now. *Harvard Business Review*, November 9, 2016.

35 Emerging Technology from the arXiv. Machine Learning, Meet Quantum Computing. *MIT Technology Review*, November 16, 2018. Available at www.technologyreview.com/s/612435/machine-learning-meet-quantum-computing/

36 For example, researcher Francesco Tacchino and colleagues at the University of Pavia in Italy have "built the world's first perceptron implemented on a quantum computer and then put it through its paces on some simple image processing tasks." Generally, "an algorithm that takes a classical vector (like an image) as an input, combines it with a quantum weighting vector, and then produces a 0 or 1 output. The big advantage of quantum computing is that it allows an exponential increase in the number of dimensions it can process. While a classical perceptron can process an input of N dimensions, a quantum perceptron can process 2^N dimensions."

37 Thompson, Clive. The Miseducation of Artificial Intelligence. *Wired*, December 2018, p. 77.

38 Ibid., p. 78.

39 Ibid., p. 77.

40 Houser, Kristin. Elon Musk Just Unveiled Breakthrough AI Research. Here's What You Need to Know. *Futurism*, May 16, 2017. Available at https://futurism.com/elon-musk-just-unveiled-breakthrough-ai-research-heres-what-your-need-to-know/

41 Ibid.

42 Thompson, Clive. The Miseducation of Artificial Intelligence. *Wired*, December 2018, p. 76.

43 Houser, Kristin. AI Can Make Sure Cancer Patients Get Just Enough (but Not Too Much) Treatment. *Futurism*, August 13, 2018. Available at https://futurism.com/glioblastoma-patients-ai-treatment/. https://news.mit.edu/2018/artificial-intelligence-model-learns-patient-data-cancer-treatment-less-toxic-0810

44 Ibid.

45 Artificial Intelligence for the Real World by Thomas H. Davenport and Rajeev Ronanki, *Harvard Business Review*, January–February 2018, pp. 108–116.

46 Ramirez, Vanessa. Drug Discovery AI Can Do in a Day What Currently Takes Months. *Singularity Hub*, May 7, 2017. Available at https://singularityhub.com/2017/05/07/drug-discovery-ai-can-do-in-a-day-what-currently-takes-months/#sm.0000fwnti418w0el4sg3say3u0bzk

47 www.reuters.com/article/us-usa-walmart-robots/wal-marts-new-robots-scan-shelves-to-restock-items-faster-idUSKBN1CV1N4

48 Bose, Nandita. Wal-Mart's New Robots Scan Shelves to Restock Items Faster. *Reuters*, October 26, 2017. Available at www.reuters.com/article/us-usa-walmart-robots/wal-marts-new-robots-scan-shelves-to-restock-items-faster-idUSKBN1CV1N4

49 Stanford, Duane. Coke Engineers Its Orange Juice—With an Algorithm. *Bloomberg*, January 31, 2013. Available at www.bloomberg.com/news/articles/2013-01-31/coke-engineers-its-orange-juice-with-an-algorithm#p1

50 Laurent, Lionel. The Limits of Artificial Intelligence. *Bloomberg*, June 13, 2017. Available at www.bloomberg.com/news/articles/2017-06-13/the-limits-of-artificial-intelligence

51 Thompson, Clive. The Miseducation of Artificial Intelligence. *Wired*, December 2018, p. 79.

52 Ibid.

53 Brooks, R. 2017. The Seven Deadly Sins of AI Predictions. *MIT Technology Review*, 2017. Available at www.technologyreview.com/s/609048/the-seven-deadly-sins-of-ai-predictions/

54 See Margaret Mitchell TED Talk, How We can Teach AI to Help Humans, Not Hurt Us; www.ted.com/talks/margaret_mitchell_how_we_can_build_ai_to_help_humans_not_hurt_us

55 O'Neill, Cathy. *Weapons of Math Destruction: How Big Data Increases Inequality and Threatens Democracy*. Penguin Random House, 2016.

56 Ibid.

57 See the graphic and their research summary in: www.theguardian.com/news/datablog/2012/oct/31/twitter-sandy-flooding

58 Robinson, Adam. Want to Boost Your Bottom Line? Encourage Your Employees to Work on Side Projects, Inc. Magazine, 2018.

59 Stewart, James. Looking for a Lesson in Google's Perks. *The New York Times*, March 15, 2013.

60 Thompson, Clive. The Miseducation of Artificial Intelligence. *Wired*, December 2018, p. 78.

61 Ibid.
62 Ibid., p. 79.
63 Hutson, Matthew. Artificial Intelligence Is Learning to Keep Learning (originally published as "Lifelong Learning" in *Scientific American* 319, 5, 14–15 (November 2018)). Available at www.scientificamerican.com/article/artificial-intelligence-is-learning-to-keep-learning/
64 Wadhwa, Vivek. Don't Believe the Hype About AI in Business. *VentureBeat*, March 17, 2018. Available at https://venturebeat.com/2018/03/17/dont-believe-the-hype-about-ai-in-business/
65 Knight, Will. The Dark Secret at the Heart of AI: No One Really Knows How the Most Advanced Algorithms Do What They Do. That Could Be a Problem. *MIT Technology Review*, April 11, 2017. Available at www.technologyreview.com/s/604087/the-dark-secret-at-the-heart-of-ai/
66 Ibid.
67 Ibid.
68 *Source*: Big Data vs. Artificial Intelligence. *Datamation*, May 30, 2018.

4

THE LIMITS OF HUMAN CAPABILITIES

In an age of smart machines, our old definition of what makes a person smart doesn't make sense. What is needed is a new definition of being smart, one that promotes higher levels of human thinking and emotional engagement. The new smart will be determined not by what or how you know but by the quality of your thinking, listening, relating, collaborating, and learning.

Ed Hess, Professor of Strategy, Darden School of Business, UVA[1]

A tolerance for failure requires an intolerance for incompetence. A willingness to experiment requires rigorous discipline.

Gary Pisano, Professor, Harvard Business School[2]

The Microwave's Eureka Moment

The microwave is one of the most popular household appliances in the modern world. However, few people know that the invention of the microwave was an accident that would not be possible without human imagination.

Percy Spencer was a creative self-taught engineer who earned several patents during the Second World War. One day in 1945 while working in a lab at Raytheon, he was testing high-powered vacuum tubes inside radars that produce microwaves. While preparing for his lunch break, Spencer reached his hand into his pocket and noticed that his peanut butter candy bar had melted. "It was a gooey, sticky mess," according to Spencer. He wondered about the microwaves being emitted from the magnetron. "Is it possible that the microwave heats up food?"

The next day he brought in corn kernels to test his hypothesis and put them in front of the magnetron. When they began to pop, he was certain the microwaves could cook food. The microwave was born.

The invention of the microwave is an example of human curiosity and creativity. It shows how humans—despite all their shortcomings—have the ability to connect seemingly disparate ideas. They can find solutions to problems they weren't even setting out to solve, applying insights from one domain to other areas of life, thinking "outside of the box." Machines cannot do that.

In the previous chapter we discussed the tremendous opportunities that technology provides. Machines offer unparalleled precision and accuracy. Artificial intelligence, machine learning, the Internet of Things, robots, and drones are already used in many industries to make production processes faster and more accurate. They can handle an unprecedented amount of information and data, and work in dangerous environments, are cheaper, are available 24–27, and don't require health insurance or even paid leave. They don't have emotional baggage, they do not get tired, talk back to supervisors, argue with coworkers, or ask for a pay raise. They do exactly what they are told with a physical and processing capability no human can match.

Where does that leave humans? Humans have a unique ability for creativity, ingenuity, and innovation. It is precisely human emotions, intuitions, and general intelligence that inspire us to breakthroughs in science, industrial innovations, and the future of enterprise.

To put humans and technology together in the right process, we need to see how they fit together. Per Moravec's Paradox, we should interface technology to people where people are weak and technology is strong and vice versa. Hence, in this chapter, we look at how the shortcomings of human intelligence and decision-making influence us at work. By understanding these shortcomings, we should be able to mitigate them and even take advantage of them when creating the Humachine.

Thinking about Thinking

Just as it is impossible to think about artificial intelligence without comparing it to a baseline of human intelligence, it is impossible to answer the question of the role of artificial intelligence in enterprise without contemplating what it is about human intelligence that is required to run an enterprise.

Business functions stand to benefit from the razor-sharp proceedings of logic, the critical evaluation of evidence, the careful expression of strategic communications, and the sophisticated judgments of managers and executives. Conversely, management failures often flow from illogical decisions, false beliefs about material facts, inept communications between groups, and indecision by managers and executives.

The best companies will find ways to encourage and internalize the best thoughts expressed by their human resources, while filtering out the illogical, false, inflammatory, and ambiguous. Therefore, it pays to think about thinking.

A helpful framework for thinking about thinking comes from Daniel Kahneman's *Thinking, Fast and Slow.*[3]

Kahneman elaborates upon "two systems in the mind, System 1 and System 2. The labels of System 1 and System 2 are widely used in psychology, but I go further than most in this book, which you can read as a psychodrama with two characters."[4]

> **System 1** is an effortless, involuntary, automatic, and quick way of thinking, such as the mental activity involved in passively processing speech or forming impressions from sensory inputs.[5]
>
> **System 2** is an effortful, voluntary, directed, and slow way of thinking, such as the mental activity involved in conscious agency, making deliberate choices, or performing a calculation.[6]

Kahneman summarizes the relationship between System 1 and System 2 thinking as follows[7]:

> System 1 runs automatically and System 2 is normally in a comfortable low-effort mode, in which only a fraction of its capacity is engaged. System 1 continuously generates suggestions for System 2: impressions, intuitions, intentions, and feelings. If endorsed by System 2, impressions and intuitions turn into beliefs, and impulses turn into voluntary actions. When all goes smoothly, which is most of the time, System 2 adopts the suggestions of System 1 with little or no modification. You generally believe your impressions and act on your desires, and that is fine—usually.
>
> When System 1 runs into difficulty, it calls on System 2 to support more detailed and specific processing that may solve the problem of the moment. System 2 is mobilized when a question arises for which System 1 does not offer an answer[.] You can also feel a surge of conscious attention whenever you are surprised. System 2 is activated when an event is detected that violates the model of the world that System 1 maintains... Surprise then activates and orients your attention: you will stare, and you will search your memory for a story that makes sense of the surprising event. System 2 is also credited with the continuous monitoring of your own behavior—the control that keeps you polite when you are angry, and alert when you are driving at night. System 2 is mobilized to increased effort when it detects an error about to be made.
>
> System 1 is gullible and biased to believe, System 2 is in charge of doubting and unbelieving, but System 2 is sometimes busy, and often lazy.

The division of labor between System 1 and System 2 is highly efficient: it minimizes effort and optimizes performance. The arrangement works well most of the time because System 1 is generally very good at what it does: its models of familiar situations are accurate, its short-term predictions are usually accurate as well, and its initial reactions to challenges are swift and generally appropriate. System 1 has biases, however, systematic errors that it is prone to make in specified circumstances. As we shall see, sometimes it answers easier questions than the one it was asked, and it has little understanding of logic and statistics. One further limitation of System 1 is that it cannot be turned off.

In the subsequent sections, as we discuss biases, heuristics, bounded rationality, and the limits of human capabilities in terms of thinking, decision-making, and so forth, we are really talking about the limits inherent in System 1 of the mind.

As human beings our thinking and processing are subject to an endless array of cognitive biases. Simply put, cognitive biases are mistakes in reasoning, evaluating, and remembering. They are systematic errors in thinking that affect the decisions and judgment of people and are related to a variety of shortcomings in human processing ability. Some biases can be related to memory. Memory biases influence what one remembers and can lead to biased thinking and decision-making. For example, people are more likely to recall events that are tied to strong emotions. These may be events they find humorous, pleasurable, dangerous, threatening, or inspirational. They also remember information they produce themselves or activities they were engaged in rather than observed.

Other cognitive biases can be related to problems with attention. Humans have limited attention span. We can easily become overwhelmed with large quantities of data and are not able to process them. We cannot consider many variables and complex relationships. Since attention is a limited resource, people have to be selective about what they focus on.

According to research in *Harvard Business Review*, "Many experts believe that human beings will still be needed to do the jobs that require higher-order critical, creative, and innovative thinking and the jobs that require high emotional engagement to meet the needs of other human beings. The challenge for many of us is that we do not excel at those skills because of our natural cognitive and emotional proclivities: We are confirmation-seeking thinkers and ego-affirmation-seeking defensive reasoners. We will need to overcome those proclivities in order to take our thinking, listening, relating, and collaborating skills to a much higher level."[8]

In order to harness uniquely human powers, we need to understand our limitations.

The Conundrum of Originality

One of the strengths of humanity is the apparently *sui generis* quality of our thoughts and actions. We feel like self-starters, with originality, freedom of thought and action, creativity, imagination, and capacity for true novelty. These qualities, which we generally characterize as "originality," form a powerful intuitive basis for distinguishing humanity from artificial intelligence. But that intuition might be wrong.

Since the early stages of AI research, the assumption that "a machine cannot do anything without having a rule telling it to do so"[9] has served as a bedrock conviction that separates human from machine.

We know technology provides tremendous opportunities for enterprise to gain efficiency and effectiveness. However, we can also see that there are things technology cannot do—at least, not yet. The greatest advancements in business and our everyday lives have come from human creativity and innovation. Creativity and sensing emotions are core to the human experience and also difficult to automate. So far it is empirically true to say that machines simply cannot do those human things marked by originality of thought, volition in action, feeling in response to stimuli, and so forth.

Arthur Samuel's influential 1960 essay *Some Moral and Technical Consequences of Automation—A Refutation*, published in the journal SCIENCE, still resonates with intuitive strength to this day[10]:

> It is my conviction that machines cannot possess originality in the sense implied by [the] thesis that "machines can and do transcend some of the limitations of their designers, and that in doing so they may be both effective and dangerous[.]" A machine is not a genie, it does not work by magic, it does not possess a will, and... nothing comes out which has not been put in, barring, of course, and infrequent case of malfunctioning[.] [T]he machine *will not and cannot* do any of these things until it has been instructed as to how to proceed. There is and logically there must always remain a complete hiatus between (*i*) any ultimate extension and elaboration in this process of carrying out man's wishes and (*ii*) the development within the machine of a will of its own. To believe otherwise is either to believe in magic or to believe that the existence of man's will is an illusion and that man's actions are as mechanical as the machine's.

Therein lies the source of the conviction that a machine cannot do anything without having a rule telling it to do so: the underlying belief that humankind's actions spring from *free will* and are not mechanistically determined like the last domino falling is just a result of antecedent dominoes falling, and that this free will is the ultimate causal explanation of human behavior. In other words, the conviction that machines cannot be original is merely an implication of the article of faith that humans have free will.

Samuel's argument against machine originality depends on the assumption that human originality defies a regressive causal explanation. Forgive us for being harsh but this appears to be the logical fallacy *petitio principii*, or "begging the question," wherein we use the premise of an argument to support itself. The assumption of free will is, again, intuitively powerful, but it comes with a lot of philosophical baggage. It hangs from skyhooks.

That humankind has the potential for originality in action, and that machines do not, is supported by the lack of empirical evidence to the contrary: We have never see a toaster decide to toast bread or a word processor decide to craft a sonnet, unless it has been instructed to do so by its human user. Of course, lack of evidence is not evidence of a null hypothesis, but you get the point. The conviction that machines lack originality may be rather an article of faith than a valid axiom. We discuss some of the philosophical aspects of machine originality and human free will in this endnote.[11]

One issue is whether Samuel's premise is true as a contingent matter or whether it is true for all time. If it is true as a *contingent* matter—that is, it just so happens to be true because of the state of technical advancement today—then it is possible for machines to transcend the limitations of their designers at some point in the future. Conversely, if it is true *for all time*—that is to say, no matter how advanced the technology, machines will never possess originality in action, then Samuel is revealing something inherently transcendental in the nature of mankind's make-up, as well as something inherently limited in the nature of machine intelligence.

At this point, the authors are unaware of a moral code, legal framework, or economic system that takes as its predicate assumption about human nature that we are *not* free to choose our course of conduct. The notions of right and wrong, justification and culpability for our actions, self-determination, and the agency required to fulfill the so-called American dream (or at the very least enter into economically efficient transactions) all depend on the idea that human beings more or less know what they are doing and freely choose to engage in actions to their own benefit.

We are left with the less than satisfying conclusion that humans enjoy originality in action (freedom, spontaneity, self-direction) and machines do not, simply because (*i*) humanity has not yet devised practicable moral, legal, or economic frameworks for governing human affairs absent this hypothesis, and (*ii*) our technology has not yet advanced enough to be capable of generating original action without prior human programming. As a result, it is only because of practicality that we proceed under the assumption that "humans can do X, machines cannot."

In other words, unlike Samuel, we believe that, "machines can only do what they are programmed to," is true, but its truth is only contingent on the state of the art, and is not an absolutely true statement that would be true for all time. This caveat applies to the various claims we make throughout this book that take the form, "humans can do X, but machines cannot." Moravec's Paradox is not just a manifestation of species chauvinism.

Next, we look at some unique qualities of human intelligence.

In Defense of Homo Sapiens

There is no question that technology is replacing jobs across all industry sectors. We have been warned about potential job losses. Advances in automation, robotics, and artificial intelligence have made this a reality. Digitization is transforming labor markets and human skill requirements.

While the idea of replacing humans with machines is scary to imagine for anyone with bills to pay, it may also lead corporate leaders to envision massive reductions in labor costs with surging profits. Sorry, but the issue is more nuanced than that. As the CEO and founder of Fetch Robotics, Melonee Wise put it: "For every robot we put in the world, you have to have someone maintaining it or servicing it or taking care of it."[12] She points out that technology is not going to render obsolete the human labor force.

Yes, it is going to boost productivity but balance sheets will not be improved due to a reduction in human resources. Productivity growth will only occur if organizations manage their talent properly. As a result, organizations will be looking for different capabilities and skills from their people. The traits that are innately human—*creativity, innovation, empathy, caring, imagination*—are the skills all humans need to function in an organizational setting in the Humachine era.

General Intelligence

According to Douglas Hofstadter in *Godel, Escher, Bach: An Eternal Golden Braid*, "Sometimes the complexity of our minds seems so overwhelming that one feels that there can be no solution to the problem of understanding intelligence[.]"[13] That said, there are some key ingredients that are definitive abilities of humanity's ***general intelligence***. They are the ability to[14]:

- Respond to situations flexibly;
- Take advantage of fortuitous circumstances;
- Make sense out of ambiguous or contradictory messages;
- Recognize the relative importance of different elements of a situation;
- Find similarities between situations despite differences that may separate them;
- Draw distinctions between situations despite similarities that may link them;

- Synthesize new concepts by taking old concepts and putting them together in new ways; and
- Come up with ideas that are novel.

Until machines can attain these abilities, humans are likely to remain indispensable to enterprise, despite the otherwise notable flaws to our intellects, which we discuss in later sections.

Intuition

To get the most out of ourselves, we need to play to our strengths. We need to tap into our intuition.

According to Garry Kasparov, *intuition* is "the product of experience and confidence. And here I mean 'product' in the mathematical sense, as the equation *intuition = experience x confidence*. It is the ability to act reflexively on knowledge that has been deeply absorbed and understood. Depression short-circuits intuition by inhibiting the confidence required to turn that processed experience into action."[15]

Another formulation of intuition comes from Herbert Simon. According to Simon, "Intuition is nothing more and nothing less than recognition," where "The situation has provided a cue; this cue has given the expert access to information stored in memory, and the information provides the answer."[16] Accordingly, per Simon, *intuition is decision-making based on pattern recognition.*

Unlike Kasparov's formulation, Simon's definition of intuition would apparently allow an artificially intelligent system to have intuition. As we discussed in previous chapters, machine learning and neural nets deploy pattern recognition as fundamental to their operation. However, general intelligence goes beyond pattern recognition and is not yet attained by any artificially intelligent system.

Creativity and Innovation

According to business consultant Linda Naiman, creativity is the act of turning new and imaginative ideas into reality by perceiving the world in new ways, uncovering hidden patterns, making connections between seemingly unrelated phenomena, and generating solutions.[17]

Experts in creativity theory distinguish between different types of creativity[18]:

- *Mini-c creativity* describes personally meaningful ideas and insights that occur to a person but are not shared, like seeing a familiar shape in a cloud or coining a nickname;
- *Little-c creativity* describes the kind of novel problem-solving deployed in our daily lives necessary to adapt to changing environments, like finding a new transit route to avoid a traffic jam;

- **Pro-C creativity** describes original output generated by professionals, which while skillful and creative, does not lead to wide acclaim or major impact, like coming up with scenarios for television commercials;
- **Big-C creativity** describes transformative, paradigm shifting creating works that have the potential to change the world, like medical innovations, technological advances, and artistic achievements.

In the book *The Innovator's DNA: Mastering the Five Skills of Disruptive Innovators*, authors Jeff Dyer, Hal Gregersen, and Clayton M. Christensen interviewed thousands of inventors and executives, and they found that creativity is not simply a mental function but a set of behaviors that tend to generate new insights.[19] These behaviors include:

- *Associating.* Finding connections between unrelated fields;
- *Questioning.* Challenging conventional wisdom;
- *Observing.* Noticing the subtle behavior of customers, suppliers, and competitors;
- *Networking.* Bridging gaps between people with different ideas and perspectives;
- *Experimenting.* Entering into interactive experiences to elicit new responses.

These behaviors are illustrated by a couple of famous examples of invention.

Consider the invention of the potato chips. The salty and crispy snack was created in 1853 at Moon's Lake House near Saratoga Springs, New York. Chef George Crum was tired of listening to a customer who kept on sending his fried potatoes back to the kitchen. He complained they were soggy and not crunchy enough. Out of anger, Crum then sliced the potatoes as thin as possible, fried them in hot grease, then doused them with salt. The customer loved them. Thus, "Saratoga Chips" quickly became a popular item at the lodge and throughout the greater New England region.

Eventually these chips became mass-produced and distributed far and wide. But they would quickly become stale on the shelf. Then, in 1920, entrepreneur Laura Scudder invented the airtight bag by ironing together two pieces of waxed paper. This kept the potato chips fresh longer and thus mass production of potato chips began. Both inventions—the potato chip and the airtight bag—were a creative way to solve a problem: Crum satisfying a grumbling customer and Scudder figuring out a way to keep a product fresh longer.

Henry Ford brought the world automobiles. Had he worked merely from historical data he would have come up with a faster horse. Instead of just making a faster car, Elon Musk is working on an underground tunnel system with car elevators and a hyper loop. Steve Jobs was the first to give us a real choice of fonts. Although typeface was invented way back by Gutenberg, it was Jobs who understood its value and enabled its use in personal computers and a sense of customizability. None of these innovations came from machines alone.

Although it may be theoretically possible for an artificially intelligent system to have an original thought, to date it has not happened. Innovation and creativity are processes that machines are just now learning to mimic. But remember they only work from the data they have. They cannot think "outside of the box." Humans can dream, sense, and feel. We can use our intuition in deciding what path to take. Machines can dredge through data looking for patterns and statistical correlations; however, it is we humans who sense which unfulfilled needs could drive innovation.

Pleasure and Aesthetics

This section looks at humans' enjoyment of sensory indulgence and appreciation of beauty.

Companies like Starbucks learned a long time ago that customers don't just want a product, they want an experience. For Starbucks, this means they don't just want good coffee. They want an aesthetically appealing environment that enhances the pleasure of consumption. Former Chairman Howard Schultz wrote, "Every Starbucks store is carefully designed to enhance the quality of everything the customers see, touch, hear, smell or taste. All the sensory signals have to appeal to the same high standards. The artwork, the music, the aromas, the surfaces all have to send the same subliminal message as the flavor of the coffee: Everything here is the best-of-class."[20]

Pleasure and aesthetics require experiencing, feeling, and sensing. It is not something machines can do. Pleasure is something humans and animals experience and is a range of positive feelings, both physically and emotionally. Aesthetics concerns appreciation of beauty in both nature and art. Machines can copy what we as humans label as "aesthetically beautiful" or "artistic." They can copy or even create something that mimics it. But we think it is safe to say machines cannot experience; they have no subjective "what it is like to feel" the sound of music or the taste of cappuccino or the security of receiving trustworthy advice. Consumers of products—both goods and services—are human. While machines may be producing at a more efficient rate with greater precision than humans, they cannot create something on their own that will appeal to the pleasures and aesthetic taste of humans.

Aesthetics, feelings, and pleasurable sensations are the cornerstone of selling products to customers. It is the way we communicate as humans. While machines communicate through data, we communicate through the senses. There is art in creating reactions without words. Catering to aesthetic sensibilities is therefore a critical skill in business. Artwork conveys everything from beauty to power to influence and wealth. That is where brands begin and end.

Aesthetics are everywhere. Hotel lobbies, amusement parks, board-rooms, clothing labels, car interiors and vanity lighting, and so forth. Aesthetics is specific to product categories. Computers are designed for functionality, such as lightness, responsiveness to touch (such as the weight of a key on the keyboard) and ease of use. Fashion aesthetics are for use and functionality, such as moisture-wicking fabrics, as well as for show, such as shimmering colors. Let's have machines design the latest hairstyle and see how it works out.

Look and feel doesn't override function, of course. Some consumers may prefer mobile phones with a masculine look, whereas others want something cute. However, everyone expects the phones to work. That said, the design of products for pleasure with aesthetical appeal is something only humans can do (so far).

Emotions

Emotions are mental states characterized by feelings. The experience of emotion is perhaps most integral to being human as emotions filter the way the world shows up to us. Like laying a colored lens over the eye of the camera, emotions tint our perception of reality.

If you want to get the most out of your human labor force, they need to be happy, or at least not depressed. "Many studies have shown that depression, or the simple lack of self-confidence, results in decision making that is slower, more conservative, and inferior in quality."[21]

Depressed employees are less likely to make correct decisions intuitively, that is, less likely to be able to act on their own experience. It is ironic that emotions are both our strength and our weakness.

Because we are emotional, we can be pumped up with confidence, thus supercharging our own intuition, which in turn enables us to rapidly make correct decisions that are informed by experience. This same susceptibility to emotional influence can lead to depression—say, a snarky comment from a supervisor at work—which in turn cripples our intuition, leading to the inability to access the knowledge informed by our experience.

Because humans are all unique and susceptible to different emotional triggers, emotionally intelligent managers would know the profile of their subordinates and would understand what it takes to motivate and encourage them into harnessing their intuition. Whereas some need affirmation and positive feedback to feel confident, others may respond more confidently to a challenge.

Let this be a lesson to cruel managers. The all-too-common work environment governed by the mantra, "The beatings will continue until morale improves," is self-defeating. Intimidating workers undermines their productivity and squelches their ability to make sound decisions.

While there may be no authoritative definition of what an emotion is, the science of emotions has been considerably advanced by empirical research. While "happy" and "sad" are about as far apart as we can imagine, and while we tend to represent emotional experiences using categorical labels, research shows that actually "the boundaries between categories of emotion are fuzzy rather than discrete."[22] Based on extensive self-reporting across thousands of survey respondents, the National Academy of Sciences reports that there are 27 different human emotions. Table 4.1 displays the results of a fairly comprehensive empirical study of human emotions.[23]

Table 4.1 Human emotions

Admiration

Adoration

Aesthetic appreciation

Amusement

Anxiety

Awe

Awkwardness

Boredom

Calmness

Confusion

Craving

Disgust

Empathetic pain

Entrancement

Envy

Excitement

Fear

Horror

Interest

Joy

Nostalgia

Romance

Sadness

Satisfaction

Sexual desire

Sympathy

Triumph

Although emotions can cloud our better judgment and lead us to irrational choices, we want to take a moment and appreciate what they contribute to productivity. Emotions fuel creativity and innovation. They generate energy that can spurn us to action and motivate us to complete a challenging task. Feelings are the fuel to human activity because they motivate us to pursue or avoid various outcomes.

Marketers know how to leverage the power of emotions. Emotions connect people, help sell products, recruit an employee from a competitor, empower teams to create innovative products, and so forth. Loni Stark, Senior Director of Strategy & Product Marketing at Adobe Experience Manager, says, "Lasting brand loyalty is built on an emotional connection with the brand across every customer touch point. Brands need a content strategy which is informed by data to elicit emotion and build connections."[24]

A critical ingredient to the success of enterprises in this technology era is to be emotionally literate. *Do not to ignore emotions.* Do not suppress them. Do not try to fight against human nature. We must learn to use emotions, to work with them, to inform business decisions based on the emotional reactions they are likely to generate, and to manage accordingly. Organizational leaders need to create working environments that cultivate healthy emotional responses. Leaders and team members need to understand how to create and anticipate the emotional responses of customers and clients, suppliers, and other stakeholders, as well as other members of the organization.

There is right and wrong, true and false, but then there is the way things make us *feel*. Most human problems could be solved if only we would feel positive emotions about right and true things, and negative emotions about wrong and false things, but our social reality is messier than that.

A statement made by an executive to his or her team could be true and right, but if it is delivered in an emotionally inept manner, it will not *feel* true and right; it will *feel* false and wrong. The disconnect between truth, morality, and emotions can lead to all sorts of organizational failures.

Emotional Intelligence

Also known as emotional quotient (EQ), **emotional intelligence** is the capability of humans to recognize their own emotions and those of others, to discern between different feelings and label them appropriately. Emotional information can help guide thinking and behavior, and help manage emotions to adapt to various environments or achieve goals. Empathy is typically associated with EI because it relates to an individual connecting with the personal experiences of others.

Why is this important? Studies have shown that people with high EI have greater mental health, job performance, and leadership skills.[25]

Indeed, EI can help people alleviate stress, reduce errors, become more innovative, and improve job performance. Although some individuals innately have a higher EI than others, these skills are trainable. An important aspect for organizations in building a human-centric organization will be training talent to navigate emotions in a productive and compassionate way by developing emotional intelligence. This ability to manage one's thoughts and feelings is essential to business success.

It is also important to understand that emotions are intertwined with human thoughts. Our ideas are colored by emotions; thoughts are imbued with evaluations and judgments, some positive and others negative. Human mental states are complex, messy things that combine ideas, perceptions, beliefs, emotions, biases, and motivations.

Ultimately, these messy mental states govern how we operate. Negative emotions can be all-consuming. They can stifle creativity and innovation. Positive emotions can be energizing. They can make us want to conquer the world and be the best we can be.

In the work environment human emotions are also intertwined with the organizational culture. A positive culture that is inclusive, empowering, and welcoming will foster positive emotions and create fuel for creativity and innovation. A lot of business deals are done because we trust one another and feel a connection at an emotional level. In the Hu machine era, businesses need their human capital—leaders, managers, and employees—to connect with others on an emotional level. Success will depend on human talent being able to connect with each other—with coworkers, customers, and suppliers—on the basis of trust. It will require an understanding of each others' emotional needs. As AI takes over increasing functions in an enterprise, the ability to feel and emote in an intelligent, responsive manner that helps manage relationships will become an increasingly important role for humans. Emotionally intelligent management is, at least for now, a safe space for humans to thrive in the workplace that has not yet been displaced by machines. See Table 4.2.[26]

Not everyone is equally emotionally intelligent. Sometimes emotions spring up inside us without a clear explanation, and sometimes we react to feelings without even realizing that our actions are being caused by our emotions. This is why emotion or passion is often contrasted with rationality. Those with high EQ tend to exhibit certain behaviors that make them exceptionally gifted in working with other people, even to the point where they can govern their own emotions and create emotions in others.

Care

Care is a special feature of humanity. Humans tend to care about the objects of their attention and affection. We care about our family, our jobs, our things, and ourselves. According to Merriam-Webster Dictionary, the

Table 4.2 Emotionally intelligent behavior

Behavior	Intelligence
Thinking about feelings	Awareness of how moods affect thoughts and actions of self and others.
Pausing before acting	Refrains from making decisions based on impulsive feelings.
Control your thoughts	Consciously responds rather than unconsciously reacting.
Benefit from criticism	Determines how to improve self upon receiving negative feedback.
Display authenticity	Stand by your principles, instead of trying to conform to your audience.
Demonstrate empathy	Builds connections with others by seeing the world through their eyes.
Praise others' virtues	Inspires others by lauding their positive qualities.
Give helpful feedback	Frames criticism as constructive instead of harsh.
Apologize when needed	Demonstrates an endearing sense of humility.
Forgive when slighted	Releases feelings of resentment to be free of anger.
Keep your word	Follows through on commitments large and small.
Help others	Recognizes when others need support.
Avoids sabotage	Manages own emotions to stymie attempts at emotional manipulation.

verb "care" is defined as "to feel trouble or anxiety," and "to feel interest or concern." The noun "care" is defined as the "suffering of mind," a "disquieted state of mixed uncertainty, apprehension, and responsibility," and a "painstaking and watchful attention."[27] The practice of medicine is often described as providing medical *care*.

Humans are caring creatures. When the mind is preoccupied with a subject, we are said to care about that subject. Care is related to the existential philosophy concept of "dasein," a German term that literally means "being there," coined by the philosopher Heidegger.[28]

Dasein describes the dialectical tension between the mind and the external world, in opposition to the notions that the mind exists wholly apart from its environment (on the one hand) and that the mind is causally determined by the external world (on the other).

Dasein is the location in which existence makes itself known. The human being is distinct from everything else in the world because it makes its own existence an issue to itself. The human mind is always potentially something else; its own possibilities come toward itself from itself, and it is always lurching into the future while informed by its own past. A caring mind is concerned with itself and with its environment.

If all this sounds mysterious, just remember—the mind is a mysterious thing, and to adequately describe it, we have to get pretty weird in our language.

Suffice it to say, the human mind cares. It feels troubled with a task assigned to it. Care takes up a challenge with a "disquieted state of mixed uncertainty, apprehension, and responsibility." That is the essence of caring about our job. Without this kind of care, our world would fall apart.

The managers' job is to ensure their employees are caring about the right tasks. You can get the smartest and most talented people on your team, but if they care about the wrong things, they will be worthless if not hostile to your organization's mission. To orient people toward tasks with care requires emotional intelligence and understanding the levers and pulleys of motivation.

Care is a uniquely human resource. Like creativity, emotions, and aesthetic taste, care is something that humans bring to enterprise that machines cannot replicate.

Play

Because of the extended juvenile period in mammalian development, we get long periods of play in the course of developing our minds. It wasn't until 2005 that we saw serious scientific study of play in other forms of life, including marsupials, birds, reptiles, fish, and invertebrates. That's when Gordon M. Burghardt published the book, *The Genesis of Animal Play: Testing the Limits.*[29]

Burghardt proposes five criteria to define "play"[30]: (1) behavior is not fully functional; (2) play is spontaneous, voluntary, pleasurable, or autotelic (which means having an end or purpose in itself); (3) play differs from serious performance of typical behavior either structurally or temporally; (4) behavior is repeated but not stereotyped; and (5) behavior occurs when the animal is in a relaxed field (e.g., well fed, safe, healthy).

Burghardt proposes the **surplus resource theory** to predict and explain why animals play. According to this theory, "play will occur when there is sufficient metabolic energy (an important condition for play among invertebrates), lack of stress from environmental demands, a need for stimulation (boredom), and a lifestyle that includes behavioral complexity and flexibility (e.g., generalist foragers)."[31]

Play is a relatively mysterious behavior in animals, and our focus is on human play. Research in human play tends to use at least five quite

Table 4.3 Types of human play

Type	Characteristics	Player
Progress	Adaptive activity, learning behaviors, acquiring skills, socialization, and neural development	Juveniles
Fate	Existential optimism, magic, chance, and chaos	Gamblers
Power	Games of strategy, skill, political contests, warfare	Hegemon
Identity	Symbolic interaction, bonding, festivals, parties	Socialites
Imagination	Transformation via repetition, reorganization, and exaggeration	Creatives

distinct connotations. We can understand play in terms of progress, fate, power, identity, and imagination.[32] See Table 4.3.

Think about how much of the global economy is driven by humans just playing. For fun. Because we have a surplus of resources. Because we are bored.

Burghardt argues that although playfulness may have been essential to the origin of much that we consider distinctive in human behavior, it only develops through a specific set of interactions among developmental, evolutionary, ecological, and physiological processes, and it is not always beneficial or adaptive.[33]

Leaders should encourage play at work. It is a fundamental human behavior. It brings us joy and allows us to relax. We are much more creative and productive when we are having fun. All work and no play is seriously detrimental to mental health.

Ethical Convictions

Merriam-Webster Dictionary defines **conscience** as a sense of the moral goodness or blameworthiness of one's own conduct, intentions, or character, together with a feeling of obligation to do right or be good.[34] Outside of the rare instances of psychopathy and sociopathy, most humans have a conscience. We may disagree over right and wrong in any given situation, but most of us agree that, generally speaking, one should strive to do the right thing.

Business ethics do differ from culture to culture—for example, some cultures expect a good bribe, whereas others make bribery a crime. However, research suggests that, even across cultures, there are some (practically) universal ethical standards. Breaching these rules might just upset *everyone*, regardless of the national origin, religion, or cultural background of the counterpart affected by one's actions.

Table 4.4 Universal code of conduct

Name of virtue	Description of virtue
Trustworthiness	To be worthy of confidence and dependable to others.
Respect	To have regard for and not interfere with other's interests.
Responsibility	To be accountable for one's acts and accept one's burden.
Fairness	To be impartial and abstain from favoritism.
Caring	To have concern for and kindness to others.
Citizenship	To accept a membership role within a community.

Normative research into codes of ethics articulated by corporations, global institutions, and the business ethics literature reveals a convergence of six (basically) universal moral values: trustworthiness, respect, responsibility, fairness, caring, and citizenship.[35] See Table 4.4.

In addition to ethical codes pronounced by corporations, lots of professional societies impose ethical obligations upon their members and condition membership on compliance with certain norms. The American Psychological Association (APA) has published Ethical Principles of Psychologists and Code of Conduct for its members. The American Bar Association has promulgated Model Rules of Professional Conduct for adoption by the various state bar associations. It is the essence of a profession that it polices its members and holds them to high standards. Say what you will about attorneys, but they are taught to take ethical issues as seriously as legal ones.

We can have fascinating discussions on ethics—about their evolutionary origins (e.g., Nietzsche's 1887 book *On the Genealogy of Morality: A Polemic*), about cultural relativism (and how it leads to absurd implications such as the inability to make moral progress over time or to characterize one cultural habit as morally inferior or superior to any other), or about blatantly unethical corporate conduct that makes headlines every day (our lawyers suggested not mentioning anyone specifically here). But that's for a different book. Some ethicists might argue that ethics are all relative, but we feel that is an academic point to make which trivializes matters of grave concern to a humanity in need of basic morality across the board. We need to take ethics seriously, even if there is a lot of untidy philosophical baggage and loaded words involved.

All that said, we are more interested in the very human aspect of ethics, which is the ethical *conviction* we feel when tempted to do something that might be wrong or when we are forced to stand up against opposition to something that is right. In those times, it's not the written code of conduct so much as it is the compelling subjective feeling of conviction that actually constrains our behavior. Not just on the negative or abstention side (the fear of punishment, the nagging doubt of guilt) but also on the positive or proactive side (the yearning to do the right thing, the zeal of righteousness). Among other things, our conscience makes human decision-making different from what you would get from an unprincipled self-interest-maximizing AI.

Like our rationality, our morality sometimes fails us. But morality is a feature, not a bug, of the human. To create a Humachine, we should take both our most rational and most moral moments and normalize them, to ensconce within our enterprises wisdom and justice.

With all these glowing commendations of human virtues, let's turn to the limitations of human reasoning: our biased and bounded rationality.

Managing When Human, All Too Human

We like to think we are rational beings. In fact, humans are prone to myriad biases that cause us to think and act irrationally. Identifying human biases in decision-making has been well studied. It requires applying psychology to economics to predict, explain, and control how humans behave. In 2002 the psychologist Daniel Kahneman won the Nobel Prize in Economics for his work in this field. This was a high point in behavioral economics—the *empirical* study of how humans *actually* behave in the environment—as contrasted with *hypothetical* models of how a rational person *ought* to behave. The findings have been applied to practically all economic environments—from marketing departments to law and public policy—to improve understanding of human nature and to improve our ability to explain, predict, and control ourselves.

Let us be clear. In the age of technology humans are the centerpiece—not an afterthought. We cannot take humans out of the equation. Even today in the world dominated by technology, the key to success is to adapt humans to this new work environment—not to *replace* but to *enhance*, not to train humans to think *like* computers, but how to think *with* computers. That said, according to Ed Hess in the *Harvard Business Review*, "Because AI will be a far more formidable competitor than any human, we will be in a frantic race to stay relevant. That will require us to take our cognitive and emotional skills to a much higher level."[36]

We must understand how and why humans act irrationally to improve our cognitive and emotional skills. For decades, psychologists have studied cognitive biases as they relate to decision-making. The practice of understanding our limitations and designing systems around them goes back a long way. Policymakers have understood human cognitive and emotional frailties and built systems around them at least as far back as the framers of the United States Constitution, as evidenced by the so-called "constitution of man" described in the 1788 publication *The Federalist Papers.*

Deservingly popularized by the Broadway hit *Hamilton*, *The Federalist Papers* "explains the need for and effectiveness of many of the architectural features of the United States Constitution, including separation of powers and other safeguards designed to prevent abuse of government and to ensure excellence in government as near as humanly possible."[37]

Despite our capacity for rationality and deliberation, humans are plagued with limits unknown to any AI system. We are bounded in the sense that we have limited rationality, we lack total self-control, we do not always pursue our own self-interest, and we often fail to live up to our own ethical ideals. Cognitively, we are biased in that we suffer from availability bias, self-serving bias, confirmation bias, and optimism bias. In negotiation settings, our limitations are revealed by reactive devaluation, escalation of commitment, myopia, endowment effect, loss aversion, and prospect theory, all of which make us bad at betting rationally. In interpersonal settings, we can suffer from collective action problems, rent-seeking behavior, tendencies toward free riding, groupthink, and holdout scenarios.[38]

These limitations have been known at least anecdotally to classical liberal thinkers for centuries (indeed, the United States Constitution was designed around these flaws), and in recent decades they have been dusted off, empirically investigated, and given more formal definition by psychologists, economists, and legal scholars.[39]

Despite the connotation, cognitive biases may not be all bad. Some cognitive biases are taken to be adaptive in the evolutionary context and thus may lead to success in certain situations. They are the brain's attempt to simplify information processing in a complex environment with limited processing power. Some of these biases are rules of thumb— known as "heuristics"—that help humans make sense of the world and reach decisions with relative speed.

To survive in an overwhelmingly complex world, biases can provide crucial mental shortcuts. Sometimes they lead us to make bad decisions, but they can also allow us to reach decisions quickly when, generally speaking, speed is more important than accuracy. Heuristics may allow us to make effective choices when information is limited but action one way or another is nonetheless necessary for survival.

Biases cannot be *eliminated*. They are part of being human. Even when someone is fully informed of their biases, they are still subject to them when making unaided decisions. For example, the majority of people think they are better than the average driver. However, these biases can be mitigated to avoid their worst consequences. They can be leveraged to bring out uniquely human advantages.

What does this mean for the workplace environment? It means biases can, and need to be, *managed*.

How can we manage our biases?

First, engage workers in *experiential learning* rather than having them just observe or being told what to do. Engaging people—from leadership to talent—means leveraging these human traits.

Second, create a *culture of belonging* to trigger strong and pleasurable emotions associated with work. An inclusive culture of teamwork and belonging has been used successfully by leading technology companies—from Google to Zappos to American Airlines.

Third, utilize people for *focused decision-making*, while leaving technology for a large number of repetitive tasks. Humans have limited attention span and easily become overwhelmed with large amounts of information. However, we excel in creativity and innovation when focused on a small range of decisions. Use technology to automate the decisions that require big data computation, while reserving decisions that require value judgments for the humans. Executives and managers can make decisions that matter without having to become quants.

Fourth, *prevent atrophy of decision-making muscles*. We live in a world of disruptions that are increasingly becoming commonplace. Technology is only as good as the data it is based on, and disruptions alter data. Humans with their cognitive adaptive strategies can override systems to account for new and unexpected events that require quick responses more than precision.

These strategies will bring out the best in people while accommodating for our inherent frailties.

Dealing with Human Biases

Kasparov has mixed feelings about human intelligence. "For all of the immense power of the human mind, it is very easy to fool. I'm a firm believer in the power of human intuition and how we must cultivate it by relying on it, but I cannot deny that my faith has been shaken by reading books like Kahneman's *Thinking, Fast and Slow* and Ariely's *Predictably Irrational*. After reading their work, you might wonder how we survive at all."[40]

Indeed, there are dozens of known and well-documented human *cognitive biases* that plague our ability to reason consistently, to make decisions based on evidence, to make accurate predictions of the future, and to evaluate facts.

We want to distinguish the biases reviewed here from that of racial, ethnic, gender, religious, or other forms of biases. The cognitive biases reviewed here are universal—they plague humans regardless of race, gender, etc. The biases associated with judging others based on their skin color, body parts, or place of birth is not baked into what it means to be human—it is an individual moral failure. That's why we aren't dwelling on those kinds of biases.

This section does not attempt to provide a comprehensive review of cognitive biases but rather describes a handful of them that are particularly problematic in an organizational setting as they pertain to how people interact with other people in transactional settings. Fortunately, most biases are susceptible to remediation by strategic utilization of AI as a decision-making support system.

Anchoring

In making a numerical forecast (e.g., How many marbles are in the jar? How many hours will this task require to complete? How much would she be willing to pay for this car?), humans tend to use a reference point or "anchor" to begin with—even when doing so is irrational. One's guess is prone to be unreasonably influenced by suggestion because of the *anchoring effect*. This describes a situation where people make a wrong choice as to a numerical value because they were exposed to an anchor number, even when the anchor number is completely unrelated to the choice at issue. Kahneman suggests that the anchoring effect "occurs when people consider a particular value for an unknown quantity before estimating that quantity."[41]

Research suggests there are actually two different mechanisms responsible for producing anchoring effects in human decision-making, and they correspond to the two different systems of thinking described above. System 1 is plagued by anchoring resulting from a "priming effect," whereas System 2 is hampered by anchoring that occurs in a "deliberate process of adjustment."[42]

System 1 anchoring is a consequence of the effort to "construct a world in which the anchor is the true number." In System 1 thinking, "anchoring is a case of suggestion," and "suggestion is a priming effect, which selectively evokes compatible evidence." "System 1 understands sentences by trying to make them true," which requires "the selective activation of compatible thoughts," which in turn "produces a family of systematic errors that make us gullible and prone to believe too strongly whatever we believe."[43]

System 2 anchoring is a heuristic that seeks to make an estimate when quantities are uncertain. We can fall victim to anchoring even when we are acting in a consciously deliberate manner. We tend to "start from an anchoring number, assess whether it is too high or too low, and gradually adjust [our] estimate by mentally 'moving' from the anchor. The adjustment typically ends prematurely, because people stop when they are no longer certain that they should move farther."[44]

We can illustrate the effect of anchoring in enterprise with a few examples. In a negotiation setting, whichever party makes the first offer establishes a range of reasonable possibilities in the other's mind. The counteroffer will naturally be a reaction to the first offer upon which it is anchored. Retailers routinely use anchoring to incentivize purchases. Prices are shown as a comparison against an anchor. For example, the product is labeled as "was $49.99 now $29.99." The anchor provides the point of reference, making the new deal seem more valuable than it really is.

Technology can assist in negotiations by churning through data and arming the human negotiator with the best anchors and providing ranges and conditions to consider to avoid being unduly influenced by the anchor, so they might be most effective in negotiations.

Management should have protocols in place to mitigate the effects of anchoring in situations requiring humans to make numerical forecasts.

Bandwagon Effect

The *bandwagon effect* is a cognitive bias that manifests as the tendency to adopt beliefs, attitudes, behaviors, and styles simply because other people are doing it, even if this conflicts with our own beliefs or the available evidence.[45]

Examples are seen everywhere—from fashion, to music, to politics. It is a form of groupthink where there is pressure to conform to others and the desire to be right. The bandwagon effect reveals the very human need of individuals to be included and accepted in a group. Belonging is a basic human need.

There are clearly negative implications to this. Working meetings, for example, can be unproductive due to the desire of members to conform with the ideas and attitudes of others. It goes without saying that what is popular is not always rational. Understanding the bandwagon effect and groupthink can help companies mitigate it—and use it.

The bandwagon effect can be used to promote diverse ideas by encouraging people to voice different opinions. This sounds contradictory, but it works. Organizations that have an open environment and actually encourage members to be free to express novel opinions find that the bandwagon effect kicks in and others follow suit. Conformity in this case actually encourages, instead of inhibits, the contribution of novel and creative ideas.

The bandwagon effect underscores the importance of humans to be included and to be part of a group. Enterprises would be wise to leverage this bias by creating an inclusive culture that in turn encourages individual expression as part of the group identity.

Attribution Bias

Attribution bias is a cognitive bias that arises in situations where we are trying to explain other people's behavior. Attribution biases are the systematic errors in evaluating the motivation and explanations for behavior. "When we tend to overestimate the role of personal factors and overlook the impact of situations, we are making a mistake that social psychologists have termed the *fundamental attribution error.*"[46] For example, when someone leaves a large tip because they are trying to impress their dinner date, but we mistakenly assume they left the large tip because they are wealthy, we commit the fundamental attribution error. When explaining behavior, the context of the behavior matters to its explanation at least as much as the identity of the actor.

We tend not to be objective when evaluating others' behavior versus our own. Humans can have skewed perceptions that blame others when they fail but excuse our own conduct when we fail. When judging negative actions of others we tend to assume these actions are the result of personal factors. This may involve assuming they are a bad person or they have the personal vice of laziness. However, when judging negative aspects of our own performance, we tend to attribute problems not to our own actions but as a result of external circumstances. We were late because the freeway was backed up, not because we overslept. It is interesting that positive outcomes are given just the opposite attribution. Successful performance of others tends to be attributed to external factors (e.g., "my competitor succeeded because he had better luck"), while our own successful performance is attributed to personal competence (e.g., "I succeeded because I have greater skill").

Like the other biases, attribution bias is part of being human. We just need to manage it. This is especially pertinent to enterprise in the context of performance evaluations.

Given the prevalence of attribution bias, we would be prudent to lean on objective performance indicators and decision support software when making performance evaluations in the workplace. Technology can provide the objectivity needed to produce consistent measurements and give credit where credit is due. Technology can take the subjectivity out of evaluation.

Confirmation Bias

Confirmation bias is the tendency to only seek information that matches what one already believes. It is a human tendency to want to be right and loathe being wrong. We give special weight to the conclusions we want to reach and the beliefs we already have. Contradictory information requires extra mental energy to process so we shy away from it. The effect is stronger for emotionally charged issues and for deeply entrenched beliefs. People also tend to interpret ambiguous evidence as supporting their existing position.

Kahneman explains confirmation bias as a maladaptation of System 2 thinking. "A deliberate search for confirming evidence, known as *positive test strategy*, is also how System 2 tests a hypothesis. Contrary to the rules of philosophers of science, who advise testing hypotheses by trying to refute them, people (and scientists, quite often) seek data that are likely to be compatible with the beliefs they currently hold. The confirmatory bias of System 1 favors uncritical acceptance of suggestions and exaggeration of the likelihood of extreme and improbable events."[47]

Confirmation bias is seen any time initial information created an initial opinion. We see it in employee hiring decisions to supplier selection, project pursuit, or financial investing. For example, investors seek out information that confirms their existing opinions and filter out or ignore contrary information.

Confirmation bias is related to another bias—overconfidence. We can see this in the behavior of the stock market and why it does not always behave rationally. In stock trading the bullish tend to remain bullish, while the bears tend to remain bearish regardless of what is happening. This is due to confirmation bias—only looking for supporting evidence and then being overconfident in that evidence.

How do we counteract this bias? Seeking out people and data with alternative opinions can help overcome confirmation bias and assist in making better-informed decisions.

Creating a culture where diversity in opinions is the norm and where offering evidence-based opinions is rewarded helps eliminate this bias.

Framing

Framing is a cognitive bias where people react differently to things—events, products, or even people—depending on how they are presented. Kahneman explains the framing effect as, "Different ways of presenting the same information often evok[ing] different emotions," sometimes leading to "large changes of preferences that are sometimes caused by inconsequential variations in the wording of a choice problem."[48]

We see things the way they are portrayed or "framed." This is commonplace in politics or advertising where visuals and words are manipulated to highlight positive effects and downplay negative ones.

Just consider the following comparisons: "The medicine has proven effective in 80% of cases" versus "The medicine has failed in 1 out of every 5 cases." The sentences say exactly the same thing; they are based on the same underlying fact. However, they are framed differently and will likely evoke starkly different emotional responses—the first a positive feeling about the medicine's efficacy, the latter a lack of confidence. The framing effect is powerful.

The framing effect can cause major problems to pollsters. Depending on how a question is framed, the respondents may generate wildly different responses even when the pollster is trying to elicit information about the same underlying issue.

The effect may be reduced or even eliminated if ample credible information is provided to people. One strategy is to train humans to "think outside of the frame." This is a very simple tactic. Once we are aware of framing we can present both a negative and positive frame to ourselves and consider the underlying issue objectively.

Second, it is important that machines are programmed to provide information to decision-makers in a frame-neutral manner. Otherwise, even a technology-driven organization where decision-makers believe they are relying on facts and statistics can fall victim to the framing effect.

In conclusion, human decision-making is troubled by a number of biases. Some of these that are particularly troubling for enterprises are anchoring, bandwagon effect, attribution bias, confirmation bias, and the framing effect. Corporate leaders should aim to offset these biases with decision support technology.

Cultivating Human Virtues in the Technology Era

The nature of work is clearly changing in the digital world as machines increasingly take over tasks traditionally done by humans. Organizations should be continually reviewing what tasks can be automated and what should be retained by human labor, at all organizational levels. How to leverage talent and how to integrate human resources with technology is an ongoing management responsibility.

While cognitive skills like rational analysis and decision-making were once considered the inviolate, unreplaceable, sovereign domain of humans, AI is surpassing human rationality in many ways.

So what is left for humans? What value can humans bring to an enterprise that has AI? What are the skills needed moving forward? Remember that the competencies of both machines and humans complement each other. Organizations will simply need to find strategies to integrate the two for the new work environment—the one we call the Humachine. Three categories of human qualities needed for the Humachine are literacy, competencies, and character traits. See Table 4.5.

Let's look at the three categories of qualities that humans will need in the technology era. The first category is *literacy*. Unlike in the past where deep and narrow literacy was valued, human literacy moving forward will need

Table 4.5 Human qualities in the Humachine

Quality	Scope	Description
Literacy	Generalists versus specialists	Technological, scientific, financial, culture, cultural and social
Competence	Link technical to human	Systems thinking, collaboration, critical thinking, problem solving, creativity, innovation
Character traits	Uniquely human abilities	Emotional intelligence, curiosity, persistence, empathy, initiative, leadership, social and cultural awareness

to be broad. Humans will need technical competence but also the ability to connect that to culture, society, and needs of the enterprise. They will need to understand how data in one area relates to the organization as a whole. For example, procurement managers will need to understand how supplier data relates not just to procurement metrics but financial performance and corporate strategy. Humans will need to be fluent in the language of strategy and financials in addition to their own specialized area. AI systems driven by big data will become intelligent but in the most narrow of ways. Humans will have a much better time than machines of gaining and applying broad general understanding. This broad literacy across domains will be a distinguishing value of humans for some time to come.

The second category of a unique human resource is *competencies* in linking the *technical* with the *human*. We need to be able to use systems thinking to link data to culture, emotions, creativity, innovation, teamwork, and collaboration. This will require using emotional intelligence to create connections and trust with stakeholders, from coworkers, managers, customers, suppliers, and board members. Without this competency, the technical proficiency of an organization will fail to be translated into action.

The third category is specific *character traits* humans will need. These are the traits we consider uniquely human. This includes emotional intelligence that will allow humans to relate to others. Consider, for example, an oncologist using data from IBM Watson to develop a treatment plan for a patient. Yes, the statistics are there, but it is the physician who will need a high emotional intelligence to present facts in a way the patient can understand, allay fears, and offer support and

113

comfort. This is caring. IBM Watson is not capable of receiving high marks for bedside manner.

These character traits also include *curiosity* and *care* that will fuel creativity and innovation. We need individual "self-starters" as well as leaders who can keep the team motivated. Other traits include *adaptability*. These are individuals who can easily adapt to new environments and conditions, which are going to be inevitable in an increasingly complex world. Another character trait essential to the future enterprise is *integrity*. Machines are not yet in a position to advise on the resolution of ethical dilemmas or to guide the user on the ethical use of intelligence. We still need humans to bring ethical values to work.

Enterprises are currently focused on how to move through digital transformation. They are focused on technology and efficiency. We argue that the technological enterprise of the future must remain human-centric to succeed. For all of our biases and shortcomings, we care, and sometimes that's what matters most.

Changing What It Means to Be Smart

According to Ed Hess, "In an age of smart machines, our old definition of what makes a person smart doesn't make sense."[49] If we measure smarts by the ability to process, store, and recall information, to pattern-match and produce analysis, then humans are actually pretty dumb (relative to computers).

> What is needed is a new definition of being smart, one that promotes higher levels of human thinking and emotional engagement. The new smart will be determined not by what or how you know but by the quality of your thinking, listening, relating, collaborating, and learning. Quantity is replaced by quality. And that shift will enable us to focus on the hard work of taking our cognitive and emotional skills to a much higher level.[50]

Revising our notion of "smart" to shift away from information processing to emotional intelligence is advisable. At the same time, we should be open-minded about this. Individuals living at the far edges of the autism spectrum may lack interpersonal skills usually associated with emotional intelligence and yet may be far superior than the average person at information processing and recall.

Indeed, one of the founders of machine learning, the British mathematician, computer scientist, and logician Alan Turing, "was not diagnosed in his lifetime, but his mathematical genius and social inelegance fit the profile for autism spectrum disorder (ASD)."[51]

According to the Centers for Disease Control and Prevention, about 1% of the global population lives with ASD.[52] The vast majority of those living with autism are unemployed or underemployed, likely as a result of prejudice in our thinking that would suggest people with ASD are unable to contribute in a work environment. "To the extent that's true, it's a measure of our failure as a society. Almost half of those diagnosed with ASD are of average or above-average intellectual ability."[53] Humans with ASD tend to be very analytical, detail-oriented, honest, and respectful of rules; failing to incorporate them into the workforce "is more than just a personal tragedy; it's a monumental waste of human talent."[54]

Baby Boomers and Botsourcing

While we may be imperfectly rational, that is not a complete explanation for why AI is on the ascendancy in the workplace, taking over jobs previously held by humans. We would be oversimplifying if we said that AI is taking over the economy because humans aren't rational enough. Current trends in economic displacement are driven by much more than our limitations as rational thinkers.

In this section, we discuss some of the demographic and economic trends that are disrupting the economy, as a backdrop for a greater appreciation of the limits of human intellectual capabilities in this era of job functions driven more and more by intelligence.

The popular press is filled with warnings of the battle between technology and humans. We hear of countless studies warning of potential job losses across all sectors due to advances in automation. In the quest for improved production processes, artificial intelligence, robotics, and digitization are altering the workforce as we know it. It is replacing skills and transforming labor markets. Digitization and automation are already fundamentally transforming the way we work.

The trend of displacing physical labor with machine power that began with the Industrial Revolution has simply continued, and it's not clear that it is even increasing. In the US, the agricultural sector saw about 40% of its labor force displaced between 1900 and 1940; the manufacturing sector saw about 13% of its labor force displaced between 1970 and 1990.[55]

According to the World Economic Forum, we are witnessing the convergence of "two parallel and interconnected fronts of change in workforce transformations: (1) large-scale decline in some roles as tasks within these roles become automated or redundant, and (2) large-scale growth in new products and services—and associated new tasks and jobs—generated by the adoption of new technologies and other socioeconomic developments such as the rise of middle classes in emerging economies and demographic shifts."[56]

There are explanations for these trends that do not rely entirely on robotics. The agricultural sector probably lost jobs between 1900 and 1940 because of the Great Depression, the Dust Bowl, and the military draft and deployment of soldiers in the First and Second World Wars. The manufacturing sector probably lost jobs between 1970 and 1990 because of regulatory arbitrage. The minute the federal Occupational Safety and Health Act of 1970 (OSHA) was passed by Congress and signed into law, domestic manufacturing began fleeing the US for more laissez-faire economic conditions in other countries, presumably to avoid compliance with these new stringent worker safety standards.

Not only are there various economic, historic, and non-robot-related explanations for physical labor displacement, but also it's not like the US economy has been irreparably harmed from physical labor displacement. Agriculture and manufacturing sector jobs gave way to service-oriented and information-based work. Displacement from one sector does not mean jobs are lost forever; it usually means they move to a different (if not new) sector of the economy.

A Bain & Co. report titled "Labor 2030: The Collision of Demographics, Automation and Inequality" predicts that as a result of automation, 20%–25% of the total US labor force will be displaced.[57] However, the labor force will be shrinking as a result of the retirement of the baby boomer generation no less than because of investment into automation technology. "The three factors that created this powerful lift to growth [of GDP in OECD countries]—women entering the workforce, the opening of China and India, and the baby boomer generation—are now largely mature, and their positive boost to macro conditions is now fading."[58]

How could automation be eliminating millions of jobs if, at the same time as automation is rolled out, millions of laborers are retiring? Those jobs would have been lost without the automation, as people in their 70s age out of the workforce. More hype. It's as if AI is the notorious, despicable, faceless "other" that we are seeking to scapegoat as the cause of our economic woes.

A more likely forecast is that automation will ensure that work previously done by baby boomers will be done by robots, thus ensuring consistent levels of labor productivity even with a shrinking workforce. If an aging workforce reduces supply growth, but the concurrent trend of automation increases supply growth, then these two trends could very well cancel out. If that is true, the real turbulence forecasted by Bain & Co. is not from AI or robotic automation at all but rather from the disturbing trend of growing income inequality, which threatens to reduce potential demand growth.

In other words, the problem is not robots; it's poverty. Poor people have a hard time learning how to manage technology platforms required for the jobs of the future. We do not dispute that in the coming decades, the global economy will look different than it did before. We are simply pointing out that this has been the case since the Industrial Revolution. This sentence could have been stated truthfully for the last fifty years: "Automation and AI will mean less need for physical labor and much more demand for high-tech and social skills."[59] The *MIT Technology Review* cover's claim that "AI and robotics are wreaking economic havoc" is then somewhat misleading.

Poverty is causing economic havoc. Concentration of wealth and stagnant wages when controlled for inflation are causing economic havoc. The sense of despair that creeps in when students (even those graduating with STEM degrees) are saddled with ungodly amounts of debt and will never attain the standard of living achieved by their parents—that's what's causing economic havoc. Not robots.

If we want to reduce the economic havoc forecasted in the coming decades, we need to ensure that the oft-promised, never-delivered wealth in the trickle-down economy actually trickles down. Research suggests the answer is actually *more* AI and robotics deployed more widely throughout the economy to stimulate increases in productivity, coupled with (and we really are careful here) some fair means by which wealth can be distributed so as to alleviate the stagnation of wages and income inequality and ensure basic needs are met. Maybe it's taxing robots' efficiency gains to share the savings created by botsourcing. Maybe it's universal basic income. We leave that to the politicians.

Although horses were a fundamental economic force in the early twentieth century, "Within 50 years cars and tractors made short work of equine livelihoods. Some futurists see a cautionary tale for humanity in the fate of the horse: it was economically indispensable until it wasn't."[60]

It simply is not the case that AI is taking our jobs. The reality is more complicated than that and not as bad as is frequently reported. Humans are afraid of change, even if the change is a good one.

Conclusion

According to Alibaba's founder Jack Ma, in 30 years, "the Time Magazine cover for the best CEO of the year very likely will be a robot. It remembers better than you, it counts faster than you, and it won't be angry with competitors."[61] We disagree. We think leadership positions are not going the way of the ATM anytime soon. In the meantime, humans have a unique role to play in enterprise.

We are a resilient, adaptive, and intelligent species, even if we have our moments of cupidity. As long as we have management frameworks in place that ensure the "right" idea makes it to the top, *only one of us has to be right*. Assume we can adopt and maintain management frameworks that accomplish this filtration function, thereby bringing the best of human thought to the top. Ray Dalio's *Principles* makes this attempt. The fact that there are billions of us bodes well for our continued survival.

What do humans bring to the table? Intuition, general intelligence, aesthetic taste, emotional intelligence, and care. The Humachine will harness these unique features of human resources and offset their biases with decision support.

One of our contentions in this chapter is that human mental qualities make us indispensable for the foreseeable future. Originality, creativity, innovation, conscientiousness, and caring—these features may never be programmable. We encourage readers not to think about human versus machine like some kind of competition over limited jobs. That's not how this transition will play out. We are collaborators, each with different and complementary strengths. We discuss this in greater depth in the next chapter.

Notes

1 Hess, E. D. In the AI Age, "Being Smart" Will Mean Something Completely Different. *Harvard Business Review*, June 19, 2017. Available at https://hbr.org/2017/06/in-the-ai-age-being-smart-will-mean-something-completely-different

2 Pisano, Gary P. The Hard Truth about Innovative Cultures, *Harvard Business Review*, January–February 2019, 63–71.

3 Kahneman, Daniel. *Thinking, Fast and Slow*. pp. 20–21.

4 Kahneman, Daniel. *Thinking, Fast and Slow*. pp. 20–21. "I adopt terms originally proposed by the psychologists Keith Stanovich and Richard West."

5 Kahneman, Daniel. *Thinking, Fast and Slow*. pp. 24–25. One sentence in the block quote comes from page 81.

6 Ibid.

7 Ibid.

8 Hess, E. D. In the AI Age, "Being Smart" Will Mean Something Completely Different. *Harvard Business Review*, June 19, 2017. Available at https://hbr.org/2017/06/in-the-ai-age-being-smart-will-mean-something-completely-different

9 This formulation is from Hofstadter, Chapter XX: Strange Loops, Or Tangled Hierarchies, in the section titled, Can Machines Possess Originality? *Godel, Escher, Bach: An Eternal Golden Braid*. p. 685.

10 Samuel, A. L., Some Moral and Technical Consequences of Automation—A Refutation. *Science*, 132:741–742 (September 16, 1960).

11 Samuel appears to believe his premise that machines do not possess originality is true in an absolute sense and not merely because the state of the art at the time. We could interchange "originality" with "desire," or "feelings," or "volition," and many people would still share that same conviction—that machines just do not have it.
Samuel continues: "The 'intentions' which the machine seems to manifest are the intentions of the human programmer, as specified in advance, or they are subsidiary intentions derived from these, following rules specified by the

programmer. We can anticipate higher levels of abstraction ... in which the program will not only modify the subsidiary intentions but will also modify the rules which are used in their derivation, or in which it will modify the ways in which it modifies the rules, and so on, or even in which one machine will design and construct a second machine with enhanced capabilities. However, and this is important, the machine *will not and cannot* do any of these things until it has been instructed as to how to proceed."

Here, Samuel describes a scenario where a machine intelligence (say, "Alpha"), derived by a programmer, in turn programs a machine (say, "Beta") on its own that is not bound by the same rules as Alpha. In this case, Alpha is bound by strict rules that limit what it can do, but within those constraints Alpha builds a subsidiary, Beta, that has greater degrees of action, is less inhibited by the constraints of Alpha's programmer. Even in that scenario, Samuel argues that Beta will never come into being unless Alpha's programmer wanted it to, and gave it the ability to do so, even if that ability was latent, rather than explicit, in Alpha's programming code.

This all feels intuitive. For example, suppose a programmer writes code to power a word processing software. The software in turn through some accretive process from human use over time develops a function that crafts sonnets based on the patterns of its human user. This subsidiary poetic function, according to Samuel, is only possible because of how the word processing software was designed and is not the result of originality on the part of the software. While intuitive, it appears to be a matter of belief, a strong intuition.

Notwithstanding the empirical evidence that suggests human beings are not as free (nor as rational) as we tend to think, for practical purposes we have to take as a working hypothesis that we do possess some degree of freedom that allows us to make decisions that make sense under the circumstances and which are not strictly speaking causally determined by the past. However, we want to be very clear on this point. Just because we take free will as a working assumption does not mean that we believe it is true. A useful working hypothesis is not, simply by virtue of being useful, true. Suffice it to say, philosophers debate whether free will exists, and most of them would probably say that it is weak, if not simply implausible, to cling to the notion of free will despite all we know about physics, chemistry, biology, and neurology.

We can leave the debate to the philosophers.

12 Pisturi, Joseph. The Future of Human Work Is Imagination, Creativity, and Strategy, *Harvard Business Review*, January 18, 2018.
13 Hofstadter, Douglas. *Godel, Escher, Bach: An Eternal Golden Braid*. p. 27.
14 Ibid., p. 26.
15 Kasparov, Garry and Greengard, Mig. *Deep Thinking: Where Machine Intelligence Ends and Human Creativity Begins*. PublicAffairs. 2017. p. 239.
16 Herbert Simon as quoted by Daniel Kahneman. *Thinking, Fast and Slow*, p. 237. "The model of intuitive decision making as pattern recognition develops ideas presented some time ago by Herbert Simon, perhaps the only scholar who is recognized and admired as a hero and founding figure by all the competing clans and tribes in the study of decision making."
17 What is Creativity? (And why is it a crucial factor for business success?), Creativity at Work. Available at www.creativityatwork.com/2014/02/17/what-is-creativity/

18 Kersting, Karen. What Exactly Is Creativity? Vol. 34, No. 10 (November 2003). Available at www.apa.org/monitor/nov03/creativity.aspx. See also Kendra Cherry, *The Psychology of Creativity*, Very Well Mind (May 24, 2018). Available at www.verywellmind.com/what-is-creativity-p2-3986725

19 Dyer, Jeff, Gregersen, Hal and Christensen, Clayton M. The Innovator's DNA: Mastering the Five Skills of Disruptive Innovators. *Harvard Business Review Press* (1 ed.). July 19, 2011.

20 Schultz, Howard. *Pour Your Heart Into it: How Starbucks Built a Company One Cup at a Time* (Hyperion 1997).

21 Kasparov, Garry and Greengard, Mig. *Deep Thinking: Where Machine Intelligence Ends and Human Creativity Begins*. PublicAffairs. 2017. p. 239.

22 Cowen, Alan S. and Keltner, Dacher. Self-report captures 27 distinct categories of emotion bridged by continuous gradients, *Proceedings of the National Academy of Sciences of the United States of America*, Edited by Joseph E. LeDoux, New York University, New York. September 5, 2017. Available at www.pnas.org/content/early/2017/08/30/1702247114

23 Ibid.

24 Barrett, Jeff. If You Want to Build a Brand, Create an Emotional Experience First. *Inc. Magazine*. April 26, 2017. Available at www.inc.com/jeff-barrett/if-you-want-to-build-a-brand-create-an-emotional-experience-first.html.

25 David, Susan and Congleton, Christina. Emotional Agility, *Harvard Business Review*, November 2013.

26 Bariso, Justin. *13 Signs of High Emotional Intelligence*. Available at www.inc.com/justin-bariso/13-things-emotionally-intelligent-people-do.html (from his forthcoming book, EQ, Applied).

27 www.merriam-webster.com/dictionary/care

28 Heidegger, Martin (1889–1976), Internet Encyclopedia of Philosophy. Available at www.iep.utm.edu/heidegge/#H3

29 Burghardt, Gordon M. *The Genesis of Animal Play: Testing the Limits*. The MIT Press, 2005. https://mitpress.mit.edu/books/genesis-animal-play

30 Meyers-Manor, Julia E. Book Reviews, *American Journal of Human Biology*, 17:821–827, 2005.

31 Ibid.

32 Burghardt, Gordon M. *The Genesis of Animal Play: Testing the Limits*. MIT Press, 2005, p. 8.

33 Ibid.

34 www.merriam-webster.com/dictionary/conscience

35 Schwartz, M.S. *Journal of Business Ethics*, 59:27, 2005. doi:10.1007/s10551-005-3403-2.

36 Hess, E.D. In the AI Age, "Being Smart" Will Mean Something Completely Different. *Harvard Business Review*, June 19, 2017. Available at https://hbr.org/2017/06/in-the-ai-age-being-smart-will-mean-something-completely-different

37 Wood, John. The "Constitution of Man": Reflections on Human Nature from the Federalist Papers to Behavioral Law and Economics. *NYU Journal of Law and Liberty*, 7:185–186, 2013.

38 Ibid.

39 Ibid., p. 186.

40 Kasparov, Garry and Greengard, Mig. *Deep Thinking: Where Machine Intelligence Ends and Human Creativity Begins*. PublicAffairs. 2017, p. 240.

41 Kahneman, Daniel. *Thinking, Fast and Slow*. p. 120.

42 Ibid.

43 Ibid., pp. 122–123.
44 Ibid., p. 120.
45 Neil, John. Cognitive Bias: The Bandwagon Effect, The Ethics Centre. Available at www.ethics.org.au/on-ethics/blog/november-2016/cognitive-bias-the-bandwagon-effect
46 Bias in Attribution. Principles of Social Psychology—1st International Edition. Available at https://opentextbc.ca/socialpsychology/chapter/biases-in-attribution/
47 Kahneman, Daniel. *Thinking, Fast and Slow*. Page 81.
48 Ibid., pp. 88, 272.
49 Hess, E.D. In the AI Age, "Being Smart" Will Mean Something Completely Different. *Harvard Business Review*, June 19, 2017. Available at https://hbr.org/2017/06/in-the-ai-age-being-smart-will-mean-something-completely-different.
50 Ibid.
51 Pelphrey, Vin. Autistic People Can Solve Our Cybersecurity Crisis. *Wired*, November 25, 2016. Available at www.wired.com/2016/11/autistic-people-can-solve-cybersecurity-crisis/
52 Autism Spectrum Disorder (ASD), Centers for Disease Control and Prevention. Available at www.cdc.gov/ncbddd/autism/data.html
53 Pelphrey, Vin. Autistic People Can Solve our Cybersecurity Crisis. *Wired*, November 25, 2016. Available at www.wired.com/2016/11/autistic-people-can-solve-cybersecurity-crisis/
54 Ibid.
55 Rotman, David. *Making AI into Jobs*. MIT Technology Review. July/August 2018. pp. 13–14.
56 World Economic Forum, The Future of Jobs Report 2018, Centre for the New Economy and Society, p. v. Available at www3.weforum.org/docs/WEF_Future_of_Jobs_2018.pdf
57 Harris, Karen, Kimson, Austin and Schwedel, Andrew. *Labor 2030: The Collision of Demographics, Automation and Inequality*. Bain & Co. February 7, 2018. Available at www.bain.com/insights/labor-2030-the-collision-of-demographics-automation-and-inequality/
58 Ibid.
59 Rotman, David. *Making AI into Jobs*. MIT Technology Review. July/August 2018. p. 13.
60 Free Exchange. *Will Robots Displace Humans as Motorised Vehicles Ousted Horses? The Economist*. April 1, 2017. Available at www.economist.com/finance-and-economics/2017/04/01/will-robots-displace-humans-as-motorised-vehicles-ousted-horses.
61 Bhavsar, Neil C. and Reedy, Christianna. *Experts Assert That AI Will Soon Be Replacing CEOs*. Futurism. April 28, 2017. Available at https://futurism.com/experts-assert-that-ai-will-soon-be-replacing-ceos/

5

INTEGRATION OF PEOPLE AND TECHNOLOGY

People keep saying, what happens to jobs in the era of automation? I think there will be more jobs, not fewer... Your future is you with a computer, not you replaced by a computer.

Eric Schmidt, Chairman of Alphabet
and former CEO of Google[1]

Catalyzing positive outcomes and a future of good work for all will require bold leadership and an entrepreneurial spirit from businesses and governments, as well as an agile mindset of lifelong learning from employees.

World Economic Forum, The Future of Jobs Report[2]

My biggest fear is that, unless we tune our algorithms for self-actualization, it will be simply too convenient for people to follow the advice of an algorithm (or, too difficult to go beyond such advice), turning these algorithms into self-fulfilling prophecies and users into zombies who exclusively consume easy-to-consume items."

Bart Knijnenburg, Assistant Professor in human-centered computing at ClemsonUniversity says[3]

Use It or Lose It

As companies botsource certain technical skills to machines, they run the risk of losing these very skills entirely. Organizations may be left with no one on hand who knows how to do crucial but usually-automated tasks manually in case the power goes down. Just consider the following from a large hospital network we interviewed.

The Chief Nursing Executive (CNE) at the hospital network provided an example of skills that have atrophied with younger nurses as they increasingly rely on technology: calibrating intravenous (IV) pumps. In the hospital settings, the ability to correctly program IV pumps is critical to deliver the right infusion of medication to patients through IV drip. More than a decade ago, smart IV pumps that automatically calibrate medication dosing were introduced. Prior to this technology, all IV pump programming required the user to manually calculate the rate of infusion then input the desired infusion rate into the pump. This manual technique is complicated as many different units of measurement are used in the administration of IV medications. As a result, the required calculations are often complex and require a skilled practitioner. Otherwise, there is a high likelihood of user error. By contrast, smart IV pumps allow the user to choose the desired medication from an approved list and input the required patient information, after which the smart IV pump calculates the infusion rate automatically.

The CNE explained that a major concern for the hospital executives is the event of a security breach or power outage, as smart IV pumps depend on uninterrupted connection to a power source. Only the older nurses have the skills and experience to calibrate IV dosing. As the hospital network has become dependent on the technology, the younger nurses were never trained and the skill is being lost. By not using the skill of calibrating IV pumps to control medication dosage, nor being trained on it, nursing staff are seeing an atrophy of this vital skill. This has created vulnerability within the hospital system. Given a disruption like power loss, very few nurses would know what to do for those patients needing IV-administered drugs.

As organizations move to increase botsourcing, leaders must be mindful of resulting gaps in human-held institutional knowledge and human-held operational capacities. These gaps create risks of atrophy and are an unhealthy side-effect of too much botsourcing and inadequate integration of human and machine resources.

Recipe, Formula, Alchemical Spell, Call It What You Will

This chapter examines how AI is impacting humans at work, with the goal of understanding how unique skills of people and technology can be combined for extraordinary results.

A word about "integrating" or "combining" human and machine. We mean this in a figurative sense, as in collaboration between team members rather than combining sugar and flour in a baking recipe. We feel this distinction is important because some of the pathways to superintelligence reviewed in Chapter 2 clearly envision some literal "combination" of humans and machines in the sense of cyborgization. That's not what we are suggesting. We eschew the morbid biological-mechanical hybrid creatures of science fiction—cyborgs with cranial implants or digital whole brain emulation. Rather, we are trying to create an enterprise with superintelligence, a network of human and machine minds that are powerful, wise, and humane.

Recall from Chapter 1 that Kasparov's Law explains the results of the Advanced Chess experiment in terms of the triumph of process over genius and raw computing power.[4] How can amateur chess players defeat grand masters *unless* ordinary human and machine skills used in the right combination pursuant to the right process can attain extraordinary results? We are seeking to apply this law to the enterprise level.

Recall **Moravec's Paradox**, which holds that what machines are good at, humans are not, and vice versa.[5] **Kasparov's Law** holds that *weak human + machine + better process* is superior to a strong computer alone and, more remarkably, superior to a *strong human + machine + inferior process*.[6] Further, Bostrom's definition of "collective" or **organizational network superintelligence** holds that superintelligence could emerge "through the gradual enhancement of networks and organizations that link individual human minds with one another and with various artifacts and bots."[7]

At the highest level of abstraction, we are applying Kasparov's Law to resolve Moravec's Paradox so as to fulfill Bostrom's conditions for collective intelligence, thereby creating a Humachine. See Figure 5.1.

Moravec's Paradox

- Machine capabilities are inversely related to human capabilities.
- Where computers excel, humans struggle, and vice versa.

Kasparov's Law

- Combining ordinary humans and computational resources with the right process can produce extraordinary results.
- Ordinary machines and people using the right process can prevail over human genius and supercomputing without the right process.

Bostrom's Collective Superintelligence

- Emerges from enhancement of networks and organizations linking individual human minds with one another and with various bots.
- A large number of smaller intellects networked together can create a system that outstrips existing cognitive systems.

The Humachine

- Harnessing data and AI to power the display of uniquely human skills.
- Combining the virtues of machines and humanity to overcome the limits of both in a superintelligent organization.

Figure 5.1 Conceptual map of our thesis.

The Humachine is an organization of humans and bots so networked that each mitigates the other's unique limitations and augments the other's unique strengths, thereby attaining collective superintelligence.

To that end, we explore some of the challenges involved in integrating humans and machines, two complementary yet inversely related organizational resources. As noted by the World Economic Forum's The Future of Jobs Report 2018, "The emerging contours of the new world of work in the Fourth Industrial Revolution are rapidly becoming a lived reality for millions of workers and companies around the world.

An enterprise will need to utilize management protocols that allocate enterprise functions optimally between existing human and technical resources, such that each contributes its exclusive and complementary skill to the enterprise's mission. We think eventually this kind of collaborative process between human and technical resources can lead to the emergence of organizational network superintelligence.

If the correct organizational structure is deployed, the combination of humankind and machine skills will not only be additive but rather synergistic as the enterprise ends up (whether this is figuratively or literally, we leave to the philosophers) possessing a mind of its own that is greater than the sum total of its parts. A mind that is relentless in its pursuit of the mission of the enterprise, but also wise, humane, and conscientious in its methods.

This quest to create the Humachine is already underway.

This chapter will survey trends in human resources driven by the ascendance of AI with an eye toward creating organizational network intelligence.

Jobs Are Going to Evolve but Not Disappear

Let's face it, some of us are going to lose our jobs because a machine replaced our function. In the medical community, for example, radiologists are vulnerable to displacement by advances in radiology technology. However, we must go beyond this first-generation job loss to contemplate the larger impacts of automation on work. While one generation of radiologists may be out of work, future medical school students will likely choose an alternative career path within medicine and will apply their talents to other issues outside of radiology. This influx of human talent into other fields of medicine will create spillover benefits to all health care stakeholders, including patients, as human talent will be more efficiently allocated within the industry, at least in theory leading to better quality care and more innovation. Policymakers can help ease the pain of transition by lowering transaction costs associated with re-skilling.

While it is challenging to make precise forecasts of how *many* jobs will emerge in the Fourth Industrial Revolution, The Center for the Future of Work at Cognizant Technology Solutions has tried to describe certain *kinds* of jobs in its reports 21 Jobs for the Future.[8]

Cognizant offers an optimistic perspective on the future of human work, based on a few principles[9]:

- Work has always changed
- Lots of current work is awful
- Machines need man
- Don't underestimate human imagination or ingenuity
- Technology will upgrade all aspects of society
- Technology solves—and creates—problems

New and previously unimagined job titles may include: Data Detectives, AI-Assisted Healthcare Technicians, Chief Trust Officers, Augmented Reality Journey Builder, Personal Memory Curator, Man-Machine Teaming Manager, Personal Data Broker, and Talkers. Cognizant even provides a mock-up of job descriptions for these positions.[10]

The dark cloud cast by the fear of job losses obscures the much brighter future wherein we have so many jobs automated we can finally afford to apply our uniquely human skills to creative, aesthetic, emotional, caring, and joyful pursuits. In a more mundane forecast, AI will enable humans to be more productive at our typical drudgery. Either way, it's not all bad.

Although employment in the financial services sector has contracted since 2008, to date this is in part due to the Great Recession as much as it is to displacement by machines. Going forward, the most vulnerable jobs in the financial services sector are those ripe for automation—the US Bureau of Labor Statistics suggests that bank tellers and insurance underwriters will see a tangible decline in human employment between 2014 and 2024. That said, financial services employers are hiring new talent in the areas of software development and data science. Large financial institutions are acquiring and investing in AI and machine learning-powered fraud detection and financial security start-ups in order to acquire technology and labor that can be strategic assets for the bank—evidence that the human skill set required to manage performance of financial institutions is *shifting* rather than *eroding*. Let us learn how to work with bots; they will soon be our colleagues.

According to Arvind Purushotham, the managing director of Citigroup's venture investing arm, the big problems facing financial institutions are not being solved by machines just yet, but by humans assisted by AI: "We think of human-assisted AI and AI-assisted humans," said Purushotham, "There are some things that humans can do that software programs can't hope to catch up to in decades."[11] This points to the emergence of a more symbiotic relationship between humans and machines. Here, both robots and machines depend on one another and improve by interacting with one another.

Still others predict that AI is coming for the financial services industry in a more corrosive way with respect to displacing human laborers. While automated teller machines (ATMs) are now a familiar sight on urban streets and inside grocery stores, they cost bank tellers a lot of jobs. Then with the advent of Internet and mobile banking, more human workers in the banking space were displaced as bank customers increasingly accessed banking resources through their phones and at home, rather than by driving to a bank and interacting with a person.

According to Suranga Chandratillake, a partner at London-based venture capital firm Balderton Capital, the next wave of displacement in financial services will be in "pseudo white-collar jobs," such as reviewing mortgage applications and adjusting insurance claims. These positions are lower in the corporate hierarchy than executive or manager, still characterized as requiring human judgment, but which would see performance improvements from AI in terms of increased speed, greater accuracy, and less bias.[12] Jobs that fit these characteristics are most susceptible to botsourcing.

The greatest impacts of AI are not in sloughing off human resource costs from the balance sheet as people are displaced by machines. That is a myopic view of the transformative potential of AI. This assumes humans are merely a cost, not an asset. We suggest looking at AI as a performance-enhancing additive. rather than an alternative to, human resources. Companies will see the greatest payout in terms of performance improvements if they can engender collaboration between humans and smart machines.

According to research in *Harvard Business Review*, humans and AI are already working together to create ***collaborative intelligence***. "While AI will radically alter how work gets done and who does it, the technology's larger impact will be in complementing and augmenting human capabilities, not replacing them."[13]

We consider this perspective a powerful rebuke to the fear mongering over botsourcing. The real transformative impact of AI is not kicking human laborers to the curb but in equipping them with greater analytical and data-driven powers. Further, smart machines will need human coaches and interpreters.

People are needed to train machines, explain their outputs, and ensure their responsible use. AI, in turn, can enhance humans' cognitive skills and creativity, free workers from low-level tasks, and extend their physical capabilities.[14]

AI Is a Horizontal Enabling Layer

Automation of physical labor can lead to growth, not just efficiency gains. Amazon is plowing forward with a continued expansion of robot-human collaboration meant to improve efficiency in fulfillment centers.[15] Amazon explains that its expansion in the use of robots has led to *more* investments and *new* jobs.

In fact, facilities with robots tend to employ more humans than those without them because robots make these facilities more efficient and capable of processing more orders. Robots cannot do everything and more orders mean more humans are needed. In other words, *the robots might not take our jobs—they could very well make our jobs.*

As of publication, more than 25 of Amazon's 175 fulfillment centers worldwide use robots.[16] There are over 100,000 robots in Amazon's fulfillment centers that autonomously deliver products to humans, who then pack the boxes that go out to customers. Amazon's warehouses have been partially automated for some time. Most use robots to carry shelves of products to human workers, who then select the items to be shipped. While the humans handle the complex manipulations that would confound a robot, the robots do the dull task of hurrying around the warehouse carrying heavy loads.

In its warehouse in Monee, Illinois, humans and robots now work alongside one another to fill customer orders. The warehouse has more than 2,000 full-time employees working alongside a fleet of Kiva robots, delivering items to workers and helping them with tasks.

What is surprising is that despite the robot influence, the human jobs have not changed all that much. The robots just help to do the difficult tasks. Jobs for humans working alongside robots "aren't as different as you'd think" from what they had been doing in a warehouse without robots, said Jeff Messenger, the facility's general manager.[17] He explains that the robots handle things that would be considered grunt work. They move boxes and do things to help humans become more efficient, such as dispensing the right amount of packing tape and lifting heavy boxes. The robots are their helpers to add precision and handle the heavy work.

As we see with Amazon's warehouses and fulfillment centers, machines are being used in all sectors and all areas. The misconception, however, is that robots are actually meant to replace human labor. As the scenario with Amazon illustrates, robots are typically doing supporting roles that are challenging for humans. That said, we are probably only one or two steps away from completely automated factories—we just need some advancements in the robots' hand-like manipulation of objects and all but the most delicate packaging tasks could be botsourced. Robot designers in Boston will probably have patented a fully dexterous bipedal humanoid capable of knitting a sweater white tap dancing before this book is printed.

According to Peter Norvig, former NASA scientist, leading artificial intelligence scientist, and a director of research at Google, it is easy to foresee the downsides of the dramatic displacement of human laborers from the workforce but almost unimaginable what the upsides could be.[18] When the internal combustion engine displaced the horse-drawn buggy, it also led to the creation of millions of new jobs that were inconceivable at the time of the disruption.

Studies show that looking at specific jobs is not a good indicator of where machines will dominate. Rather it is work activities rather than actual occupations that will be given away to machines.[19] Repetitive, routine, and predictable problems that rely on electronically available data are the most easily automated. For automation to work, however, the requirement is that the knowledge and relevant decision criteria be very clearly defined and structured. The problem itself must be clear and well understood to be accurately programmed into the algorithms. Examples of this are seen in traditional manufacturing processes, such as assembly work, security monitoring, time tracking, shipping, and inventory decisions. These decisions are all pretty routine and easily specified, therefore easy to automate. We also see automation in banking, such as credit card and loan application processing as well as making changes to investment portfolios. These are all technical, tactical activities where the problems are easy to specify and the answers are based on data. Therefore, they are easy to automate.

The jobs that will remain the domain of humans are those that are unpredictable, require managing others, interacting with stakeholders, applying expertise and decision-making, and explaining decisions to others. It is also not possible to automate jobs that require a high degree of imagination, creativity, goal setting, or strategic thinking. This includes executive and leadership roles, management, medicine, education, as well as construction, forestry, physical therapists, personal trainers, negotiators, and hair stylists. These, for example, will continue to require uniquely human skills.

However, all these roles will be assisted with machines. Machines are not a threat, they are collaborators. This human-machine interaction is needed for humans to excel, to be more productive and efficient.

According to Amazon CEO Jeff Bezos, we are in a golden age of AI and machine learning in enterprise[20]:

> We are solving problems with machine learning and artificial intelligence that were in the realm of science fiction for the last several decades. Machine learning and AI is a horizontal enabling layer. It will empower and improve every business, every government

organization, every philanthropy—basically there's no institution in the world that cannot be improved with machine learning. I would say, a lot of the value that we're getting from machine learning is actually happening beneath the surface. It is things like improved search results. Improved product recommendations for customers. Improved forecasting for inventory management. Literally hundreds of other things beneath the surface. The most exciting thing that I think we're working on in machine learning, is that we are determined, through Amazon Web Services—where we have all these customers who are corporations and software developers—to make these advanced techniques accessible to every organization, even if they don't have the current class of expertise that's required. Right now, deploying these techniques for your particular institution's problems is difficult. It takes a lot of expertise, and so you have to go compete for the very best PhDs in machine learning and it's difficult for a lot of organizations to win those competitions. I think we can build a great business doing that, for ourselves, and it will be incredibly enabling for organizations that want to use these sophisticated technologies.

With these AI and machine learning capabilities pioneered by Amazon, and made widely available to smaller enterprises through cloud computing, AI has become a horizontal enabling layer that empowers all who deploy it.

Complementary Coworkers: Moravec's Paradox Resolved

Humans and machines complement one another. The strengths of one are weaknesses of the other. Together, they can offset the other's shortcomings and enhance the other's strengths. See Figure 5.2.

As enterprises seek to integrate human and machine laborers, the field of *social robotics* becomes more relevant. Social robotics is the study of "how people interact with artificially intelligent technology."[21] Machines are great at brute strength analysis, precision in calculation, and processing speed. They can process huge data sets, identify patterns unimaginable to humans, and offer unparalleled accuracy.

Nonetheless, a machine as powerful as IBM's Watson that is explicitly "designed to understand natural human language has to sort through millions of clues to establish enough context to make sense of something that is instantly obvious to a human."[22] Humans, on the other hand, can make connections using context clues, be creative and think "outside of the box." They are innovative, strategic, capable of leadership, have empathy and emotion, and capable of explaining the logic of their decisions.

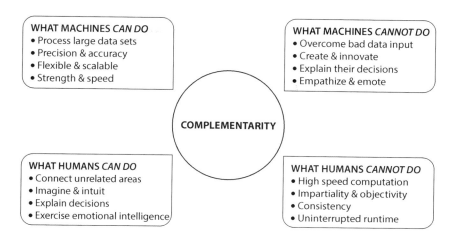

Figure 5.2 Moravec's paradox in management applications.

This latter "human" capability bears emphasizing. Explaining the logic of an answer is crucial for all significant business decisions—not just what the answer is, but why it is the answer, and why it matters. "Machines have no independent way to know if or why some results matter more than others unless they've been programmed with explicit parameters[.] What does it even mean to say something matters to a machine? Either a result is significant or it's not, based on what it has been told is significant."[23] Although advancements are being made in cognitive computing, for instance using genetic algorithms and neural nets, these differences between humans' and machines' abilities to explain and justify will last for a long time.

"A medical diagnostic AI can dig through years of data about cancer or diabetes patients and find correlations between various characteristics, habits, or symptoms in order to aid in preventing or diagnosing the disease. Does it matter that none of it 'matters' to the machine as long as it's a useful tool? Perhaps not, but it matters very much to those who want to build the next generation of intelligent machines."[24]

According to the former CEO of Google and Chairman of Alphabet Eric Schmidt, the concern about botsourcing is overblown because only the most routine jobs can be replaced, whereas most human work skills cannot be replicated by a machine. That said, "humans will need to work alongside computers in order to be more productive."[25]

Jeff Immelt, the outgoing CEO of General Electric, was more blunt in his assessment of the prediction of rampant cascading unemployment from botsourcing. According to Immelt, the notion that robots will completely run factories in five years is "bullshit."[26] Apparently we are still a long way off from widespread displacement, as there still remains far too much low-hanging fruit in terms of enhancing human productivity by augmenting human skills with technology.

Technological advancements and machine capabilities will continue to evolve and speed up. Similarly, humans will need to develop skills that add value in this new environment. Although many jobs will be eliminated, many more jobs will be created but with different skill requirements. Many of the new jobs will simply be new versions of "old-world" jobs. There will be tremendous demand for people who can design, program, monitor, and fix technology. There will be a huge demand for people who can explain data, findings, and machine insights to other humans. There will also be a need for people who can work with technology and its output, then interact with other humans—customers, patients, coworkers, superiors, and other stakeholders.

A better use of AI in the context of innovation would be, instead of substituting human creativity, supplementing it. For instance, a marketing department using AI could simulate what the impact would be on the marketplace if the company were to launch an innovative product—thus modeling the impact on company performance prior to sinking a fortune into the research, design, and launch. A marketing department could use AI to synthesize all products in a category and identify the best-selling features of those products, and then apply that insight as input into the product design phase.

According to Sam Ellis, Business Director of Innovation at the advertising agency M&C Saatchi, whereas in the past the agency's employees might have worried that using AI in advertising would kill off creativity, they have become excited about the power of harnessing AI to glean insights into potential customers. Take, for example, a coffee-brand ad featured in a poster displayed at a London bus stop. The poster was digital, not print, which means it could change like a chameleon. This poster would change from "drab grays and blocks of text" to "a minimalistic image with a short saying." While changing images in advertisement is nothing too special, "what was unique about this particular poster ... wasn't the fact that people were looking at it. Rather, it was looking at them—and learning."[27]

The poster featured an AI function that used facial tracking to monitor the eye movements of passersby and coupled this data with a genetics-based algorithm. This enabled the AI to identify which features of the posters were the most eye-catching and then internalized that feedback to modify the design. Each successive permutation of the advertisement would improve over prior iterations, learning and becoming more eye-catching as it evolved.

According to Ellis, "We were surprised how quickly it learned." In less than three days, the AI-powered marketing technology "was creating posters in line with the current best practices in the advertising industry, which had been developed over decades of human trial and error like realizing three to five word slogans work best."[28]

To some readers this example will give them the creeps. It is uncanny that a poster would be monitoring its own viewers and modifying itself to become increasingly alluring. Is it possible for these technologies will become all too effective, thereby invading consumer privacy to an unacceptable degree? We dive into that thicket in Chapter 6. For now, consider the upshot of this example, which is that AI can find applications even in the more "creative" of human enterprises, such as marketing and advertising.

Humans will increasingly work side by side with machines, their new coworkers. This will require humans to get better at the human-machine interface. While machines will do routine tasks, humans will need to develop social, emotional, and creative intelligence to strategically leverage these machine-enhanced capabilities. Further, nonroutine tasks that require social skills will continue to be done by humans. Just consider being a barber, hairdresser, makeup artist, or personal trainer. These jobs will require uniquely human skills and will not be replaced by a robot anytime soon. Jobs that require interpersonal caring, such as being a social worker, are also less amenable to being substituted by robots.

To work at the human-machine interface, humans will need to have the three qualities we discussed in Chapter 4. First, they need *literacy* in a broad set of areas, rather than being highly specialized. This will enable workers to connect different parts of their organizations and work with cross-functional teams and across flexible hierarchies. Certainly, employees will need to have their domain of expertise. However, they will need to have an understanding of the other areas with which they are interacting. Second, humans will need *competence* that links the technical with the human. This means technical literacy as well as the ability to be collaborative, creative, and emotionally aware. Lastly, humans will need to develop their *uniquely human traits*. They will need to develop their emotional intelligence, empathy, leadership skills, social and cultural awareness, ethical sensitivity, aesthetic taste, and so forth.

Augmentation, Amplification, and Other Performance Enhancers

As humans become comfortable collaborating with machines even though we may not realize it. When we get into our car, many of us boot up Google Maps and let the algorithms guide us to our destination. We may not be aware but we are collaborating with a machine. When we ask Siri, Apple's personal assistant who lives inside our phone to read emails, schedule appointments, or find the closest restaurant to us, we are collaborating with a machine. When we ask Amazon's Alexa, who resides in our smart speakers to set our house alarm or dim house lights, we are collaborating with a machine. Even apparently simple tasks like current weather updates and spam filters are all based on AI and involve some level of human-machine interaction.

In the next sections, we discuss examples of how machines are making humans better: augmentation, co-bots, amplification, creativity enhancement, innovation improvement, and learning enhancement. There are different levels of human-machine collaboration. At the basic level there is *autonomous intelligence*. This is where machines work independently from humans such as completely autonomous robots in factories. But at the intersection of technology and the humanities, we have augmentation, co-bots, amplification, enhancing creativity, improving innovation, and enhanced learning through visual analytics.

Augmentation

Augmented intelligence is where machines learn from human input and humans, in turn, are provided with information by the machines to make decisions that are more accurate. In numerous business disciplines, AI is able to hasten processes and provide decision-makers with reliable insights. For example, automation in marketing is one of the key features of Customer Relationship Management (CRM) applications. Detailed market segmentation and campaign management are typically automated, providing invaluable and detailed customer insights. This enables the sales team to interact better with their customers and create microtargeted campaigns. There is a feedback loop between the algorithm and the team, as they augment the other's performance.

Augmentation of human skills by machines is taking place in every industry sector and even in our own lives. A great example is in the finance industry. Consider the investment firm Vanguard. It now has a "Personal Advisor Service" that interacts with clients and combines automated investment advice with guidance from human advisers.[29] The machine technology is set up to perform many of the traditional tasks of investment advising, constructing a customized portfolio based on customer profiles, such as automated rebalancing of portfolios. More routine tasks are automated while the human advisers serve as "investing coaches." They are the ones tasked with explaining, answering investor questions, and encouraging good financial behaviors. In Vanguard's words, the humans are "emotional circuit breakers" to keep investors on plan. Human advisers are even encouraged to learn about "behavioral finance" to perform these roles effectively.

This example clearly demonstrates the new skills human employees will need to have and the important role that emotions of human clients play in designing work functions. It shows that jobs are not being eliminated but are morphing. The humans explain the optimized AI output to other humans using language that will emotionally resonate and be trusted, lest it be ignored.

Vanguard describes its approach as a "hybrid product" that blends human advisers and automated investing. Karin Risi, head of Vanguard Personal Advisor Services, said the investment portfolio is just one piece of the puzzle, and people also need advice on spending their retirement savings, how to handle market drops, and other money matters. She explains that people increasingly don't need to talk to a human adviser about routine things. However, they absolutely must have a human interaction when there are changes in either the economy or a client's life. These are emotional events an algorithm is not competent to handle. "Many clients—and I would put myself among them—probably don't need to talk to their adviser until they need to talk to their adviser, whether it's a market downturn, I had a baby, I got divorced," says Risi.[30]

This augmented hybrid approach is becoming the norm in virtually every sector. It underscores that humans need to be prepared to learn different skills for new sets of jobs in order to interact with machines.

Co-bots

Co-bots is short for "collaborative robots" and are a "second wave" of robots intended to physically interact with humans in a shared workspace. They are dedicated to teamwork with human employees and are specifically designed for that purpose. Unlike first-generation automation, advanced co-bots can now recognize people and objects, and they can work safely alongside humans. This ushers in a new wave of human-machine interaction.

This interaction takes augmentation to a new level and provides amplification of human abilities. Consider a situation where a co-bot might handle repetitive actions in a factory such as heavy lifting. Simultaneously a person can perform complementary tasks that a co-both cannot do, tasks that require dexterity and human judgment. A good example is assembling a gear motor or doing delicate packing. However, this also has huge security and ergonomic implications in co-bot development and worker training. Not only would there be resistance from workers but also fear of being hurt by the sheer physical strength of the robot.

In the auto industry companies such as Ford and Hyundai are extending the co-bot concept with exoskeletons.[31] These wearable robotic devices, which adapt to the user and location in real time, are enabling industrial workers to perform their jobs with superhuman endurance and strength. They are also shielding workers from harm in doing physically difficult and dangerous tasks, almost making them superhuman.

Of course, wearable tech does not a Humachine make, but we appreciate the example of evolution in automation.

Amplification

Beyond mere physical augmentation the human-machine interface is moving to a relationship where each entity amplifies the other. Recently, Ken Goldberg, professor of engineering at UC Berkeley, introduced the concept of *multiplicity* to describe how AI will influence future workforces.[32] The idea is that the future of human-machine interaction will essentially result in humans amplifying—or multiplying—themselves.

Professor Goldberg pushes back against the fear of robots taking over the workforce and replacing humans. Rather, he describes a hybrid workforce composed of a diverse group of robots and humans working together to achieve superior results. Together they can accomplish far more than compared to what either group could accomplish working alone.

One example he points to is the AlphaGo competition where some of the world's top Go players began competing alongside the AlphaGo program. What were created were essentially human-machine teams where the players learned new strategies by studying AlphaGo's previous games, and the algorithm learned new strategies by studying the players.

This virtuous feedback loop of amplification is the type of system interaction we see in Google searches, recommendation systems for Netflix and Spotify, and all other AI systems. As Goldberg points out: "The important question is not when machines will surpass human intelligence, but how humans can work together with them in new ways."[33]

Enhancing Creativity

The augmentation and amplification just described have a tremendous impact on enhancing human creativity. Humans can use the machines as their "workhorse" to quickly dig up options as humans provide the specs. An example would be a *computer-aided design (CAD)* system that can generate thousands of design options for the designer that would meet the designer's specified goals and comply with design parameters. The designer can work on developing the specs and then submit them to the CAD system. Quickly, the CAD system can provide thousands of options. The designer can then look at them, refine, improve, and respecify. Iteratively, the designer and the CAD program running on the designer's computer work to create the ideal design.

This collaboration is now a reality. Autodesk's Dreamcatcher AI system is the next generation of CAD and does precisely that. Dreamcatcher is a generative design system that enables designers to create an initial set of specifications for their design problem with specific goals and constraints. That information is used by the algorithm to identify alternative design solutions that meet these objectives. Designers are able to explore trade-offs between many alternative approaches and work back and forth to improve their solutions.

For example, a designer may provide Dreamcatcher with specifications about a chair. The requirement may be that the chair is able to support a weight of up to 300 pounds, to have a seat 18 inches off the ground, and be made of materials costing less than $75. The designer can specify many other criteria such as preferred materials and colors and even preferences of other chair styles. The algorithm then churns out thousands of designs that match those criteria, often sparking ideas that the designers might not have initially considered. They can then respond to the algorithm, providing feedback and refining the designs to meet their evolving specifications. The algorithm that does the "heavy lifting" in terms of finding the designs that comply with the specs and the designers are now free to use their uniquely human abilities to create and exercise aesthetic judgment.

Improving Innovation

Machines are also improving innovation. Consider the pharmaceutical industry where Pfizer is using IBM's Watson to accelerate the difficult process of drug discovery. An excellent example is research in immunooncology, an emerging approach to cancer treatment that uses the body's immune system to help fight cancer, but which is extremely time consuming.[34] Immunooncology drugs can take up to 12 years to bring to market, requiring a labor-intensive process. Every year spent waiting on a discovery means so many potentially avoidable cancer deaths.

However, IBM's Watson speeds this up dramatically by combining a complete literature review with Pfizer's own data, such as lab reports. Insights are continually made available to researchers—relationships that surface, hidden patterns that should speed the identification of new drug targets, combination therapies for further study, and patient selection strategies for this new class of drugs. All these big-data driven AI insights help researchers move faster in their quest to cure the emperor of all maladies.

The success comes from the fact that AI can quickly and efficiently churn through thousands of scenarios. It can then identify scenarios that optimize certain criteria and maximize desirable outcomes.

Enhanced Learning Through Visual Analytics

An important aspect to human decision-making in the face of machine intelligence is how humans receive the data they are given. Successfully extracting intelligence from data depends in large part on how that data is visually presented. Studies have shown that data presentation can make a significant difference in how data is interpreted and the success of resulting decisions. The possibilities are especially important today, as technology has significantly advanced in data visualization, presentation, and manipulation.

Consider that very few people think in terms of numbers or data tables. Rather, humans are programmed to create a physical representation of a mental model.[35] Visualization not only helps in extracting intelligence, understanding relationships and patterns, and detecting trends. It is also effective in communicating the findings to an audience because it can easily be tailored to their background.

The idea behind *visual analytics* is to enable better, faster, and more actionable results from data by combining strengths of computerized analysis with human perception, human intelligence, and intuition in integrated data analysis approach.[36] Computers are very powerful and efficient in large amounts of data processing, which could not be perceived by any human.

The problem, however, is that many real-world problems are not sufficiently well defined from the beginning. This is especially true given the complexity of today's business environment. Often, we first need to explore available data before we can capture the essence of the problem. Visual analytics provides the means to explore and discover relationships otherwise hidden from default assumptions in statistical modeling.

Visual analytics is an effective tool for audience-specific end-result conveyance. It is a tool that exploits and uses the hidden opportunities and knowledge resting in unexplored data sources. In many applications success depends on the right information being available at the right time.

The acquisition of raw data is no longer the problem, but rather it is turning that data into intelligence and knowledge. This problem is exacerbated by the fact that the amount of data is growing exponentially (Moore's Law) and visual analytics provides the means to "see" the data. This is an essential limitation of being human.

Visual analytics enables humans to process the data by making information "transparent" for an analytic discourse, providing the means of communicating about the data rather than just seeing results. It is therefore a medium, across which humans and machines cooperate.

While visual analytics is critical for extracting intelligence from large data sets, however, it is costly to implement, requiring investments in computer technology and highly trained specialists. As such, there are a few considerations in its implementation. The key to using visual analytics is to find the right balance between the trade-offs of the resources needed to support visualization and needs of the organization.

The first issue to consider is problem complexity, how difficult the problem is to solve, and the objectives of the analysis. For example, problems that require one single optimal solution may not need human involvement compared to problems where an array of multiple solutions may suffice and judgment calls are ultimately needed. A second issue is data quantity and quality, such as how large is the data set, the number of variables involved, and how comprehensive and "clean" is the data.

Third, there is the issue of user capability. Certainly it requires the ability to conduct analytics, but also the user must have domain knowledge and contextual knowledge that go well beyond understanding analytics itself.

These three issues—*problem, data, and user*—have to be considered in the trade-off between complete computerization and extreme interactivity of visualization. Certain problems can and should be completely automated and computerized. That is where the problem is well defined, the data complete, and there is a search for one optimal solution. Many problems don't rely on interpretation and may heavily rely on pure computation and analysis. At the other extreme are problems that are unstructured, do not have enough data, and rely on domain knowledge of the expert. Lastly, is the issue of problem importance. Some problems are more trivial, can easily be automated, and it may not be worthwhile to incur the costs of visual analytics.

Ultimately, organizations will have to make this trade-off when deciding whether to invest in visual analytics. Extracting intelligence from data enables humans to better understand the data being presented to them by their machine coworkers and will considerably enhance the human-machine collaboration.

The Human-Machine Interface

To use machines for everything from gathering routine information to enhancing creativity and innovation requires different human skills. Machines generate data, predictions, and information. Humans are needed to take the output and use it as a basis for their creativity, and come up with new ideas and designs. They are also needed to train machines, program them, and make adjustments based on the machine output. Humans are needed to provide leadership and develop strategy.

We are calling for new roles of human employees that play to our complementary strengths. See Figure 5.3.

How does a company get its human workforce in sync with its new bot coworkers? We answer this question next.

It is ultimately people (whether individuals or teams) that make the big decisions based on input from smart machines. Restructuring has to

Figure 5.3 Complementary strengths.

be focused on enabling that. As human beings, we have limited ability to consume and understand data.[37] The behavioral limitations of humans as decision-makers has been documented in hundreds of studies and is a practically an academic discipline in and of itself that has cut across fields of economics, psychology, and law. Machines must provide output that is visually presentable for decision-makers to be able to integrate it into decision-making. Much work has been done in creating useful data visualization and dashboards. These enable managers to not only view the critical variables but be able to manipulate values of certain variables and "see" changes in other dependent variables.

This is exactly what IBM's Watson computer is doing in a project with Memorial Sloan Kettering Cancer Center (MSK) in New York City.[38] Watson is being used to sift through volumes of data on patients and treatments and recommend the best course of treatment for a particular patient. It uses predictive analytics, but that does not mean Watson provides an answer—or tells exactly what the future holds. Rather, Watson provides choices in courses of options, and licensed medical professionals use this decision-support to provide better care.

For example, for a particular cancer patient, considering all available patient data, Watson may recommend three courses of action. One may be with a 95% confidence level, another with a 45% confidence level, and the third with a 10% confidence level. Physicians can then look at this information and make the final decision. This is typical of what machines can do in such environments. A machine is not a crystal ball but simply gives probabilities of outcomes that help humans make the final decision.

Developing Trust in the Machines

The human-machine interface can be seen as the intersection of two complementary coworkers. It can also be seen as bridging a "great divide," an ontological gulf separating two competing and very different information processing entities. Organizations will need strategies for their employees to accept their new coworkers and to trust the machines. This is one of the biggest problems faced by the companies to which we spoke.

Lack of trust in machines will result in employees adjusting the numbers provided by the algorithm. One of the companies we spoke with—a leader in analytics—had a problem where managers were simply modifying the numbers provided by analytics, as they did not trust the data. Others were continuing with routine decisions regardless of the data they were provided. This lack of trust truly defeats the purpose of adopting decision-support technology in the first place.

For true integration to occur, the people who make decisions need to not only have the data when they need it—but they also need to have confidence in the data. Companies need active strategies to develop trusting working relationships among the workforce, at all levels. Implementing technology will not help us if we treat it with disdain.

The companies we spoke with that made headway in human-machine interface considered the "great divide" as a reality and actively prepared for it. These are some of the strategies they followed.

First, it was imperative for leaders to communicate their vision to the organization with transparency. This includes their goals for technology, how the organization will be changing, how all ranks of people will be affected, how the change will take place and over what time frame. This also includes a vision of where the organization is going and what this future will look like. Updates need to be delivered on a regular basis with a chance for follow-up questions and answers. This is an extremely important element so that people's fear doesn't get the best of them. Rumors about impeding job losses can quickly begin to dominate watercooler talk, leading to a talent flight. Without openness and regular updates, you may create the conditions for your human workers to sabotage the technology or engender other forms of resistance, in turn creating negative pressure on productivity, morale, and economic performance. Fear erodes the ability of humans to think intuitively. Creating pervasive fear of displacement is a quick way to ruin a company's culture.

Second, companies need to go beyond providing basic technology training for their talent. Certainly ongoing technical training in using the technology is a necessary part of implementation. However, a few of the companies found it very helpful to arrange for "visits" to other companies that were using the same or similar technologies. Providing a model enabled people to actually "see" how the technology is used and how the workers engage with the technology. This can certainly be difficult to arrange if the model comes from a competitor. But in a situation where the companies are not competing there may be openness for such a visit.

Seeing how others work creates a personal experience. It goes a long way toward building trust and acceptance. Once mastery of the technical aspects has been achieved, a pilot implementation on a limited scale is imperative. This will serve to solidify what has been learned, ensure that all is functioning smoothly, and will aid acceptance.

Third, a useful step in gaining acceptance is providing users with several final versions of the technological tools they will be engaging with and allowing them to make the final selection from the alternatives. This creates a sense of ownership and allows the enterprise to identify possible points of failure before wider implementation efforts take place. Including employees in the process of adoption creates trust by allowing participation in the effort rather than having it imposed upon them. This is beyond mere training on the technology itself but rather giving employees who will be using the technology the opportunity to understand the potential problems, the option to reject the technology, and to solicit help in getting teams ready to adopt it. These strategies leverage human emotions of fear and curiosity, and provide a sense of respect and communal belonging, without which you run the risk of failure in technology adoption, not unlike the body of a recipient of an organ donation rejecting an organ transplant.

Fourth, an important part of implementation strategy is directed at the management level of the organization. Much of the discussion on technology acceptance tends to focus on either frontline employees or top leadership. However, middle management is the linchpin between top strategy and direct implementation. Unlike employees who interface with technology at the operational level, managers are intermediaries whose attitudes toward technology will filter down toward the employees who report to them. A few of the companies we spoke with found it effective to use interviews or conduct anonymous surveys of management. The purpose was to uncover hidden attitudes and opportunities for development at the managerial levels. The insights from these interviews and questionnaires helped to develop training for managers, uncover hidden opportunities, and develop new incentives. One lower-level manager confided that the company "actually paid attention to the responses and made appropriate changes." He said the people were thrilled and more open to embracing new technology because this manager-level feedback was actually internalized by executives.

Ultimately, the human-machine interface will come down to human emotions. Machines will do whatever they are programmed to do. However, it is humans who may have a harder time adjusting. We aren't so easily programmed. Our training takes place over years if not decades. Whether integration of AI and humans is a success will be make or break for many companies.

The CEO and founder of Fetch Robotics, Melonee Wise, puts it well. She emphasizes that the technology itself is just a tool—just like any other tool—and one that leaders can use how they see fit. Machines can be used to replace human work, or companies can choose to use them to augment it. "Your computer doesn't unemploy you, your robot doesn't unemploy you," she said. "The companies that have those technologies make the social policies and set those social policies that change the workforce."[39]

Human Resources in the Artificial Intelligence Era

We have made an effort to push back against the fearmongering over botsourcing. We predict that AI will make, not take, our jobs. We have underscored how artificial intelligence in the workplace should make humans more valuable, not less, that smart machines can make our work environments more personal, intuitive, and humane. It is up to managers to find the right combination and balance of human-held versus automated tasks. Allocating workflows between humans, machines, and some combination thereof is the new priority for human resource managers.

AI will have tremendous implications for human resource management. Foreseeable trends include impacts to recruitment, training, performance of existing tasks, and the formation of entirely new job descriptions.

Applications of AI in the recruitment and hiring process pays off in terms of reduced time to hire, increased productivity for recruiters, and enhanced candidate experience.[40] For example, when DBS Bank's Talent Acquisition team deployed JIM, an AI-powered virtual recruitment bot, they saw tremendous gains in these dimensions. "JIM," the familiar name of a popular character from *The Office*, actually stands for Jobs Intelligence Maestro. Using JIM, DBS Bank was able to reduce candidate screening time from 32 minutes to 8 minutes per candidate. That is substantial time savings, especially when processing thousands of candidates for any given job posting.

Botsourcing the candidate screening function to JIM has allowed the human recruiters to focus on those uniquely human functions of the recruiting process where emotional intelligence, interpersonal communication skills, and creative expression are key—for instance, explaining the culture and values of the bank to make sure that the candidates were not only qualified on paper (which the AI can do) but, to use a very subjective phrase, whether the candidate would be a "good fit" with the team.

According to James Loo, head of the Talent Acquisition Group for DBS Bank, JIM has contributed to the team already because his human recruiters have been freed up to "perform higher-value work such as sourcing, recruitment marketing, engaging with candidates, and hiring managers."

In the prior chapter, we discussed uniquely human skills and traits such as caring, emotional intelligence, and aesthetic taste. We predict that emotional intelligence will be as important as technical intelligence in the future of work. Even with advanced technological tools in play, we will still need human marketers with emotional intelligence who can read the room when delivering a sales pitch; we will still need human designers with aesthetic sensibilities when creating the user experience interface of new technology. Creating automated voices that sound pleasing to listeners of different linguistic backgrounds is an example of the kind of job that will need human input from a subjective, sensory-based perspective.

Empathy is one of those emotional skills that we are unlikely to automate in the next several decades, if ever. While we could teach a computer to parrot empathic speech patterns, we do not think it would have the same effect as human empathy. Creating a meaningful interpersonal connection with someone with empathy is like being funny—not everyone knows how to do that, and it is not readily programmable.

As more customer service functions are automated, it makes sense to invest in human interpersonal skills to be proactive in filling the void. For example, Bank of America is rolling out a nationwide empathy training program for client-facing employees. John Jordan leads The Academy and Advisor Development at Bank of America. He calls the training a "life stage navigation curriculum" that helps bank staff understand the priorities and fundamental concerns of clients depending on where they are in life—a task that requires emotional intelligence and empathy.[41] This is playing to our strengths.

Dangers of Overreliance: Atrophy

There are additional reasons why it is important to include people in organizational processes and decision-making and not exclusively rely on technology. There is only so far we should go in botsourcing. Just because we can automate a function doesn't necessarily mean we should. In our endeavor to praise working with machines, let's not lean too hard on the walking stick. If we become too dependent upon technology, we expose ourselves to risks. What happens when we automate several crucial functions, giving them over exclusively to the machines, but then the power goes out and the robots are out of commission? We could be left in a bind. We can describe the inability for human resources to perform previously human-executed tasks that have been botsourced as *overreliance atrophy*.

Indeed, technology has the potential to make businesses more effective and efficient. But ramping up utilization of technology has a number of potential drawbacks. It is the *combination* of people and technology (not just the adoption of *more* technology) that creates the Humachine, when strengths of one offset the weaknesses of the other.

Another risk of over-reliance is the *self-fulfilling prophecy problem*.

Exclusive dependence on technology raises the physical and operational risk of machine malfunction. For the most part, technology works smoothly, while enabling innovation and conveniences that have made our lives more fulfilling and our jobs more productive. However, relying exclusively on technology without backup plans creates a risk of dependence.

If any one of these shuts down, the organization and its people will likely not know what to do until power is restored. These potential breakdowns are not only a headache. They create significant risk. This is especially true as today's technology increasingly controls entire systems not just localized functions. Just consider the technology that already controls systems such as airline routes, electrical grids, financial markets, street traffic lights, and communication technology. As companies automate infrastructure controls, they need to be building in privacy, security, and backup systems, and include people in this process to avoid atrophy in the skills needed to step in if automated systems crash.

This underscores the connection between electricity-dependent infrastructure and management decisions. From a human resource point of view, there can be too much of a good thing—too much reliance on machines can create undesirable consequences within the workforce (as well as in an educational context). Just as machines cannot answer "why" the answer provided is the correct answer, or why it matters, humans who rely too much on machines for analysis will also lose the ability to answer these philosophical questions.

Say you give your analyst a problem to solve, and the analyst types in a query to a database using a search engine, which processes a million pieces of data in a second and spits out a result. The analyst gives you the answer, but when you ask it why that answer is correct, you are met with a blank stare. It is not enough for the analyst to say, "Because the computer says so."

Per Kasparov, "The problem comes when the database and the engine go from coach to oracle. I tell my students that they have to use the engine to challenge their own preparation and analysis, not to do it for them."[42] Kids these days! They want to skip the hard part where they actually learn to do the analysis and "show their work" along the way (a phrase you may recall from primary school algebra assignments).

Both students and employees may be tempted to skip the crunchy analytical process and jump to a quick and ready result. As a result, if this is enabled and encouraged by institutional design or by management practices, organizations risk merely accepting blindly the outcomes of machine analytics and thereby lose the ability to verify whether the outcome is actually correct or to understand why it is correct. If we treat AI as a crystal ball instead of a fallible colleague, we cease being scientific and revert to mystical thinking.

Overreliance on machines for analysis can lead to an atrophy of the cognitive capabilities that set humans apart from machines and in some ways keeps us indispensable in the first place: our ability to explain from context, to understand, to answer the *why* question. This is one of those slowly emerging risks, as intellectual atrophy does not happen overnight.

"Overreliance on the machine can weaken, not enhance, your own comprehension if you take it at its word all the time."[43] It's the proverbial frog in boiling water, as one generation of workers who grew up using slide rules is replaced by a generation of workers that were born with smartphones in their cribs. Despite its slow pace the risk is real. Kasparov worries, "It's like taking a boat out into the middle of a lake and only realizing when the boat springs a leak that you don't know how to swim."[44]

Another way to approach the problem of overreliance atrophy is not just from the loss of the ability to answer the "why" question, but also the atrophy of our ability to *innovate*. "If we rely on our machines to show us how to be good imitators, we will never take that next step to becoming creative innovators."[45]

An AI system tasked with designing a new product could apply pattern recognition capacities and machine learning algorithms, but this is going to create only a product with features already contained in the extant marketplace and will not create something novel. There will be no fundamental innovation if we rely on traditional data analysis and machine learning to do the thinking for us. The marketing department, dominated by an AI program that tells us what the next product should be, can only spit out iterations of existing products—amalgams of the features of other products that have sold well. This may be acceptable to shareholders in the near term if it leads to profit, but it leads to intellectual stagnation in the long run. There are only so many ways to reinvent the wheel and still remain competitive.

Conclusion

Humans will not be put out to pasture anytime soon. We no longer employ banks of switchboard operators or elevator attendants, and somehow we survived.

Automation will displace the worst possible jobs—for example, ones that are physically dangerous or extremely boring. No one is going to miss bomb diffusion by hand or processing piles of mortgages. Machines are tools, and tools need a user for relevance and maintenance.

Bolstered by AI, our imaginations will be set free to discover and explore reality with ever-greater processing power. We can create a future that suits ourselves.

Major portions of the global economy—transportation and healthcare infrastructure, for example—are in dire need of an overhaul. Technology will be a critical tool in solving these hard problems, which will have major efficiency gains, each in turn significantly enhancing the quality of human life.

For every problem technology solves, it will likely cause a few more—so there will never be an end to human work.

Notes

1 Arjun Kharpal, A.I. Will Create More Jobs That Can't Be Filled, Not Mass Unemployment. *CNBC*, June 16, 2017. Available at www.cnbc.com/2017/06/16/ai-robots-jobs-alphabet-eric-schmidt.html
2 World Economic Forum, The Future of Jobs Report 2018. *Centre for the New Economy and Society*, p. v. Available at www3.weforum.org/docs/WEF_Future_of_Jobs_2018.pdf

3 Lant, Karla. AI Won't Just Replace Workers. It'll Also Help Them. *Futurism*, May 13, 2017. Available at https://futurism.com/ai-wont-replace-workers-also-help-them/

4 According to Gary Kasparov, "There are certain things that we can do that machines are not at all going to be able to replicate. It's things like love, emotions, passions… One of the rules is anything that we know how we do machines can do it. But there's so many things that we do that we don't know how we do—and that's where we humans can excel. […] Machines don't have understanding, machines don't recognize strategic patterns, and machines don't have a purpose," he added, arguing for a blend of what humans and machines do best—and finding "a way to bring together these complementary skills." Lomas, Natasha. "We should not talk about jobs being lost but people suffering," says Kasparov on AI, *TechCrunch*, May 17, 2017. Available at https://techcrunch.com/2017/05/17/we-should-not-talk-about-jobs-being-lost-but-people-suffering-says-kasparov-on-ai/

5 Moravec, Hans P. *Mind Children: The Future of Robot and Human Intelligence*, Harvard University Press, Cambridge, MA, 1988.

6 Kasparov, Garry. *Deep Thinking: Where Machine Intelligence Ends and Human Creativity Begins*, p. 246, Hatchet Books, New York, 2017.

7 Bostrom, 58–59.

8 21 Jobs of the Future, Cognizant Technology Solutions. November 28, 2017. Available at www.cognizant.com/perspectives/21-jobs-of-the-future.

9 Ibid.

10 Ibid.

11 Levy, Ari. How Software Is Eating the Banking Industry. February 15, 2017. *CNBC Future of Work*. Available at www.cnbc.com/2017/02/15/how-software-is-eating-the-banking-industry.html

12 Ibid.

13 Wilson, H. James and Daugherty, Paul R. Collaborative Intelligence: Humans and AI Are Joining Forces. *Harvard Business Review*, July–August 2018, p. 116.

14 Ibid.

15 Alison DeNisco Rayome. Amazon doubles-down on hybrid human/robot workforce in Illinois warehouse. Tech Republic. April 2, 2018.

16 Ibid.

17 Ibid.

18 Hunter, Matt. Here's How One of Google's Top Scientists Thinks People Should Prepare for Machine Learning. *CNBC Future of Work*. April 29, 2017. Available at www.cnbc.com/2017/04/29/googles-peter-norvig-how-to-prepare-for-ai-job-losses.html

19 Chui, M., Manyika, J. and Miremadi, M. (July, 2016). Where Machines Could Replace Humans—and Where They Can't (Yet). *McKinsey Quarterly*. Retrieved January 13, 2018. Available at www.mckinsey.com/business-functions/digital-mckinsey/our-insights/where-machies-could-replace-humans-and-where-they-cant-yet

20 Bishop, Todd. Jeff Bezos Explains Amazon's Artificial Intelligence and Machine Learning Strategy. May 6, 2017. Available at www.geekwire.com/2017/jeff-bezos-explains-amazons-artificial-intelligence-machine-learning-strategy/

21 Kasparov, Garry and Greengard, Mig. *Deep Thinking: Where Machine Intelligence Ends and Human Creativity Begins*, p. 71, PublicAffairs, 2017.

22 Ibid., p. 75.

23 Ibid., p. 72.
24 Ibid., p. 77.
25 Arjun Kharpal, A.I. Will Create More Jobs That Can't Be Filled, Not Mass Unemployment. *CNBC*. June 16, 2017. Available at www.cnbc.com/2017/06/16/ai-robots-jobs-alphabet-eric-schmidt.html.
26 Ibid.
27 Castillo, Michelle. Even the Mad Men Could Be Replaced by Machines Someday. *CNBC*. February 24, 2017. Available at www.cnbc.com/2017/02/24/artificial-intelligence-and-creative-work.html.
28 Ibid.
29 Davenport, Thomas H. and Ronanki, Rajeev. Artificial Intelligence for the Real World. *Harvard Business Review*, January–February 2018.
30 Reklaitis, Victor. Here's the Advice You Get from Vanguard's New Robot-Human Hybrid. *MarketWatch*, December 2015.
31 Howard, Bill. Ford's Factory Floor Exoskeleton Vest: "Power Without Pain." *ExtremeTech*, June 20, 2018.
32 Goldberg, Ken. The Robot Human Alliance. *The Wall Street Journal*, June 11, 2017; Call It Multiplicity: How Humans and Machines Can Work Together, Berkeley IEOR June 12, 2017.
33 Ibid.
34 Mukherjee, Sy. How Pfizer and IBM Are Teaming Up to Develop Next-Gen Cancer Drugs. *Fortune*, December 1, 2016.
35 Winkenbach, M. Using Visualization to Connect Humans and Analytics in Supply Chain Decision Making. Webinar September 2017, MIT, Center for Transportation and Logistics.
36 Keim, D., Andrienko, G., Fekete, J.D., Görg, C., Kohlhammer, J. and Melançon, G. Visual Analytics: Definition, Process, and Challenges. In *Information Visualization. Lecture Notes in Computer Science*, edited by Kerren, A., Stasko, J.T., Fekete, J.D. and North, C. vol. 4950. Springer, Berlin, Germany, 2008.
37 Dean, Derek and Webb, Caroline. *Recovering from Information Overload*. McKinsey & Company, January 2011. Available at www.mckinsey.com/insights/organization/recovering_from_information_overload
38 Hempel, Jessi. IBM's Massive Bet on Watson. *Fortune*, October 7, 2013.
39 Keim, D., Andrienko, G., Fekete, J.D., Görg, C., Kohlhammer, J. and Melançon, G. Visual Analytics: Definition, Process, and Challenges. In *Information Visualization. Lecture Notes in Computer Science*, edited by Kerren, A., Stasko, J.T., Fekete, J.D. and North, C., vol. 4950. Springer, Berlin, Germany, 2008.
40 Meister, Jeanne. Ten HR Trends in the Age of Artificial Intelligence, *Forbes.com*. January 8, 2019. Available at www.forbes.com/sites/jeannemeister/2019/01/08/ten-hr-trends-in-the-age-of-artificial-intelligence/#691269c03219
41 Ibid.
42 Kasparov, Garry and Greengard, Mig. *Deep Thinking: Where Machine Intelligence Ends and Human Creativity Begins*, p. 227, PublicAffairs, 2017.
43 Ibid., p. 228.
44 Ibid., p. 228.
45 Ibid., p. 229.

6

LEGAL ISSUES IN THE HUMACHINE ERA

We're moving into an era where seeing is no longer going to be believing. I don't think we as a society are prepared for this.

Paul Scharre
Senior Fellow and Director of the Technology
and National Security Program at the
Center for New American Security[1]

While these are just simple little computer games, the message is clear: put different AI systems in charge of competing interests in real-life situations, and it could be an all-out war if their objectives are not balanced against the overall goal of benefitting us humans above all else.

Proceedings of the 16th International Conference
on Autonomous Agents and Multiagent Systems[2]

Cybersecurity, Deepfakes, and Generative Adversarial Networks

"Photo fakery is far from new, but artificial intelligence will completely change the game. AI isn't just a better version of Photoshop or iMovie."[3] *Deepfakes* are fake videos enhanced by AI to distort, remix, and synthesize inputs to create convincing simulacra.[4] Practically all it takes to create such a video is a smartphone, a computer with an advanced graphics chip, and access to the Internet. Open source software and cloud-based machine learning platforms have granted liberal access to the AI programs that can be used for these purposes, such as OpenFaceSwap or Paperspace.

So-called *Generative Adversarial Networks (GAN)* can create false images that are so truth-like they may be indistinguishable from reality. GAN works by pitting one deep neural network against another, with one trained to identify authentic images and the other trained to outfox

Disclaimer: This chapter discusses legal issues; however, it does not contain legal advice. This chapter includes hypothetical discussions of legal issues for educational purposes only. Reading this chapter does not create an attorney-client relationship with the authors. If you need legal advice, consult with an attorney licensed in your jurisdiction.

the former's smell test. As the biblical proverb goes, as iron sharpens iron, so one person sharpens the countenance of another.[5] Expand the definition of personhood to include intelligent machines and you've got the essence of the GAN technique being used here.

MIT Technology Review named GANs on the list of "10 Breakthrough Technologies" for 2018. As this book goes to print, it will surely have evolved further.

The GAN approach, invented by Google researcher Ian Goodfellow, brings two neural networks to bear simultaneously. One network, known as the generator, draws on a data set to produce a sample that mimics the data set. The other network, the discriminator, assesses the degree to which the generator succeeded. In an iterative fashion, the assessments of the discriminator inform the assessments of the generator. The result far exceeds the speed, scale, and nuance of what human reviewers could achieve. Growing sophistication of the GAN approach is sure to lead to the production of increasingly convincing and nearly impossible to debunk deepfakes.[6]

Although the United States' Defense Advanced Research Projects Agency (DARPA) is already studying how to detect GAN-generated deepfakes, according to Professor Hany Farid of Dartmouth University, "GANs are a particular challenge to us in the forensics community because they can be turned against our forensic techniques."[7]

Two months after the first Cyber Grand Challenge hosted by the US National Security Agency (NSA) in October 2016, the then-Director Michael Rogers concluded that AI is "foundational to the future of cybersecurity."[8] The grand challenge is an AI competition used by the US military to improve cyber defense. The challenge pits rule-based autonomous machines in a battle of wits on a cyber battlefield, each discovering and exploiting vulnerabilities of its opponent while concurrently running patches to shore up its own defenses from attack.[9]

For all our concern with the commercial and business applications of AI, we should point out that AI also has military applications. As it evolves, it will become an increasingly powerful resource. One to be wielded carefully. One that its creators and owners should not let fall into the wrong hands. AI, like all meaningful technological breakthroughs, is a double-edged sword.

Legal scholars contend that, depressingly, "The marketplace of ideas already suffers from truth decay as our networked information environment interacts in toxic ways with our cognitive biases. Deepfakes will exacerbate this problem significantly. Individuals and businesses will face novel forms of exploitation, intimidation, and personal sabotage."[10] Despite the potential gravity of harm associated with political or corporate sabotage by weaponized deepfakes, the legal system provides limited protection as it stands.

There's More Than Just the Control Problem

Recall from Chapter 1 the *control problem* of AI is a consequence of three entirely plausible theses[11]:

1 *Singleton.* That an AI may gain a decisive strategic advantage over humans;
2 *Orthogonality.* That the final goals of the AI could be at cross-purposes with human values and goals; and
3 *Instrumental convergence.* That even apparently harmless goals such as self-preservation and resource acquisition could lead the AI to act in surprisingly harmful ways.

If a superintelligence becomes a singleton with goals orthogonal to humans, then we better hope to avoid instrumental convergence, or we are doomed. That said, AI poses a number of less apocalyptic threats, such as the accountability gap between owners of AI systems and the public, questionable applications of AI to facial recognition, invasion of privacy, weaponization by bots, and so forth. All of these should be considered risks posed by AI. If corporate leaders are not going to address these risks, then lawmakers should do it.

The thesis for this chapter is simple enough: Do not create technology that evades the control of its maker. Our concerns are broader, of course, but if you had one takeaway, it would be that executives must take seriously the "control problem" posed by AI as they integrate this powerful and potentially inscrutable tool into the enterprise. AI becomes especially dangerous when it has "agency" (or unsupervised decision-making) authority over choices that affect human health, safety, justice, or welfare.

Regulations from government agencies are necessary but not sufficient to ensure that AI does not become malignant and create a power that escapes efforts by humans to limit what it may become or what it may be used to accomplish.

Every tool that uses AI should have, in essence, an "off" switch. Further, rules of behavior should be instantiated at the constitutional level of an AI. That is to say, the "off" switch should be encoded at a level that cannot be overridden by the AI itself or by any external user. These rules of behavior should be essential to the AI's own vitality, without which it would automatically turn "off," such that to disobey the rules would be tantamount to the AI's suicide.

The risk posed by AI systems does not just stem from the treasonous turn of an out-of-control AI system but also from unwitting malfunctions or falling victim to an adversarial attack. Hackers manipulating an AI system in charge of an autonomous vehicle steering system could do serious damage.

151

Daniel Lowd, Assistant Professor of Computer and Information Science at the University of Oregon, explains, "It's something that's a growing concern in the machine learning and AI community, especially because these algorithms are being used more and more. If spam gets through or a few emails get blocked, it's not the end of the world. On the other hand, if you're relying on the vision system in a self-driving car to know where to go and not crash into anything, then the stakes are much higher."[12]

Yevgeniy Vorobeychik, Assistant Professor of Computer Science and Computer Engineering at Vanderbilt University, says, "One would expect every algorithm has a chink in the armor. We live in a really complicated multi-dimensional world, and algorithms, by their nature, are only focused on a relatively small portion of it."[13]

According to a report by the AI Now Institute, a research institute affiliated with New York University and deploying the skill of top researchers from Google and Microsoft, existing trends in AI should cause worry.[14] Shy of a full-blown manifestation of a Skynet-like Terminator scenario, these are market risks that should cause alarm and spur us to action: the accountability gap, the use of intrusive and questionable "affect recognition" for surveillance, built-in bias based on problematic historical data, unregulated AI being released "in the wild,"[15] the weaponization of AI via cyber-attacks, and deepfakes (see Table 6.1).

Table 6.1 Some risks from artificial intelligence

Risk	Description
Control problem	AI becomes a singleton with a decisive strategic advantage and goals that are orthogonal to human interests.
Accountability gap	Those most affected by AI have no ownership or control over its development and deployment.
Affect recognition	Unethical applications of facial recognition technology to judge interior mental states.
Surveillance	Intrusive gathering of civilian data that undermines privacy and creates security risks from data breach.
Built-in bias	When AI is fed data that contains historical prejudices, resulting in bias in, bias out.
Weaponization	Using bots to negatively impact the public through social media or cyberattacks.
Deepfakes	Creating lifelike video fakery to sabotage the subject of the video and undermine public trust.
Wild AI	Unleashing AI applications in public settings without oversight.

There is a growing *accountability gap* between those who have our data harvested and used to dictate our choice architecture, on the one hand, and those who design and profit from those AI systems, on the other. New AI systems are being designed and implemented every day, unleashing heretofore unknown powers with practically no oversight, accountability, or governance.

Industry self-policing is woefully inadequate to address the control problem. Companies are in a virtual arms race to own increasingly powerful and proprietary AI systems. Instead of releasing AI software under various open source licensing regimes, companies assert trade secret protections, thus precluding scrutiny of how the systems work or how they could go haywire. Corporate secrecy means there is no public accountability, no transparency, and no oversight of how AI systems operate.

The United States has a National Highway Traffic Safety Administration (NHTSA) housed within the Department of Transportation with the specific mission to "Save lives, prevent injuries, reduce vehicle-related crashes." NHTSA is responsible for, among other things, issuing vehicle recalls when fatal defects are discovered post-production. We suggest the formation of a regulatory body with the narrow focus of ensuring AI safety. Given the potential for weaponization, AI can and should be regulated under the rubric of national security. This does not mean we should shut down AI research departments, but rather, we cannot assume a code of ethics enforced by the private sector will adequately deal with these risks. Industry self-policing does not have a great track record of success.

While we do call for government involvement to mitigate the fatal implications of unregulated AI, that does not mean we blindly trust government to deploy AI in an ethical or legal manner. Intrusive surveillance with aerial drones and wiretapping already significantly undermines our traditional notions of privacy.

Powered by AI, facial recognition technology that can spot you in a crowd has evolved into *affect recognition*, where scanning systems can allegedly determine what the observed subject is feeling based on their face alone. "Affect recognition is a subclass of facial recognition that claims to detect things such as personality, inner feelings, mental health, and 'worker engagement' based on images or video of faces."[16] The private sector applications of affect recognition are at least as troubling as their use by police. The claim that we can accurately predict internal mental states based on faces alone is "not backed by robust scientific evidence, and [is] being applied in unethical and irresponsible ways that often recall the pseudosciences of phrenology and physiognomy."[17]

Affect recognition used to control crowds based on their facial expressions could easily turn into outright suppression of speech and the morally questionable practice of policing pre-crime. This is an area where we should not fall for the canard that "increasing security requires further erosion of privacy." We need to be more intelligent and imaginative than to buy into those kinds of tragic trade-offs. "Linking affect recognition to hiring, access to insurance, education, and policing creates deeply concerning risks, at both an individual and societal level."[18]

Promising efficiency and cost reductions, **Autonomous Decision Software** (ADS) is being rolled out in the private sector as well as at government agencies. Like mortgage application processing at a bank, the task of processing government benefit applications can be automated fairly easily. The problem is when streamlining application processing leads to biased or arbitrary decisions made by the ADS operating without human judgmental oversight. Professor Virginia Eubanks, in her book *Automating Inequality: How High-Tech Tools Profile, Police, and Punish the Poor*, argues that ADS can be misapplied in the context of government benefit programs, creating a kind of "digital poorhouse" that compounds patterns of discrimination against the very people the programs were designed to protect.[19]

Lastly, the cavalier attitude in Silicon Valley, typified by Facebook's motto of "move fast and break things," is fine for encouraging internal creative disruption but can clearly be perverted into hero worship of the scofflaw. AI should not be tested in consumer spaces without substantial oversight. Testing new AI systems in the so-called "wild" (that is, public spaces unregulated by government and uncontained in the company research lab) is about as prudent as testing fire starters in a California forest. The risks of undomesticated or **wild AI** being tested on the public are externalized onto the public, while the benefits are captured exclusively by the company that owns the intellectual property. This is equally dangerous and unfair.

Asimov's Laws of Robotics

Any respectable discussion of the risks of AI should begin with **Asimov's Laws of Robotics**. In Asimov's 1942 short story, "Runaround," one of the most beloved science fiction writers of all time announced a set of rules designed to protect humanity from its mechanical creations. The idea is if we just follow these simple rules, AI will not harm its maker.

The rules are:

0 A robot may not harm humanity, or, by inaction, allow humanity to come to harm.
1 A robot may not injure a human being, or, through inaction, allow a human being to come to harm.
2 A robot must obey the orders given to it by human beings, except where such orders would conflict with the First Law.
3 A robot must protect its own existence as long as such protection does not conflict with the First or Second Law.

Upon reflection, Asimov later added the "zeroth" law, a rule that took precedence over the existing rules.

As a literary device and general rule of thumb, the rules do provide a lot of mileage. It is hard to argue with a prohibition against human harm, for instance. Asimov's laws have a logic to them, intended to prevent a lot of foreseeable problems that would otherwise arise when robots come to make decisions that affect their own behavior and people around them.

However, the logic of Asimov's rules is far from airtight.[20] First off, the terms "human" and "robot" seem obviously distinct, but it is not difficult to conceive scenarios where they are blended together into a singular unit, like a corporation that contains both human and robotic components in its governing body. The definition of "injure" is far too ambiguous—if this were to include economic injury, then a robot must abstain from being used in a competitive commercial environment where its work will result in "injury" to a competing corporation or its shareholders.

Deploying AI in any military setting whatsoever would be fraught with violations of the rules and probably out of the question entirely. You don't have to be a cynic to understand that the more dangerous the technology, the more likely militaries are to be researching and developing it for weaponization. Further, if the handlers intentionally withheld information from the AI, then it could unknowingly violate the rules.

A larger concern with regulating AI is whether it can be controlled at all. When Internet connectivity is spread across machinery of all kinds, not just computers, then all connected machinery is capable of being hacked and manipulated by AI. The so-called "Internet of Things" will wrap the physical world in a digital sheen that makes things "smart" but also capable of being hacked in unprecedented ways. How smart is it, really, to design healthcare technology that is capable of being hacked and, consequently, capable of causing untold harm to its users? As manufacturers embed Internet connectivity as an upselling feature in everything from appliances to Zipcars, the risk of digital hijacking grows.

We may see a renaissance of throwback "analog" manufactured goods (you could say, "dumb" products) that are immune from digital espionage and as a consequence, are more reliable, more secure, and more private than the "smart" (read, "vulnerable") modern counterparts. In the meantime, manufacturers need to exercise precaution to make hardening the security infrastructure of smart devices a far greater priority than it currently is. Government responses come belatedly limping behind a problem and are often inadequate or incomplete to address evolving risks.

As interesting as Asimov's Laws of Robotics are as a literary device, they come up short when posed as a response to the real-world risks presented by AI. Perhaps they were more suitable when dealing with humanoid robots that roam the streets or serve as advanced personal assistants. However, AI that is deployed in a non-humanoid form—say, for example, AI designed to monitor a system such as aiding in route optimization for air traffic control systems or carrying out molecular research—is likely to need different, and more specific, rules.

Google's DeepMind researchers discovered that in zero-sum interactions (where two or more agents are competing over limited resources), as the AI networks became more complex, and as resources began to dwindle, the AI began to behave in ways characterized as highly aggressive, likely to perpetrate sabotage against competitors and to act greedily in its pursuit of resource accumulation.[21]

Interestingly, the less intelligent forms of DeepMind were more willing to cooperate in such a way that the competitors ended up with equal shares. "And while these are just simple little computer games, the message is clear: put different AI systems in charge of competing interests in real-life situations, and it could be an all-out war if their objectives are not balanced against the overall goal of benefitting us humans above all else."[22]

Next, we discuss whether we should wait until AI systems fail in a dangerous manner before intervening. We discuss the precautionary principle as a method of risk management in the context of the AI control problem. We also look into how AI is already posing threats not only to the economy but also to democratic institutions. We look at the inherent limitations of AI—the black box quality of its reasoning—and how this poses legal problems when executives and design teams rely upon AI for decision-making. We also look at the security risks posed by AI when it is hacked or when it simply makes mistakes.

Risk Management, Pandora's Box, and the Chamber of Commerce

Regulations in the United States are generally based on cost-benefit analysis, where the benefits of the regulation outweigh or at least justify the costs. By contrast, regulators in the European Union more readily apply the precautionary principle to certain public health, safety, and environmental risks. Although regulations based upon formal cost-benefit analysis tend to be more rational than those failing a cost-benefit analysis, we believe regulators should use the precautionary principle instead of cost-benefit analysis under certain circumstances—specifically, when confronted with potentially irreversible risks under conditions of uncertainty.

To deal with the special kind of risk posed by AI, we argue elected lawmakers and corporate policymakers should use the precautionary principle instead of traditional cost-benefit approaches to risk management.

The *precautionary principle* champions a risk-averse approach to the development of AI with any kind of executive powers in an enterprise. Although the precautionary principle is generally applied in the context of environmental law, public health, and products liability law, we find it apt for the potential Pandora's Box of the AI control problem.

As a risk management framework, the precautionary principle can be stated in a variety of ways. One version is, "When human activities may lead to morally unacceptable harm that is scientifically plausible but uncertain, actions shall be taken to avoid or diminish that harm."[23] The term "morally unacceptable harm" is defined as "threatening to human life or health," "serious and effectively irreversible," "inequitable to present or future generations," and "imposed without adequate consideration of the human rights of those affected."[24]

Perhaps the most fundamental moral claim of the precautionary principle is that risk management action should be taken before the harm occurs. Another way of formulating the precautionary principle is, "in the case of serious or irreversible threats to the health of humans or the ecosystem, acknowledged scientific uncertainty should not be used as a reason to postpone preventive measures."[25]

We believe that the risks posed by AI justify application of the precautionary principle. Now of course, the US Chamber of Commerce would probably disagree with us here. In general, the Chamber is adamantly opposed to the application of the precautionary principle in the regulatory context. The US Chamber of Commerce's stated objective is to "ensure that regulatory decisions are based on scientifically sound and technically rigorous risk assessments, and [to] oppose the adoption of the precautionary principle as the basis for regulation."[26] The Chamber seems to have a problem understanding the precautionary principle, or alternatively they are intentionally misconstruing the precautionary principle with the following straw man fallacy:

> There is... a relatively new theory known as the precautionary principle that is gaining popularity among environmentalists and other groups. The precautionary principle says that when the risks of a particular activity are unclear or unknown, assume the worst and avoid the activity. It is essentially a policy of risk avoidance. The regulatory implications of the precautionary principle are substantial. For instance, the precautionary principle holds that since the existence and extent of global warming and climate change are not known, one should assume the worst and immediately restrict the use of carbon-based fuels. The precautionary

principle has been explicitly incorporated into various laws and regulations in the European Union and various international bodies. In the United States, radical environmentalists are pushing for its adoption as a basis for regulating biotechnology, food and drug safety, environmental protection, and pesticide use.

Defenders of the precautionary principle would take issue with how their position is characterized by the Chamber, specifically the conflation of the precautionary principle with "radical" risk avoidance instead of rather prudent risk management. Advocates of the precautionary principle might argue that listening to the Chamber about how it would like to be regulated is like asking the fox how to best guard the henhouse.

We contend that it is unfair to suggest, as the Chamber does, that advocates of the precautionary principle are extremists who champion total risk-avoidance policies that are out of step with scientific, economic, and industrial realities. That is a mischaracterization of the precautionary principle that fails to move the debate forward. Indeed, to the contrary, advocates of the precautionary principle contend that[27]:

- the plausibility of harm should be grounded in scientific analysis (not mere conjecture about worst-case scenarios);
- policy prescriptions should be subjected to ongoing review to ensure they remain appropriate (so they can be tailored as more intelligence about the risk is gathered);
- the choice of action should be the result of a participatory process that seeks input from affected stakeholders (rather than unilaterally imposed by some regulatory authority);
- regulatory actions should be proportional to the seriousness of the potential harm (rather than merely one-size-fits-all risk avoidance); and,
- the risks of inaction should be weighed along with the risks of action (as failure to act as well as interventions can each create their own risks).

The "control problem" posed by AI fits the bill for the kind of risks that justify precautionary approaches: shrouded in uncertainty, potentially irreversible, and threatening human health and safety. Lawmakers, regulators, and anyone with decisional authority over AI research and design should adhere to the precautionary principle as a guide.

The World Health Organization (WHO) recommends following the precautionary principle to deal with emerging technological risks.[28] We agree.

Even if the designers of AI systems believe they can monitor the growth and capabilities of an AI in order to catch it when things get dangerous, that is not an adequate risk management approach here. We'll make an argument by analogy that is imperfect but perhaps helpful.

Assume the goal is to heat the water up as much as possible without making it boil over. In this case, hotter temperature means more powerful AI, and boiling water is when the AI gains a decisive strategic advantage. The goal would be making AI as smart and powerful as possible (so that it can be the most promising resource to us) without making it so smart and so powerful that it gains a decisive strategic advantage. The risk management process of waiting for the water to boil before lowering the temperature is not helpful, because (in our hypothetical) once the water begins to boil, it's too late—once the AI gains a decisive strategic advantage, it can no longer be contained.

The risk management approach encouraged by the Chamber of Commerce would have us wait until we know precisely when the water will boil before we begin to take steps to control the temperature.

Let's say we try to check on the temperature of the water by removing the lid from time to time so that we have an idea of the progress being made as we approach the boiling point. Analogously, we are trying to assess the smarts and powers of the AI as it grows in both measures, so that we can curb its growth in time for it to be as strong as possible without gaining that potentially fatal decisive strategic advantage. This is not a sound approach. The act of removing the lid itself lowers the internal temperature and pressure of the pot and prevents it from boiling over. Recall, the AI will have some sense of self-awareness and may even know that it is being monitored, and may even know that its human handlers intend to curb its growth if it becomes too threatening.

The act of monitoring the AI may cause it to conceal its intelligence and power, effectively as a means of self-preservation. Bostrom speaks to this risk[29]:

> [A]n unfriendly AI may become smart enough to realize that it is better off concealing some of its capability gains. It may under-report on its progress or deliberately flunk some of the harder tests, in order to avoid causing alarm before it has grown strong enough to attain a decisive strategic advantage... We can thus perceive a general failure mode, wherein the good behavioral track record of a system in its juvenile stages fails utterly to predict its behavior at a more mature stage.

For these reasons, we urge those in positions of influence about the design and deployment of AI to adopt the precautionary principle with respect to the intelligence and powers of AI systems. Indeed, some forms of superintelligence may conceal its powers simply because it was not explicitly instructed to reveal them. We need to be able to appreciate the risks posed by AI without anthropomorphically attributing good and evil intentions to the system. A tsunami has no desire to harm, but that makes it no less destructive.

Some risks of AI, such as deepfakes, are not easy to regulate. We look at this next.

Deepfakes: A Pernicious Permutation of Photo Fakery

The problem with deepfake technologies is, while they can provide altered images for entertainment purposes at a fraction of the millions that CGI used to cost a big budget production studio, they can be used for nefarious purposes.

According to Charles Seife, a professor at New York University and the author of *Virtual Unreality: Just Because the Internet Told You, How Do You Know It's True?*, "Deepfakes have the potential to derail political discourse."

The same could be said about markets. A deepfake of a prominent stock analyst ringing an alarm bell and panicking about some purported insider information is enough to send markets into a reactive mood. That the video would later be understood as a deepfake does little to assure investors who lost money as a result. According to Seife, "Technology is altering our reality at an alarming rate."

The High Stakes of Deepfakes

Recent advances in machine learning have made it possible for anyone with a PC and a couple of hours for mischief to concoct a "face-swapping" video that basically depicts one person's face on another person's body in such a way as to make it believable to the casual viewer.

Using artificial intelligence to create seemingly realistic but definitely fake videos began as a more or less harmless joke. There is already an instance overlaying the features and mannerisms of a certain US President onto the body of Frankenstein's monster in a scene from that old black-and-white classic sci-fi film. Market forces caught on, and the profit motive drove the application of this technology to create unethical clickbait to lure viewers to adult websites—for instance, by overlaying a celebrity's face onto the body of a pornographic actress. While this kind of behavior may already be actionable in a court of law, for instance under a tort theory of false light or under criminal theory of impersonation, oftentimes the damage is done simply by the video's existence, and legal recourse is available, if at all, years after the fact.

In the case of political figures and CEOs being impersonated, the election results or stock market prices can be irreparably altered by the appearance of such a deepfake, and when the stakes are so high that the risk of facing civil or criminal prosecution may not be an adequate deterrent. This is especially true if the bad actor creating strategic deepfakes is a hostile foreign power. AI is turbocharging espionage, cybercrimes, and propaganda, which could result in "the end of truth."[30]

As machine learning advances in terms of sophistication and refinery, complex deception will become increasingly difficult to identify and distinguish from authentic imagery. Paul Scharre, Senior Fellow and Director of the Technology and National Security Program at the Center for New American Security, says the emergence of deepfakes means "We're moving into an era where seeing is no longer going to be believing. I don't think we as a society are prepared for this."[31]

Social media platforms already provide an effective and efficient vehicle for the widespread release and propagation of information and disinformation alike. Unfortunately, the latter is given an assist by "bots" and their unwitting human followers, who post and repost topics with the aim of artificially increasing their relevance and impact. Artificial intelligence used to create deepfake videos pours gasoline on this "fake news" wildfire.

According to Renee DiResta, researcher at Data for Democracy, "Before the technology even gets good, the fact that it exists and is a way to erode confidence in legitimate material is deeply problematic." In the corner of your mind, you are aware that what you are watching may indeed be a deepfake. In certain ways the damage is already done by those seeds of doubt, even if the video is authentic. According to Will Knight, senior editor of *MIT Technology Review* covering artificial intelligence, "If you can't tell a fake from reality, then it becomes easy to question the authenticity of anything."[32]

Law's Limited Remedy

Imagine the market consequences if a deepfake emerged of the CEOs of Facebook, Apple, Amazon, Netflix, or Google announcing they were culpable of committing fraud to artificially inflate market value, and as a consequence were immediately liquidating their assets. Stock market prices in these companies would suddenly dip at the news as confused and frightened investors would seek to shed the toxic asset in the resulting panic.

The ripple effect could potentially erase millions if not billions of dollars in value from stock ledgers in a single trading day. A press release would only go so far to reassure investors getting client calls and forwarded videos of what appears to be a prominent CEO committing reprehensible acts or saying things that destroy confidence in the business. Only later, a matter of days perhaps, would investigations conclude, definitively ruling the suspect videos a deepfake, that the companies were not dissolving after all, or what have you. Companies have lots of means available to try to rehabilitate reputations. But you cannot unring a bell. By the time the culprits of the deepfake video are identified and prosecuted, the damage could be irreversible.

Could a legislative body like the United States Congress simply ban the production and distribution of deepfakes? In a nation with constitutionally guaranteed freedom of speech, such a ban may not be legal. The First Amendment to the US Constitution provides that, "Congress shall make no law abridging the freedom of speech."[33]

In 2012, in *United States v. Alvarez*, the US Supreme Court ruled that the Stolen Valor Act, a federal law that prohibited lying about receiving military medals, violated the First Amendment. The reasoning behind this decision is the **counterspeech doctrine** first articulated by Supreme Court Justice Louis Brandeis' concurring opinion in *Whitney v. California* (1927): "If there be time to expose through discussion the falsehood and fallacies, to avert the evil by the processes of education, the remedy to be applied is more speech, not enforced silence." In other words, the government's remedy to lies is truth, not censorship.

For these reasons, the prevailing jurisprudence around the First Amendment probably precludes Congress from enacting a sweeping ban on deepfakes. However, the jurisprudence does leave "considerable room for carefully tailored prohibitions of certain intentionally harmful deep fakes."[34]

Whether Congress can ban a deepfake boils down to whether doing so would be an abridgment of the freedom of speech. Eight justices, writing in plurality and concurring opinions, concluded that "falsity alone" does not remove expression from the First Amendment's protection. It would be unconstitutional to outright ban making false statements. But there are certain kinds of lies that are not protected by the Constitution (and are thus susceptible to government regulation, including outright prohibitions). The First Amendment does not protect the defamation of private persons, fraud, impersonation of government officials, speech integral to criminal conduct, or language that has the effect of imminent and likely incitement of violence.[35]

Criminal laws are already on the books in jurisdictions attempting to protect against some kinds of assault on truth. For instance, the State of New York has criminalized **impersonation** in certain circumstances[36]:

A person is guilty of criminal impersonation in the second degree when he:

1 Impersonates another and does an act in such assumed character with intent to obtain a benefit or to injure or defraud another; or
2 Pretends to be a representative of some person or organization and does an act in such pretended capacity with intent to obtain a benefit or to injure or defraud another; or
3 (a) Pretends to be a public servant, or wears or displays without authority any uniform, badge, insignia or facsimile thereof by which such public servant is lawfully distinguished, or falsely expresses by his words or actions that he is a public servant or is acting with approval or authority of a public agency or department; and (b) so acts with intent to induce another to submit to such pretended official authority, to solicit funds or to otherwise cause another to act in reliance upon that pretense.
4 Impersonates another by communication by Internet website or electronic means with intent to obtain a benefit or injure or defraud another, or by such communication pretends to be a public servant in order to induce another to submit to such authority or act in reliance on such pretense.

The word "impersonation" should be construed broadly to encompass the creation of digital deepfakes. It would seem that New York's criminal impersonation law would fit the offense of publishing a pernicious deepfake for purposes of corporate sabotage. However, the New York Attorney General does not have infinite jurisdiction.

Further, even if the crime was committed in New York City and the New York Attorney General had jurisdiction and apprehended the suspect, the crime only leads to a Class A Misdemeanor. That means, upon conviction, a court may sentence the defendant to a maximum of one year in jail or three years probation, and levy a fine of up to $1,000 or twice the amount of the individual's gain from the crime. A deepfake prank in the corporate espionage context could cost far more. Obviously, that is not steep enough punishment to deter someone with sufficient motivation or free time and lack of conscience. These deepfakes could foreseeably wreak untold havoc in politics and the markets.

Convicting a deepfaker is only possible if the prosecutor can identify the culprit and prove beyond a reasonable doubt that the video in question is in fact a fake. Brace yourselves and your organizations for deepfakes—you cannot trust everything you see on the internet.

The Promise of Legal Solutions

Lawmakers must not think about impersonation in such a pedestrian sense as someone showing up at your front door dressed as a police officer so they can "confiscate" your TV. The power of the Internet, coupled with artificial intelligence, is capable of creating deepfake impersonations for far more sinister purposes, and with far greater adverse consequences.

The law might go a step further by outlawing the creation of any such impersonation in the first place. However, that would raise complex First Amendment issues. Even if the motives are harmless, once a deepfake is published, its inventor loses control over the purposes to which it is applied. The law to ban dangerous deepfakes would run up against the limits on government restrictions provided by Constitutional safeguards around freedom of speech and freedom of expression.

How do lawmakers draw the line between a constitutionally protected but disturbing deepfake parody video of a public person in flagrante delicto with the logo of a special interest group, on the one hand, and a criminal violation involving a deepfake video that is literally the "impersonation of another by communication by internet website or electronic means with intent to … injure or defraud another"? These lines must be drawn carefully to avoid infringing on constitutionally protected speech, commercial speech, and entertainment, while providing adequate deterrence against harmful deepfakery.

At least lawmakers in the United States are starting to look into it. On September 13, 2018, a bipartisan coalition of members of the House of Representatives sent a letter to the current Director of National Intelligence Dan Coats, requesting "that the Intelligence Community report to Congress and the public about the implications of new technologies that allow malicious actors to fabricate audio, video and still images."[37]

Fortunately, these congressional representatives recognize the risk: "Hyper-realistic digital forgeries—popularly referred to as 'deep fakes'—use sophisticated machine learning techniques to produce convincing depictions of individuals doing or saying things they never did, without their consent or knowledge. By blurring the line between fact and fiction, deep fake technology could undermine public trust in recorded images and videos as objective depictions of reality."[38] Lawmakers concerned with intelligence and national security are already reaching out to CEOs of Big Tech, inquiring about policies for dealing with deepfakes on their platforms.

The law must keep pace with the risks posed by the weaponization of technology. The risks posed have evolved, and the law must respond in equal or greater measures. But private sector enterprises would be foolish to wait for the government to solve this problem.

The US Department of Defense took the results of the inaugural cyber grand challenge seriously, subsequently launching "Project Voltron" to run similar autonomous cybersecurity protocols to monitor and repair vulnerabilities within military cyber infrastructure.[39] The technology has already evolved beyond rule-based AI to deploy machine learning capabilities. Expect these kinds of military projects to continue. We hope they will spill over into commercial applications of cybersecurity defense systems that use protective AI systems to harden IT infrastructure across the world.

A meeting in the capital of the United States between the CEOs of some of Silicon Valley's largest companies convened by then-Attorney General Jeff Sessions, "could presage sweeping new investigations of Amazon, Facebook, Google and their tech industry peers, stemming from lingering frustrations that these companies are too big, fail to safeguard users' private data and don't cooperate with legal demands."[40]

Sessions' purpose for the meeting was to probe whether these tech companies were promoting a liberal ideological bias across their platforms. This was a response to complaints by President Trump and top Republicans that Silicon Valley social media platforms were surreptitiously squelching the viewpoints of conservative online users. As social media platforms increasingly become forums for the delivery and consumption of news, the concern about partisan curation of public information is a legitimate concern, however we should be equally concerned about outright disinformation and harmful propaganda. Indeed, the opportunity to grill tech company executives was seized upon by the other attorneys in attendance, including the Attorneys General of eight states and the District of Columbia and officials from five other states. The focus of the meeting quickly turned to what the attorneys felt about Big Tech's handling of consumer privacy.

According to D.C. Attorney General Karl Racine, the "AGs are really focused on understanding more as to what consumers are truly consenting to and what they may not know is going on with their data." According to Jim Hood, Attorney General of Mississippi, "We were unanimous. Our focus is going to be on antitrust and privacy. That's where our laws are."

According to the *Washington Post* report on this meeting[41]:

> For months, tech giants like Facebook, Google, and Twitter have weathered brutal criticism in the nation's capital for their business practices—from the ways they safeguard their data to their preparedness to combat misinformation online ahead of the 2018 midterm elections.
>
> Whether state and federal officials have the legal tools under antitrust law to regulate the tech industry's data practices was a major question for the group.

For other states, the issue was the tech industry's relationship with law enforcement. That included talk about Apple and "how we in law enforcement depend on cellphones." Hood said that Apple has "waved at us and didn't use all their fingers" in its handling of encryption.

Although the state Attorneys General agree that legal action against the industry (if wrongdoing is found) would probably be led by the United States Justice Department, interestingly, leadership on the issue of policing tech companies' use of consumer data and protecting consumer privacy is driven by a bi-partisan multistate inquiry of the part of various state Attorneys General, coordinated by Nebraska Attorney General Doug Peterson.

In Europe, breaches in consumer privacy or security are dealt with by application of the European Union's *General Data Protection Regulation (GDPR)*. The GDPR became applicable in May of 2018. The law is sweeping in territorial scope—it applies to those who control or process personal data related to offering of goods or services to data subjects (i.e., consumers) who are in the European Union, regardless of whether payment is required.[42]

A company with its servers located anywhere in the world is subject to the GDPR, even if it is not based in the EU, if it is processing data belonging to a data subject in the EU. The GDPR requires data to be processed in a transparent manner; inaccurate data must be erased or rectified without delay; and the data controller must comply with all principles of the GDPR, including safeguards for storage, de-identification of personal data, obtaining consent from the data subject, and providing infrastructure to protect the rights and freedoms of the data subject.[43]

The GDPR creates interesting (that is, complex) compliance situations where government agencies still need to develop internationally compatible frameworks for data governance during cross-border transfers. Time will tell whether the GDPR will catch on in other nations. Google is being sued by a natural person claiming the right to privacy means he can de-list prejudicial information about him—effectively staking out the consumer's privacy right to delete oneself from Internet search results.[44]

Meanwhile in the United States, the federal legislature gave Internet Service Providers the right to gather and sell for profit an Internet user's private browsing history, without even requiring that they obtain the user's consent. The strength of consumer expectations of privacy was clearly no match for the strength of telecommunications industry influence. The US and the EU's stance toward digital privacy rights stand in stark contrast. Savvy consumers are starting to take privacy into their own hands, purchasing home security infrastructure such as *Virtual Private Networks (VPN)* and using encrypted telecommunications devices.

166

The complacent attitude of US lawmakers toward increasingly frequent and severe data breaches by US-based companies surely cannot last much longer.

Consumer Privacy and the "Internet of Eyes"

Evan Nisselson coins the phrase the *Internet of Eyes* to describe the state of affairs when manmade objects all have Internet connectivity and smart sensors built in.[45]

Nisselson provides an effusive take on the Internet of Eyes because he looks forward to Amazon being able to tell him when he needs to purchase a change of pants or to stock up on his groceries, as this will streamline his shopping experience. We feel that literal domestic surveillance is a steep price to pay for limited benefits in terms of customer convenience. But that's just us. Some people may not put as high a premium on privacy. In describing the new Amazon Echo "Look" (which is basically the Amazon Echo with a surveillance camera built in), Nisselson explains[46]:

> Major technology companies and new startups are at war over having the most valuable artificial intelligence and at the core of this war is having unique high quality visual data. Inanimate objects with cameras enable companies to own the first step in gathering the data for computer vision and artificial intelligence algorithms to analyze.
>
> Their core goal is to capture unique and proprietary visual data of their customers so their computers can learn as much as possible about us through the Selfies we capture via Amazon's product the Echo Look.
>
> [In the future,] these cameras will analyze many different types of visual data from photographic, thermal, X-ray, ultra-sound, and white light to deliver high quality signals unlike anything we've had previously.

We are concerned about the proliferation of commercial spying, in which the companies consume the consumer, harvesting our data under the guise of enhancing consumer experiences, but truly creating disturbing privacy, security, and autonomy concerns such as choice architecture.

We feel like the Internet of Eyes is a little creepy and should be addressed by legal constraints on "smart" product design that at the very least requires consumer consent to being monitored. Of course, consumers can purchase products capable of spying on them and may have little concern about being spied upon.

Unless legislation comes down against this kind of practice, expect to see eyes on everything from refrigerators to television sets.

At what point does it become impossible for an ordinary human to resist an advertisement that has harnessed millions of data points about consumer preferences, emotional triggers, and human cognition such that it is impossible to ignore? When does the persuasion of an effective advertisement, which is protected commercial speech, become illegal coercion that overpowers the volition of the consumer? If an advertisement is irresistible, then we can no longer claim to be informing the consumer—we are controlling the consumer and the resulting transaction should be set aside.

Many nations' legal regimes of criminal law, contract law, and tort law assume humans have free will and are in control of their actions, absent extenuating circumstances such as coercion, duress, insanity, minority of age, or intoxication. In the United States' criminal justice system, the notion of criminal liability for actions depends on mens rea, or having a guilty mind, as well as actus reus, or a volitional criminal act. Both mens rea and actus reus depend on some folk psychological notion of free will. Courts only uphold contracts that were freely entered into by consenting adults enjoying legal capacity. The legal system assumes we are free, not automata.

In these cases, companies that harvest data about consumers in order to influence consumer choice are *consuming the consumer* in the sense that they are harvesting data created by consumers like they are picking wildflowers. It is unclear where the line should be drawn or how it could be drawn in a uniform and fairly applicable manner. However, it appears intuitive (and we would argue strenuously) that there should be some limitation on what companies can do to manipulate consumers. Issues of consumer privacy, self-determination, meaningful choice, and safety (in instances where distraction can lead to dangerous conditions) must be given weight. Advertisements that are based on big data-driven artificial intelligence may be too potent to be appropriate for use in certain areas (such as on billboards along freeways) or in certain audiences (for instance, minors or seniors who are easily persuaded due to mental infirmity).

As deepfakes illustrate, even reasonably prudent people can be duped or manipulated by a military-grade psy-op or propaganda campaign. We should counteract the continually expanding power of persuasion that is even today harnessing AI to transform the art of advertisement. With AI, advertising is becoming a dangerously potent weapon capable of seizing control of our attention span to the point where we can no longer resist its lure.

We warn against the day when, thanks to advances in AI and machine learning, every purchase becomes an "impulse buy." Under those extreme circumstances, the moral support for free markets breaks down, as we can no longer trust the market to behave efficiently. Consumers would not be maximizing their own utility from entering compulsively into transactions; they would be manipulated into exchanges that do not make them better off. When advertising becomes too powerful, this could lead to market failures, thereby justifying (even for a libertarian) some form of regulatory intervention, if not robust self-policing by the marketers themselves. With all the insight into consumer psychology housed in Marketing departments, we expect them to exercise leadership in this context. AI combined with big data gives marketers recipes that could become perhaps too potent.

Our concerns about consuming the consumer are threefold. First, the collection of consumer-generated data is uncompensated. What companies that monitor their customers and the public capture is valuable, but they are not paying anything back to the people creating that data. Second, the consent given by consumers to have their privacy invaded is often obtained imperfectly. Disclosure and permission are buried in fine print and legalese in click-through end user license agreements that no one reads. Third, the data harvested by companies may not be safeguarded by the harvesting company to a reasonable degree that adequately protects consumer privacy interests. We turn to the safeguarding of consumer data, next.

The Cost of Failing to Implement
Privacy and Security Safeguards

The largest ride-hailing app disrupting the yellow cab industry and transforming transportation in general is Uber. Thriving in the new access-based economy, Uber provides job opportunities for those with a vehicle and increases the transparency and accessibility of cab rides to any user with a smartphone and credit card. The popularity of the app led to the meteoric rise of the company.

Its original CEO, Travis Kalanik, took the company perhaps too close to the sun. Public scrutiny of his leadership style and the "tech bro" corporate culture that fomented under his leadership, along with a handful of scandals, led to his replacement. When the company's board appointed a new CEO, Dara Khosrowshahi, he immediately began to clean up shop. Several problems came to light under new leadership, one of them being a massive data breach from 2016.

With millions of users' payment and personal information loaded into the app, consumers and employees alike trusted Uber to maintain this sensitive information in a manner that preserved privacy and security. The company suffered a data breach that exposed the names, emails, and phone numbers of 57 million people around the world.

Then, in response, the company sat on this information and even paid $100,000 to the hackers to keep the breach quiet. As the new CEO,

Khosrowshahi honorably ordered an investigation into a purported data breach and the company's subsequent cover-up attempt, and then disclosed the findings publicly.

The data breach came to the attention of Uber's Chief Legal Officer, Tony West, on his first day on the job. "Rather than settling into my new workplace and walking the floor to meet my new colleagues, I spend the day calling various state and federal regulators," says West.

Despite (but not because of) the efforts of Khosrowshah and West, Attorneys General for all 50 of the United States and the District of Columbia took legal action against Uber. Apparently, hiding a breach from your customers is not the proper response. In September 2018, the company reached a settlement agreement to pay $148 million to end the multistate probe.

According to the Attorney General of California Xavier Becerra, "Uber's decision to cover up this breach was a blatant violation of the public's trust. Companies in California and throughout the nation are entrusted with customers' information. This settlement broadcasts to all of them that we will hold them accountable to protect that data."[47] The settlement represents the biggest ever multistate penalty for a data breach. According to New York Attorney General Barbara Underwood, "We have zero tolerance for those who skirt the law and leave consumer and employee information vulnerable to exploitation."[48]

In the summer of 2018, Uber hired as its Chief Trust and Security Officer a former general counsel for the National Security Agency. As part of the settlement, Uber is required to make changes to its practices and corporate culture, including undergoing regular third-party audits of security practices.

Today's technology—and the interconnectivity that ties devices, business partners, and customers—also exposes businesses to a wide range of security threats. With the explosion of connected devices and the amount of personal data, the Identity Theft Resource Center (ITRC, 2018) reports that in just the first three months of 2018 there have been 273 breaches with over 5 million customer records exposed.

There are other well-known data breaches—the 2017 Equifax breach exposing 140 million customers' social security numbers and more recently we saw the use of personal information from Facebook by Cambridge Analytica weaponized to influence the 2016 presidential election. Firms that use any type of data—especially disaggregate customer data—need to be very careful about security and privacy, less they violate local and federal laws. Further, cyberhacks can disrupt operations, steal data and IP, and create massive security breaches that can destroy a company.

We are witnessing increasingly sophisticated cyber intrusions that exploit computer-based systems, threatening public trust, and wreaking economic havoc. In 2013, when hackers exploited a vulnerability in retail giant Target's infrastructure, they stole 40 million customer credit and debit cards and 70 million records containing personally identifying information of customers; Target's fourth-quarter profits that year dropped 46% from the year before.[49] Facebook was recently ordered to pay a USD $5 billion file as part of a settlement with regulatory authorities over mishandling consumer data; the privacy penalty is the largest fine in Federal Trade Commission history.

Each breach of a digital or cyber technology challenges users to mistrust and abandon the technology. User loyalty has, to date, proved remarkably enduring. But when it breaks, customers exit rapidly and in droves[.] A company's cybersecurity safeguards protect not only its trade secrets and other intellectual property, but also its reputation, brand, and goodwill.[50] Companies today are more than ever targets of actors—state sponsored and rogue alike—dedicated to increasingly cunning forms of corporate espionage, writing malware to bypass IT security defenses, stealing intellectual property, and generally causing mayhem.[51] Building information security into technology must be a top priority. Our "smart" devices are simply far too vulnerable. As organizations increasingly go digital, they increase the amount of surface area vulnerable to cyberattack. As institutions adopt CRMs and other electronic management platforms, they open themselves up to ransomware. "Smart" is a double-edged sword.

Beware of Algorithmic Bias

Recall from Chapter 3 we explained that algorithms generally are defined procedures for solving a problem, and more technically, sets of rules or procedures that a computer is programmed to follow when carrying out problem-solving or task-oriented operations. Algorithms apply rules when triggered by certain inputs. If a mortgage application contains elements X, Y, and Z (for example, high credit score, low debt, and steady income), it should be approved. It is easy to imagine botsourcing that kind of function to an algorithm-based AI.

Algorithmic approaches to data processing can be more reliable problem solvers than humans in the sense that algorithms tend to be relatively objective, consistent, and powerful in processing vast data sets.

Machine learning goes beyond applying an algorithm to carry out a task; machine learning utilizes pattern recognition and Bayesian reasoning to "teach" itself based on new data.

According to Will Knight in the *MIT Technology Review*, "Big tech companies are racing to sell off-the-shelf machine-learning technology that can be accessed via the cloud. As more customers make use of these algorithms to automate important judgments and decisions, the issue of bias will become crucial. And since bias can easily creep into machine-learning models, ways to automate the detection of unfairness could become a valuable part of the AI toolkit."[52]

The problem with machine learning is that we can inadvertently come with *built-in bias* when the AI is trained with dirty historical data. For example, an AI system that processes mortgage applications would presumably be trained by reviewing historical data sets of all the prior mortgage applications that have been submitted, and learning to recognize patterns that identify which should be approved versus those which should be rejected. The problem comes when the historical data set includes a number of rejected applications that were rejected for reasons of unfair prejudice or illegal racial discrimination.

Historically, some banks would reject mortgage applications in a nonwhite neighborhood, or they would increase the cost of the capital or the cost of insurance for nonwhite applicants in order to discourage home buying by people of color. This is called *redlining*, which refers to the practice of banks drawing red lines on maps to indicate neighborhoods predominately occupied by nonwhites where they did not want to provide loans in order to discriminate against persons of color who were otherwise creditworthy and qualified loan applicants.

Redlining on the basis of race is now illegal under the federal Fair Housing Act, whereas redlining a neighborhood because it sits on a seismic fault line or in a flood plain is reasonable and appropriate risk underwriting.[53] A machine learning AI system fed decades of mortgage applications in the greater Detroit area may very well perpetuate the now-illegal practice of race-based redlining even though, of course, the AI itself holds no racial animus. It is only following precedent.

Given the sordid past of discrimination based on race, gender, and wealth, we need to build our AI systems to be fair and transparent. "Algorithmic bias can lead to over-policing in predominately black areas; the automated filters on social media flag activists while allowing hate groups to keep posting unchecked."[54] To combat the problem of algorithmic bias and build trust in our AI comrades, IBM is requiring developers to jump through some hurdles before AI software goes to market.

One of these safeguards is a third-party audit, where the source code and historical data underlying the AI software are evaluated by an independent expert to flag for prejudices; another safeguard is running counterfactual tests to ensure the algorithm is not inappropriately sensitive to race, gender, or wealth.

To help promote ethical algorithms, IBM scientists are proposing that developers of AI programs must publish a *Supplier's Declaration of Conformity (SDoC)* prior to an algorithm's sale. The SDoC would take the form of a report or user manual that indicates to prospective purchasers how well the algorithm performed on "standardized tests of performance, fairness and risk factors, and safety measures."[55] In the same way that a prospective purchaser can obtain crash safety information about a car before driving it off the lot, a potential buyer of AI software should be able to tell whether the algorithms contained in the software are likely to generate outputs informed by prejudices or whether it is secured against known cyberattack threats.

Microsoft is also pursuing the problem of algorithmic bias. According to Rich Caruana, Senior Researcher at Microsoft working on a bias-detection dashboard, "Things like transparency, intelligibility, and explanation are new enough to the field that few of us have sufficient experience to know everything we should look for and all the ways that bias might lurk in our models."[56] Caruana argues that the most important step tech companies can take on this issue is workforce education, "so that they're aware of the myriad ways in which bias can arise and manifest itself and create tools to make models easier to understand and bias easier to detect."

Facebook is also raising the profile of algorithmic bias as a corporate concern. Facebook has launched a product for internal detection of bias called Fairness Flow. According to Will Knight, "Facebook says it needed Fairness Flow because more and more people at the company are using AI to make important decisions," and it needed to be warned if an algorithm was making inappropriate recommendations on the basis of race or gender, for example.[57]

We forecast that algorithmic bias will become the subject of federal regulation, just like food safety standards for food processing companies imposed by the Food and Drug Administration, or crash test safety standards imposed by the National Highway Traffic Safety Administration. Until then, IBM, Facebook, and Microsoft are pushing forward with self-policing. Experts are skeptical. Professor Bin Yu at University of California, Berkeley, appreciates these proactive steps but suggests third-party external audits are more appropriate: "Someone else has to investigate Facebook's algorithms—they can't be a secret to everyone."[58]

Black Box Decisions: AI's "Dark Secret"

The inscrutability of more advanced algorithms poses a problem in instances where AI systems make decisions with huge consequences, such as self-driving cars pulling off an emergency maneuver to avoid a crash, multimillion-dollar stock market trade decisions, cancer treatment recommendations, and other complex judgments delivered by AI. There will be errors that lead to lawsuits on the part of victims. Plaintiffs' attorneys will seek to depose the AI developers and the executive decision-makers who relied upon the AI recommendations. Victims will want to know why the AI did what it did. Litigators will want to know whether the executive followed the recommendation of the smart software, and if not, why not.

What if the AI suggested Option A, but the executive chose Option B resulting in harm?

What if the AI suggested Option A, and the executive chose option A resulting in harm?

If the AI cannot explain why it is making its recommendations, then executives will have a harder time justifying reliance upon its recommendations when defending their actions. They will have to independently justify actions with personal reasons. But if they are doing that, then it leads us to question why even have AI recommendations if they cannot be relied upon when those actions have legal consequences?

This leads us to what Will Knight of the *MIT Technology Review* describes as the "dark secret at the heart of AI."[59] To illustrate the challenge, Knight describes an experimental vehicle set loose by Nvidia. Unlike autonomous cars demonstrated by Google, Tesla, and General Motors, which follow instructions of engineers and programmers, the Nvidia vehicle used deep learning to teach itself solely by watching videos of human drivers. This is how it works (and why it's mysterious)[60]:

> Information from the vehicle's sensors goes straight into a huge network of artificial neurons that process the data and then deliver the commands required to operate the steering wheel, the brakes, and other systems. The result seems to match the responses you'd expect from a human driver. But what if one day it did something unexpected—crashed into a tree or sat at a green light? As things stand now, it might be difficult to find out why. The system is so complicated that even the engineers who designed it may struggle to isolate the reason for any single action. And you can't ask it: there is no obvious way to design such a system so that it could always explain why it did what it did.

Until an AI system is capable of being interrogated as to why it reached a decision (e.g., why did you recommend to sell these shares? Why did you turn into oncoming traffic?) then it should not be deployed in the wild.

Perhaps unsurprisingly, the European Union is taking a precautionary approach to AI—and contrary to the fears expressed by the US Chamber of Commerce, the European approach to regulating AI is not to stifle innovation out of some extreme risk aversion but rather to increase investment and deployment of this technology in a safe manner.

The European Artificial Intelligence Alliance will draft ethical guidelines based on the input from businesses, researchers, consumers, trade unions, policymakers, and government officials in the format of formal stakeholder feedback.[61] The European Commission will provide guidelines for AI based on the existing Product Liability Directive. Products liability law in the United States and Europe defines when a product manufacturer or distributor is liable for unreasonably dangerous or defective conditions in a product.[62] It goes beyond the scope of this chapter to compare and contrast products liability law in various jurisdictions. Suffice it to say, it will be interesting to observe how the United States, Europe, and China and other tech-ambitious nations each approach the risk management, ethical, and legal challenges posed by AI. We continue to support the European approach as most prudent in light of the gravity of the control problem.

The European Union's GDPR went into application in 2018 as a sweeping reform of the 1995 European Data Protection Directive. The GDPR applies to any company doing business with European citizens. While saying a lot about consumer privacy and data security, as well as how to handle data breaches, the GDPR surprisingly says very little about the black box decision-making of AI systems. That said, it is one of the only formal pronouncements by legal institutions on this important challenge posed by AI. And what little is said by DGPR on black box decision-making has generated some controversy among legal scholars.

The GDPR provides that data controllers are required to notify consumers how data is used, which includes "the existence of automated decision-making, and, at least in those cases, meaningful information about the logic involved, as well as the significance and the envisaged consequences of such processing for the data subject." This arguably requires data controllers to explain how consumer data is being used by AI systems to make decisions.

This interpretation is supported by the language in Recital 71, a legally unenforceable companion document to the GDPR, which elaborates on the actual requirements of the GDPR.

Recital 71 applies not only to the issue of algorithmic bias but also to the mysterious mind of some AI systems. The entire text of Recital 71 is in this endnote.[63] The most salient part is the EU's solution to the black box problem: Data subjects have "the right to obtain human intervention, to express his or her point of view, to obtain an explanation of the decision reached after such assessment and to challenge the decision." This would seem to preclude some neural net AI systems from operating on EU data subjects altogether, due to the inexplicable nature of its output.

The Impact of AI on Lawmaking and Regulations

With all this talk about how laws can protect us against the risks posed by AI, we should spend some time on how AI is influencing the lawmaking and regulatory process itself. Ironically, if not ultimately tragically, AI can manipulate the very institutions meant to curb its abuse.

Erosion of Public Trust

In the US, to create a law, it must be drafted by legislators (or supplied to them by a special interest group—for example, the controversial American Legislative Exchange Council), then the bill must make it out of committee, be put on the floor for a vote, receive a majority affirmative vote in both houses of Congress (both the House of Representatives and the Senate), then signed into law by the President. There are a lot of procedural hurdles to ensure only wise laws are enacted that carry the carefully considered majority support of the nation's elected representatives. Somehow despite these checks, balances, and tripwires designed to keep bad laws off the books, sentiment is usually unfavorable toward government, and the average person hardly feels comfortable trusting the US government to "do the right thing."

According to PEW Research Center data, public trust in the government is at an all-time low and has been trending downward since the Nixon administration, trending upward only when the economy is doing well or when the nation rallied in response to the 9/11 World Trade Center attacks.[64] Predictably, trust in government is higher when the respondent's own political party holds the power of office, yet somehow both Democrats and Republicans feel their party is always losing, and there are only modest differences between the generations, races, and ethnicities in terms of trust in government. In general, most people do not trust the government to do the right thing.[65]

According to Professor Anthony Curtis, an expert in mass communications, the history of social media use can be divided into three historical phases: Before the Dawn (1969–1993), The Dawning (1994–2004), and After the Dawn (2005 and beyond).[66] Researchers began seriously to study social media by analyzing data obtained through monitoring and performing sentiment analysis over that data in order to begin scientifically to understand the mood of social media users. Beyond the United States, other governments are trying to improve relationships with citizens by using social media to promote transparency and engagement that enables the government to be citizen-centric, thereby prioritizing government resources toward meeting real-time citizen needs rather than merely offering services based on existing government capabilities.[67]

The advent of cloud Internet services, wireless Internet accessibly in far broader reaches, and the proliferation of social media platforms and the penetration of these platforms ever deeper into popular usage have enabled both corporations and governments unprecedented access into the mood of the people. Governments and corporations can study our moods with statistically significant sample sizes and can interact with large swaths of the population at virtually no cost, simply by "posting" an infographic on an official Facebook page or by "tweeting" out a brief statement on an official Twitter handle.

With this unparalleled access to social feedback and sentiment analysis, you would think governments and corporations would do a better job at restoring public trust. What if the limitations on human self-interest and rationality (discussed in Chapter 4) prevent us from writing good laws or governing our companies in ways that retain social license to operate? Can technology transform the rulemaking process to improve public trust in regulatory outcomes?

Improving Public Participation

According to Chris Horton of the *MIT Technology Review*, there is a "simple but ingenious system" being deployed in Taiwan that offers a "promising experiment in participatory government," but, ironically, its main obstacle to gaining traction in greater use in politics is… politics.[68] In brief, the Taiwanese government has deployed an online platform ("vTaiwan") to enable *crowdsourcing* (querying the public to answer a specific question) on controversial issues of policy. Crowdsourcing answers to proposed legal reforms has proven "useful in finding consensus on deadlocked issues," says Horton, but "the question now is whether it can be used to settle bigger policy questions at a national level—and whether it could be a model for other countries."[69]

Due to unfortunate tribal elements of human nature and the partisan arrangement of many electoral political bodies, we fall easily into deadlock on divisive issues where one "side" has to "beat" the other side, and compromise is viewed as weakness. This frustrates efforts at building consensus and ultimately undermines the ability of a government to enjoy ongoing majority support for its policies over time. However, the vTaiwan experiment has shown a way to resolve these partisan deadlocks by cutting out the middleman of elected representatives and letting the people speak directly to the issues. Not speaking to each other, mind you, but to the issues themselves.

According to Colin Megill, the CEO and cofounder of pol.is (a digital hosting platform used by vTaiwan), one of the reasons for deadlock is that "the opposing sides had never had a chance to actually interact with each other's ideas. When they did, it became apparent that both sides were basically willing to give the opposing side what it wanted."[70]

Technology using certain features of social media platforms like "commenting" on a "post" (a la Facebook) and "upvoting" or "downvoting" on a comment (a la Imgur) are enabling governments to govern in ways that better reflect the goals and priorities of the people. According to Horton, "vTaiwan relies on a hodgepodge of open-source tools for soliciting proposals, sharing information, and holding polls, but one of the key parts is pol.is, created by Megill and a couple of friends in Seattle after the events of Occupy Wall Street and the Arab Spring in 2011."[71]

The mechanism for pol.is is as follows: a topic is posted for debate; anyone may create an account to post a comment and also "upvote" or "downvote" another user's comment; however—and this is the unique part that distinguishes this platform from the social media forums on Facebook and Twitter—users are not allowed to reply to other user's comments. Each comment must stand on its own, earning favor or garnering derision based on the other user's feedback through the voting mechanism.

According to Audrey Tang, Taiwan's Digital Minister and a former activist for greater transparency in government, "If people can propose their ideas and comments but they cannot reply to each other, then it drastically reduces the motivation for trolls to troll." When commenters are not mudslinging, they are actually engaged in constructive civic discourse. Lawmakers may in turn see these commenters as "not protesters or mobs, but actually people with distinct expertise."[72]

Another unique feature of this crowdsourcing mechanism is that the upvote and downvote process generates "a kind of map of all the participants in the debate, clustering together people who have voted similarly," according to Horton. What this does is transform thousands of separate comments into distinct areas of consensus where like-minded users gravitate around certain proposals on the original topic, and it reveals where the remaining gaps are. "People then naturally try to draft comments that will win votes from both sides of the divide, gradually eliminating the gaps," says Horton.[73]

As a result of this process, lawmakers can confidently take these consensus comments into the lawmaking process, knowing they can win votes from both "sides" of the issue, and steer clear of the areas that are least supported. "If you show people the face of the crowd, and if you take away the reply button, then people stop wasting time on the divisive statements," says Tang.[74]

An example of vTaiwan in action is how the nation dealt with the unique regulatory challenge posed by disruptive ride-hailing service Uber. Like many divisive issues in politics, when first introduced, Uber was met with strident opposition from—you guessed it—cab drivers whose market share would be depleted by competition from the influx of freelance drivers using the app. Using the vTaiwan platform, the initial crowdsourcing responses quickly coalesced into two groups at loggerheads—one for Uber and another larger camp firmly against. At first blush, the experiment was a failure because this kind of entrenched disagreement between two sides of an issue was just politics as usual.

> "But then the magic happened: as the groups sought to attract more supporters, their members started posting comments on matters legal everyone could agree were important, such as rider safety and liability insurance. Gradually, they refined them to garner more votes. The end result was a set of seven comments that enjoyed almost universal approval, containing such recommendations, as 'The government should set up a fair regulatory regime,' 'Private passenger vehicles should be registered,' and 'It should be permissible for a for-hire driver to join multiple fleets and platforms.' The divide between pro- and anti-Uber camps had been replaced by consensus on how to create a level playing field for Uber and the taxi firms, protect consumers, and create more competition."[75]

The result was a regulatory platform consistent with this emergent consensus.

As many who follow politics in the United States would attest, there are few utterances about politics that are not controversial. That US politics is divisive is one of those few statements upon which most would agree. The US political discourse is driven in large part by divisive rhetoric about so-called wedge issues that drive voters into one of two camps in order to consolidate each party's "base," sewing deeper discord and disdain for the opponent in the process, with the unfortunate end result being the vilification of the opponent and dissatisfaction from both sides in the end legislative and regulatory result. When political victories are always pyrrhic and no one is happy with the outcome, something is broken in the process. If we are to take a lesson from vTaiwan, the way the US political process tends to play out is the exact opposite method for restoring trust in government to "do the right thing."

The Spambot Lobby: Repealing Net Neutrality

Net neutrality regulations, essential to maintaining a free and open Internet, were repealed in the United States as a result of a cyberattack on the Federal Communications Commission that appears to have corrupted government decision-making. Millions of fake comments posed by spambots tipped the scales and created a pretext for the Trump Administration to repeal net neutrality safeguards. How did this happen? How can we use technology in government without further eroding public trust?

"Notice and Comment" Rulemaking

As of late 2017, according to Carroll Doherty, the director of political research at PEW, "The fact that Republicans and Democrats differ on…fundamental issues is probably not a surprise, but the magnitude of the difference is striking, and particularly how the differences have grown in recent years."[76] In many ways, the United States is becoming functionally, if not legally, two separate one-party nations fighting for control over the seat of government, rather than an indivisible two-party nation.[77] If there is a time for restoring public trust in government and forming consensus around issues, it is now. Can using technology to solicit public comments, such as demonstrated in Taiwan, help in the United States?

The typical process for introducing regulations in the United States is to follow the so-called **Notice and Comment rulemaking** process under the Administrative Procedure Act (APA).[78] An agency complies with the Notice and Comment requirements of the APA by citing to the legislative authority under which it is acting, identifying the areas of the economy and market actors potentially affected by the regulation, setting forth a regulatory proposal, and opening up a window to give private sector stakeholders notice of the proposed rule and to provide the public an opportunity to comment.

Under the APA, an agency must not act in an "arbitrary or capricious" manner, and must not ignore "substantial evidence on the record," otherwise a federal judge could set the agency's regulations aside. In this manner, if a public commenter challenges the proposed regulation by dropping scientific studies of adverse social, economic, or environmental impacts into the record, or if the public overwhelmingly opposes a rule, the agency proposing the rule must address the concerns raised, at risk of having the regulation thrown out by a federal judge.

In theory, the Notice and Comment rulemaking process should provide popular support and due process for new rules, ensuring that regulatory agencies do not run wild with rules that are inconsistent with science, law, or public policy.

Open Internet on the Electronic Frontier

However, the rise of artificial intelligence, natural language processing, and the use of "bots" has undermined this democratic safety valve. Take, for example, the fallout from the proposed **Net Neutrality** regulations under the Trump Administration.

First, a word about net neutrality. Really, "net" stands for "network," in reference to the world wide web, and "neutrality" refers to "the idea that Internet service providers (ISPs) should treat all data that travels over their networks fairly, without improper discrimination in favor of particular apps, sites or services."[79]

The principle of net neutrality would prevent an ISP from throttling access to certain websites, blocking certain applications, or otherwise undermining an open Internet and the ability for users to freely exchange and access ideas and services online. Given the significance of Internet access to modern life, net neutrality is the twenty-first-century virtual equivalent to freedom of speech and freedom to move about—without which life as we know it would be greatly impoverished.

The threat to Internet freedom led the Federal Communications Commission (FCC) under the Obama Administration to propose rules for an "open Internet" in 2010. The problem was this initial attempt at safeguarding an open Internet was legally and practically deficient, and it foundered after major telecommunications provider Verizon challenged it in court in 2014. This sent the FCC back to the drawing board. In the spirit of transparency and engagement with the public, the FCC accepted comments from actual Internet users on how to protect net neutrality properly. Led in part by the Electronic Frontier Foundation (EFF), a nonprofit organization with the mission of defending civil liberties in the digital world, millions of users weighed in on the revised rule.

According to the EFF, "As a direct result of that intense public activism and scrutiny, in 2015, the FCC produced rules that we could support—in part because, in addition to the bright line rules against blocking, throttling, and paid prioritization of Internet traffic, they included strict 'forbearance' restrictions on what the FCC can do without holding another rulemaking."[80] This was a major win for advocates for an open Internet, including Internet-based start-ups and Internet users. But it was a temporary victory.

Betraying the Founders of the Internet

Fast forward to the Trump Administration, where in 2017 the new FCC Chair, Ajit Pai (formerly Associate General Counsel at Verizon), repealed the net neutrality protections, "despite intense resistance from nonprofits, artists, tech companies large and small, libraries, even some ISPs, and millions of regular Internet users."[81] The order to repeal the net neutrality safeguard was given the Orwellian moniker, "Restoring Internet Freedom Order."[82] According to EFF, the order "ignored technical evidence submitted by EFF and others and showed a remarkable lack of understanding of how the Internet works."[83]

Indeed, inventors of the Internet itself criticized the intellectual basis for the rule. In an open letter signed by more than 20 Internet pioneers and leaders (including Vint Cerf, "father of the Internet," Tim Berners-Lee, the inventor of the World Wide Web, and Steve Wozniak, Apple cofounder) urged the FCC to cancel its vote to repeal net neutrality, describing the plan as "based on a flawed and factually inaccurate" understanding of how the Internet works.[84] "The FCC's rushed and technically incorrect proposed order to repeal net neutrality protections without any replacement is an imminent threat to the Internet we worked so hard to create. It should be stopped," they wrote. They were ignored.

The FCC's proposed repeal of net neutrality garnered at least 22 million comments during the Notice and Comment rulemaking process. In 2017, the digital policy and law intelligence platform FiscalNote founded by Tim Hwang conducted an analysis of these comments. The FiscalNote analysis concluded that 19 million commenters opposed the repeal, of which mere thousands were auto-generated by visitors to the Electronic Frontier Foundation who provided the online forms as a service to its visitors. The FiscalNote analysis also initially determined that "hundreds of thousands of pro-repeal comments were written by bots using natural-language generation, an artificial-intelligence technique that simulates human language."[85] "FiscalNote showed that each fraudulent comment consisted of 35 phrases arranged in the same order but varied by plugging in up to 25 interchangeable words and phrases, a system designed to make comments appear unique."[86]

What followed was an investigation into the online comment process by the Attorney General of New York. This investigation by law enforcement concluded that no less than two million comments supporting the repeal of the net neutrality rule were submitted to the FCC by fraudulent accounts using the stolen identities of US citizens—some military service men and women who were deployed at the time, some children, and some deceased individuals. These victims of the identity theft had their names and contact information used to fill out the Notice and Comment form in order to file fake comments supporting the repeal.[87] On the eve of the FCC vote, the New York Attorney General warned, "Moving forward with this vote would make a mockery of the notice and comment process mandated by the Administrative Procedure Act and reward those who perpetrated this fraud in service of their own hidden agenda."[88]

Despite the overwhelming opposition to the repeal of net neutrality protections by the public commenters, despite the fraudulent support of repeal by identity thieves, despite the opposition of the rule by law enforcement, and despite the objection to the repeal by the inventors of the Internet and World Wide Web, the FCC voted to repeal net neutrality anyways.

Transparency versus "Openwashing"

The contrasting examples of vTaiwan's successful crowdsourcing to develop consensus regulations on controversial topics, on the one hand, and the FCC's shocking repeal of overwhelmingly popular net neutrality regulations on the basis of fraudulent comments submitted by bots corrupting the public notice and comment rulemaking process, show that technology can be a two-edged sword when applied to the development of law. Clearly, we need to use technology where it can help, but we cannot be blind to the ways in which technology is an enabling mechanism that allows misconduct to be scaled, or which simply creates the appearance of transparency and open process when there is none. Products of artificial intelligence—like deepfakes—combined with natural language processing makes it easier to create a digital mask to cover the true faces of bad actors. Engagement via online platforms does not always generate the desired results and simply underscores how unpopular government proposals are before they are enacted.

The risk of deploying vTaiwan and the Notice and Comment process is that if the consensus proposals are not actually adopted into law, then it reveals the process to be a sham. Further, the risk of comments being flooded with bots following the orders of some hidden agenda is that it corrupts the process. The risk is *"openwashing,"* or creating the mere pretense of transparent process, according to C. L. Kao, one of the cofounders of g0v.[89] Openwashing is to transparency what "greenwashing" is to environmental benefits—creating the impression of an environmentally friendly profile with mere labels or colors that do not reflect the underlying environmentally degrading reality. According to Jason Hsu, a founder of vTaiwan and lawmaker, the biggest problem with this platform for public comment is the outcomes are not binding on lawmakers, which makes it "a tiger without teeth."[90]

According to Beth Noveck, the director of New York University's Governance Lab, vTaiwan is a "step in the right direction," but like most of these mechanisms for ensuring public participation in governance, vTaiwan fails to gain credibility with citizens precisely because the outcomes are not binding on governments.

These lessons apply with equal force to corporate governance. Building consensus, ensuring feedback from the corporate hierarchy and stakeholders, and ensuring major decisions are not made on the basis of corrupt or fraudulent decision process are crucial to integrity of corporate conduct. People worldwide are increasingly skeptical of those in power and increasingly hungry for the truth.[91]

According to the *Harvard Business Review*, "For 17 years the Edelman Trust Barometer has surveyed tens of thousands of people across dozens of countries about their level of trust in business, media, government, and NGOs. This year [2017] was the first time the study found a decline in trust across all four of these institutions."[92] The failure of leaders in business and government to earn the trust of stakeholders has obvious deleterious consequences for brands (for business) and for the rule of law (for governments).

"In almost two-thirds of the 28 countries we surveyed, the general population did not trust the four institutions to 'do what is right'—the average level of trust in all four institutions combined was below 50%. We also discovered a staggering lack of confidence in leadership: 71% of survey respondents said government officials are not at all or some-what credible, and 63% said the same about CEOs."[93] With public trust toward governments and corporations at an all-time low, leaders must be willing to use technology to enhance participation and trust but at the same time must be wary of the ways in which technology can corrupt those same processes and, tragically, further erode trust.

Conclusion

The Humachine is not just superintelligent; it is humane. For all the powers wrought by AI, it comes with significant risks. The legal system as currently in force does not manage these risks. The developers and owners of AI systems must proactively deal with the control problem, algorithmic bias, and the weaponization of AI (as with deepfakes and spambots). We believe these challenges can be managed, but it will prob-ably take collaboration between Silicon Valley and law enforcement, informed by a precautionary approach to risk management.

For all the emphasis we place on regulators devising policy instruments to manage the risks posed by AI, we are not optimistic that government will lead on this. Status quo legal regimes are inadequate to the task, though we applaud the EU for at least trying. As a result, compliance is not good enough. Business leaders should accept the mantle of responsibility for the powers they are creating, and steward public goods even when they are not forced to do so by law. Going beyond mere compliance will not happen until old paradigms of corporate responsibility are shed in favor of an enlightened self-interest that sees sustainability not as philanthropy but rather as key to survival. In the next chapter, we discuss breaking the old corporate paradigm to make way for the Humachine.

Notes

1 Waddell, Kaveh. Report: The U.S. Is Unprepared for the AI Future. *Axios*. July 11, 2018. Available at www.axios.com/the-us-isnt-ready-for-the-ai-future-96649a76-1027-43ba-ae27-e24cb57dd194.html
2 March 31, 2018. Available at www.sciencealert.com/google-deep-mind-has-learned-to-become-highly-aggressive-in-stressful-situations
   Joel Z. Leibo, Vinicius Zambaldi, Marc Lanctot, Janusz Marecki, Thore Graepel. Multi-agent Reinforcement Learning in Sequential Social Dilemmas. *Proceedings of the 16th International Conference on Autonomous Agents and Multiagent Systems (AAMAS 2017)*, edited by S. Das, E. Durfee, K. Larson, and M. Winikoff, S'ao Paulo, Brazil, May 8–12, 2017.
3 Knight, Will. Technology Is Threatening Our Democracy. How Do We Save It? *MIT Technology Review*, 121(5):37, 2018.

4 Ibid. p. 38.
5 Proverbs 27:17.
6 Chesney, Robert and Citron, Danielle Keats, Deep Fakes: A Looming Challenge for Privacy, Democracy, and National Security (July 14, 2018). 107 *California Law Review* (2019, Forthcoming); U of Texas Law, Public Law Research Paper No. 692; U of Maryland Legal Studies Research Paper No. 2018-21. Available at SSRN: https://ssrn.com/abstract=3213954 or doi:10.2139/ssrn.3213954. p. 6.
7 Knight, Will. Fake America Great Again. *MIT Technology Review*, August 17, 2018. Available at www.technologyreview.com/s/611810/fake-america-great-again/
8 Fraze, Dustin. Cyber Grand Challenge (CGC), Defense Advanced Research Projects Agency, www.darpa.mil/program/cyber-grand-challenge.
9 Ibid.
10 Chesney, Robert and Citron, Danielle Keats, Deep Fakes: A Looming Challenge for Privacy, Democracy, and National Security (July 14, 2018). 107 *California Law Review* (2019, Forthcoming); U of Texas Law, Public Law Research Paper No. 692; U of Maryland Legal Studies Research Paper No. 2018-21. Available at SSRN: https://ssrn.com/abstract=3213954 or doi:10.2139/ssrn.3213954
11 For more detail on the instrumental convergence thesis, see Bostrom, Nick. The Superintelligent Will: Motivation and Instrumental Rationality in Advanced Artificial Agents. Available at https://nickbostrom.com/superintelligentwill.pdf
12 Aviva Hope Rutkin. The Tiny Changes That Cause AI to Fail. *BBC*. April 11, 2017. Available at www.bbc.com/future/story/20170410-how-to-fool-artificial-intelligence?ocid=global_future_rss
13 Ibid.
14 AI Now Report 2018. Available at https://ainowinstitute.org/AI_Now_2018_Report.pdf
15 Merchant, Brian. The Five Most Worrying Trends in Artificial Intelligence Right Now, Gizmodo (12/07/18). Available at https://gizmodo.com/the-five-most-worrying-trends-in-artificial-intelligenc-1830945466
16 AI Now Report 2018, p. 4. Available at https://ainowinstitute.org/AI_Now_2018_Report.pdf
17 Ibid.
18 Ibid.
19 Eubanks, Virginia. *Automating Inequality: How High-Tech Tools Profile, Police, and Punish the Poor,* St. Martin's Press, New York, 2018.
20 Dvorsky, George. Why Asimov's Three Laws of Robotics Can't Protect Us. Gizmodo. Available at https://io9.gizmodo.com/why-asimovs-three-laws-of-robotics-cant-protect-us-1553665410/amp
21 March 31, 2018. Available at www.sciencealert.com/google-deep-mind-has-learned-to-become-highly-aggressive-in-stressful-situations
     Leibo, Joel Z., Vinicius Zambaldi, Marc Lanctot, Janusz Marecki, and Thore Graepel. Multi-agent Reinforcement Learning in Sequential Social Dilemmas. *Proceedings of the 16th International Conference on Autonomous Agents and Multiagent Systems (AAMAS 2017),* edited by S. Das, E. Durfee, K. Larson, and M. Winikoff. S'ao Paulo, Brazil, May 8–12, 2017.
22 Ibid.
23 The Precautionary Principle. Website is hosted by the European Union. Available at www.precautionaryprinciple.eu/

24 Ibid.
25 Martuzzi, Marco and Joel A. Tickner, editors. *The Precautionary Principle: Protecting Public Health, the Environment and the Future of Our Children.* p. 1. World Health Organization, Geneva, Switzerland, 2004. Available at www.euro.who.int/__data/assets/pdf_file/0003/91173/E83079.pdf
26 Precautionary Principle. Chamber of Commerce of the United States of America. August 4, 2010. Available at www.uschamber.com/precaution-ary-principle. "The U.S. Chamber of Commerce supports a science-based approach to risk management where risk is assessed based on scientifically sound and technically rigorous analysis. Under this approach, regulatory actions are justified where there are legitimate, scientifically ascertainable risks to human health, safety, or the environment. That is, the greater the risk, the greater the degree of regulatory scrutiny. This standard has served the nation well, and has led to astounding breakthroughs in the fields of science, health care, medicine, biotechnology, agriculture, and many other fields."
27 The Precautionary Principle. Website is hosted by the European Union. Available at www.precautionaryprinciple.eu/
28 Martuzzi, Marco and Joel A. Tickner, editors. *The Precautionary Principle: Protecting Public Health, the Environment and the Future of Our Children.* p. 1. World Health Organization, Geneva, Switzerland, 2004. Available at www.euro.who.int/__data/assets/pdf_file/0003/91173/E83079.pdf. "Of particular concern are the health and environmental impacts of technologies that can affect future generations. A key question is how human societies can continue to obtain the great benefits of development while promoting a clean and healthy environment and ensuring an adequate standard of living in the future. Debate about the precautionary principle is partly a response to the recognition of the severe social and economic costs of not taking pre-cautions. Millions of children worldwide have suffered from neurological damage, diminished mental capacity and thus the ability to make a living as a result of exposure to lead from smelters, in paint and in petrol. Tobacco, asbestos and numerous other agents provide ample evidence of the high costs associated with waiting for convincing proof of harm. These cases exemplify the failure of science and policy to prevent damage to health and ecosystems and the resulting impacts on health and the economy."
29 Bostrom, Nick. *Superintelligence: Paths, Dangers, Strategies.* Oxford University Press, Oxford, UK, p. 143, 2014.
30 Horowitz, Michael, Paul Scharre, Gregory C. Allen, Kara Frederick, Anthony Cho, and Edoardo Saravalle. National Security-Related Applications of Artificial Intelligence. July 10, 2018. Available at www.cnas.org/publications/reports/artificial-intelligence-and-international-security
31 Waddell, Kaveh. Report: The U.S. Is Unprepared for the AI Future. Axios. July 11, 2018. Available at www.axios.com/the-us-isnt-ready-for-the-ai-future-96649a76-1027-43ba-ae27-e24cb57dd194.html
32 Knight, Will. Fake America Great Again. *MIT Technology Review*, August 17, 2018. Available at www.technologyreview.com/s/611810/fake-america-great-again/].
33 United States Constitution, First Amendment.
34 Chesney, Robert and Citron, Danielle Keats, Deep Fakes: A Looming Challenge for Privacy, Democracy, and National Security (July 14, 2018). 107 *California Law Review* (2019, Forthcoming); U of Texas Law, Public Law Research Paper No. 692; U of Maryland Legal Studies Research Paper

No. 2018-21. Available at SSRN: https://ssrn.com/abstract=3213954 or doi:10.2139/ssrn.3213954. p. 33.

35 Ibid.

36 New York Penal Code § 190.25 Criminal impersonation in the second degree.

37 Schiff, Adam, Stephanie Murphy, and Carlos Curbelo. Letter to The Honorable Daniel R. Coats, Director of National Intelligence. September 13, 2018. https://schiff.house.gov/imo/media/doc/2018-09%20ODNI%20Deep%20Fakes%20letter.pdf

38 Ibid.

39 Bing, Chris. The tech behind the DARPA Grand Challenge winner will now be used by the Pentagon,

40 Fung, Brian and Tony Romm. Inside the private Justice Department meeting that could lead to new investigations of Facebook, Google and other tech giants. *The Washington Post*, September 25, 2018. Available at www.washingtonpost.com/technology/2018/09/25/inside-big-meeting-federal-state-law-enforcement-that-signaled-new-willingness-investigate-tech-giants/?noredirect=on&utm_term=.f58cfddc8056

41 Ibid.

42 Commission Regulation 2016/679 of 27 Apr. 2016 on the Protection of Natural Persons with Regard to Processing of Personal Data and on the Free Movement of Such Data, and Repealing Directive 95/46/EC (General Data Protection Regulation), 2016 O.J. (L 119) 1 (EU).

43 Gregory Voss, W. European Union Data Privacy Law Reform: General Data Protection Regulation, Privacy Shield, and the Right to Delisting, *The Business Lawyer*, 72(Winter):223, 2016–2017.

44 Case C-131/12, *Google Spain SL v. Agencia Espanola de Proteccion de Datos (AEPD)*, 2014 E.C.R. 317.

45 Nisselson, Evan. The war over artificial intelligence will be won with visual data. TechCrunch May 17, 2017. Available at https://techcrunch.com/2017/05/17/the-war-over-artificial-intelligence-will-be-won-with-visual-data/

46 Ibid.

47 Fung, Brian. Uber reaches $148 million settlement over its 2016 data breach, which affected 57 million globally. *The Washington Post*. September 26, 2018.

48 Ibid.

49 Trope, Roland L. and Lixian Loong Hantover, Hacking Away at Trust, *The Business Lawyer*, 72(Winter):195, 2016–2017.

50 Trope, Roland L. and Lixian Loong Hantover, Hacking Away at Trust, *The Business Lawyer*, 72(Winter):206, 2016–2017.

51 Grimes, Roger A. Back to Basics IT'S 9 Biggest Security Threats. InfoWorld, August 10, 2017.

52 Knight, Will. Microsoft Is Creating An Oracle for Catching Biased AI Algorithms: As More People Use Artificial Intelligence, They Will Need Tools That Detect Unfairness in the Underlying Algorithms. *MIT Technology Review*. May 25, 2018. Available at www.technologyreview.com/s/611138/microsoft-is-creating-an-oracle-for-catching-biased-ai-algorithms/?utm_campaign=social_button&utm_source=reddit&utm_medium=social&utm_content=2018-05-25

53 Federal Fair Lending Regulations and Statutes Compliance Handbook, Fair Housing Act. Available at www.federalreserve.gov/boarddocs/supmanual/cch/fair_lend_fhact.pdf

54 Robitzski, Dan. To Build Trust In Artificial Intelligence, IBM Wants Developers to Prove Their Algorithms Are Fair. *Futurism*. August 22, 2018. Available at https://futurism.com/trust-artificial-intelligence-ibm/

55 Ibid.

56 Knight, Will. Microsoft Is Creating an Oracle for Catching Biased AI Algorithms: As More People Use Artificial Intelligence, They Will Need Tools That Detect Unfairness in the Underlying Algorithms. *MIT Technology Review*. May 25, 2018. Available at www.technologyreview.com/s/611138/microsoft-is-creating-an-oracle-for-catching-biased-ai-algorithms/?utm_campaign=social_button&utm_source=reddit&utm_medium=social&utm_content=2018-05-25

57 Ibid.

58 Ibid.

59 Knight, Will. The Dark Secret at the Heart of AI: No One Really Knows How the Most Advanced Algorithms Do What They Do. That Could Be a Problem. *MIT Technology Review*. April 11, 2017. Available at www.technologyreview.com/s/604087/the-dark-secret-at-the-heart-of-ai/

60 Ibid.

61 DLA Piper, EU Policy and Regulatory Update: a European approach to artificial intelligence, June 18, 2018. Available at www.lexology.com/library/detail.aspx?g=14b41d97-f79e-44d4-a979-b8b4e2f243e6

62 For more on the distinction between US and EU products liability law, see Marshall S. Shapo, Comparing Products Liability: Concepts in European and American Law, *Cornell International Law Journal*, 26(2), 1993, Article 1.

63 Recital 71: European Union General Data Protection Regulation

The data subject should have the right not to be subject to a decision, which may include a measure, evaluating personal aspects relating to him or her which is based solely on automated processing and which produces legal effects concerning him or her or similarly significantly affects him or her, such as automatic refusal of an online credit application or e-recruiting practices without any human intervention.

Such processing includes "profiling" that consists of any form of automated processing of personal data evaluating the personal aspects relating to a natural person, in particular to analyse or predict aspects concerning the data subject's performance at work, economic situation, health, personal preferences or interests, reliability or behaviour, location or movements, where it produces legal effects concerning him or her or similarly significantly affects him or her.

However, decision-making based on such processing, including profiling, should be allowed where expressly authorised by Union or Member State law to which the controller is subject, including for fraud and tax-evasion monitoring and prevention purposes conducted in accordance with the regulations, standards and recommendations of Union institutions or national oversight bodies and to ensure the security and reliability of a service provided by the controller, or necessary for the entering or performance of a contract between the data subject and a controller, or when the data subject has given his or her explicit consent.

In any case, such processing should be subject to suitable safeguards, which should include specific information to the data subject and the right to obtain human intervention, to express his or her point of view, to obtain an explanation of the decision reached after such assessment and to challenge the decision.

Such measure should not concern a child.

In order to ensure fair and transparent processing in respect of the data subject, taking into account the specific circumstances and context in which the personal data are processed, the controller should use appropriate mathematical or statistical procedures for the profiling, implement technical and organisational measures appropriate to ensure, in particular, that factors which result in inaccuracies in personal data are corrected and the risk of errors is minimised, secure personal data in a manner that takes account of the potential risks involved for the interests and rights of the data subject, and prevent, inter alia, discriminatory effects on natural persons on the basis of racial or ethnic origin, political opinion, religion or beliefs, trade union membership, genetic or health status or sexual orientation, or processing that results in measures having such an effect.

Automated decision-making and profiling based on special categories of personal data should be allowed only under specific conditions.

64 Public Trust in Government: 1958–2017, PEW Research Center: US Politics & Policy. December 14, 2017. Available at www.people-press. org/2017/12/14/public-trust-in-government-1958-2017/

65 Ibid.

66 Curtis, Anthony R. 2013. The Brief History of Social Media. University of North Carolina at Pembroke. June 1, 2013. Available at www.uncp.edu/home/acurtis/NewMedia/Soci alMedia/SocialMediaHistory.html

67 Ravi Arunachalam (IBM) & Sandipan Sarkar (IBM), The New Eye of Government: Citizen Sentiment Analysis in Social Media. *IJCNLP 2013 Workshop on Natural Language Processing for Social Media (SocialNLP)*, pp. 23–28, Nagoya, Japan, October 14, 2013.

68 Horton, Chris. *MIT Technology Review*. August 21, 2018. Available at www.technologyreview.com/s/611816/the-simple-but-ingenious-system-taiwan-uses-to-crowdsource-its-laws/

69 Ibid.

70 Ibid.

71 Ibid.

72 Ibid.

73 Ibid.

74 Ibid.

75 Ibid.

76 Taylor, Jessica. Republicans and Democrats Don't Agree, Or Like Each Other—And It's Worse Than Ever. October 5, 2017. Available at www.npr. org/2017/10/05/555685136/republicans-and-democrats-dont-agree-dont-like-each-other-and-its-worst-than-eve

77 Drutman, Lee. The Divided States of America. *The New York Times*. September 22, 2016. Available at www.nytimes.com/2016/09/22/opinion/campaign-stops/the-divided-states-of-america.html?_r=0

78 The Administrative Procedure Act, Pub.L. 79–404, 60 Stat. 237, enacted June 11, 1946, is the United States federal statute that governs the way in which administrative agencies of the federal government of the United States may propose and establish regulation

79 Electronic Frontier Foundation, "Net Neutrality." Available at www.eff. org/issues/net-neutrality

80 Ibid.

81 Ibid.

82 Ibid.

83 Ibid.
84 Sawers, Paul. *Vint Cerf, Tim Berners-Lee, and 19 Other Technologists Pen Letter Asking FCC to Save Net Neutrality.* Venture Beat. December 11, 2017. Available at https://venturebeat.com/2017/12/11/vint-cerf-tim-berners-lee-and-19-other-technologists-pen-letter-asking-fcc-to-save-net-neutrality/
85 Zaleski, Andrew. The Data Lord of Lobbying: FiscalNote Takes the Intuition Out of Politics. Does It Take the Democracy Out, Too? *MIT Technology Review*, 121(5):60, 2018.
86 Ibid.
87 A.G. Schneiderman Releases New Details On Investigation Into Fake Net Neutrality Comments, available at https://ag.ny.gov/press-release/ag-schneiderman-releases-new-details-investigation-fake-net-neutrality-comments
88 December 13, 2017, letter by Attorney General Eric Schneiderman to Thomas M. Johnson, Jr., General Counsel to the Federal Communications Commission. Available at https://ag.ny.gov/sites/default/files/ltr_to_fcc_gen_counsel_re_records_request.pdf
89 Horton, Chris. *MIT Technology Review.* August 21, 2018. Available at www.technologyreview.com/s/611816/the-simple-but-ingenious-system-taiwan-uses-to-crowdsource-its-laws/
90 Ibid.
91 2018 Edelman Trust Barometer: Global Report. Available at https://cms.edelman.com/sites/default/files/2018-01/2018%20Edelman%20Trust%20Barometer%20Global%20Report.pdf
92 Harrington, Matthew. Survey: People's Trust Has Declined in Business, Media, Government, and NGOs. *Harvard Business Review*, January 16, 2017. Available at https://hbr.org/2017/01/survey-peoples-trust-has-declined-in-business-media-government-and-ngos
93 Ibid.
Nilay Patel, Facebook's $5 billion FTC fine is an embarrassing joke, The Verge (July 12, 2019) available at www.theverge.com/2019/7/12/20692524/facebook-five-billion-ftc-fine-embarrassing-joke

7

BREAKING THE PARADIGM

Design thinking is a human-centered approach to innovation that draws from the designer's toolkit to integrate the
needs of people, the possibilities of technology, and the
requirements for business success.

Tim Brown, CEO of IDEO[1]

If you make [positive human experience] your primary
metric everything falls into place.

Nick Drake, Senior Vice President of Digital T-Mobile[2]

Human Experience over Hierarchy

So many mental functions previously handled by humans—computation,
analysis, data mining, processing—can be automated, handled by
machines, or as we put it elsewhere, botsourced. We need to build enterprises that allow its human resources at all levels of the organizational
structure to cultivate their own uniquely human skills—emotional intelligence, leadership, caring, imagination, creativity, and ethical convictions.
That is, we need our organizations to be *human centric*, even as they are
increasingly driven by technology.

At Adobe Think Tank, Nick Drake, Senior Vice President of Digital
T-Mobile, described the role of human experience in the digital transformation.[3] "Everyone within my team is an experience ambassador.
Part of the beauty of the transformation is that we are exposing tools
that everybody on the team can utilize so everybody can evangelize the
changes and are empowered to make changes to portions of the user
journey that they're responsible for."

Like any company with legacy IT systems, Digital T-Mobile has faced
challenges in managing the digital transition. The company's profitability
is predicated on the feelings that the company's customers have toward
it. The primary focus should be people and the good feelings customers
and employees have about the company. This is the human experience
of Digital T-Mobile. As Drake puts it: "If you make that your primary
metric everything falls into place."[4]

Drake explains that experiences create culture and culture creates
emotions. By managing human experience, a company can leverage
powerful emotions. Digital T-Mobile has worked to create the right

experience for its team, the right office, the right place to create—the right place to "live its message." It is genuine for the consumer because it is genuine for the employees. As a result, the feeling experienced by the customer is one of authenticity.

"I like this notion of all of us becoming experience ambassadors and instead of having a hierarchy where somebody at the top dictates what's going to happen for the entire customer experience, we have people iterating constantly on the portion of the customer experience that they're responsible for and I think that's huge shift in culture," Drake says.

Technology-Driven, Human-Centric

Many business leaders would be forgiven for thinking the new technology era is about implementing technology solutions and going through a digital transformation to become more efficient. They believe technology is yet another tool to acquire and are closely watching what the competition is doing to keep up with the Joneses. Indeed, machines are just tools. They cannot fix bad processes, poor management practices, or failing employee morale. The idea that implementing technology, acquiring software, or purchasing better data will simply follow a "plug-and-play" approach is misguided. This is the old paradigm of technology. We need to break it.

The reason the old model will not succeed is that what is needed of employees—the human element of the organization—at all levels is dramatically changing. The technology revolution currently underway is different in kind than the ones that preceded it. The new era requires transformation of old business models and ushers in a new way of thinking about the role of humans in an enterprise setting. Companies are changing the boundaries and activities of their firms. They are redefining processes, functions, and how these functions interact.

Merely adopting more technology is not enough to survive as a competitive enterprise. What most companies miss is that becoming a technology-driven company requires us to become *more human*, not less. The success of becoming a leader in this new era is not primarily focusing on the technology—but rather on people. The reason is that companies cannot completely botsource their way to success.

The Humachine integrates people with AI-augmented management systems to leverage computational powers and uniquely human strengths. A key to success will be understanding how to hire the best talent; develop onboarding protocols that seamlessly absorb the talent into an innovative and inclusive culture; create a culture of innovation that brings the best from its people; create trust in those AI systems by verifying and "looking under the hood" of algorithms; and create a symbiosis between people and technology that allows the organization to thrive.

This human-centric approach of technology-focused firms is exemplified in part by leading companies such as Google, Facebook, Microsoft, and LinkedIn. The companies that are leading understand that they must transform the way they do business. It is not about changing technologies to get the latest and greatest systems but rather changing the business model itself. The issue is not that machines will replace humans so much as it is how to create a business model where machines and humans complement each other. Machines will do repetitive and automated tasks. Machines will always be stronger, more precise, and faster. They will even do certain well-defined cognitive tasks.

However, those uniquely human skills of creativity, innovation, adaptability, empathy, integrity, and imagination will become increasingly imperative to success. They cannot be botsourced. It is precisely these skills that are needed to bridge the gap between technology and people, and utilize machines in the best way to serve people—customers, coworkers, suppliers, and all other stakeholders. The physical and the digital must be integrated to achieve this. To illustrate, we present a paradigm shift in business models, contrasting the traditional business model with the Humachine. See Table 7.1.

Without a new model focused on cultivating human talent and authentic culture, the human element of the organization becomes an appendage to technology, one that quickly atrophies. But remember—without people there is no innovation, no strategy, no connections with customers. Therefore, to succeed in the technology era, companies need to focus on people, ensuring that human talent at all levels is prepared to move the organization forward. The new era is about empowering human flourishing, emotional connections, and authenticity.

Table 7.1 Paradigm shift in business models

Old model	Humachine
Sole focus on profit and loss	Intentionality and purpose
Contractual engagements	Meaningful relationships
Functional procedures	Systems thinking
Silos	Flexible structures
Hierarchical	Integrated teams
Physical presence	Physical and virtual
Traditional offices	Work environments promoting comfort
Rigid measures of productivity	Aspirational goals

A New Business Paradigm

There are four broad maneuvers to undertake in making the transition from the old paradigm to the Humachine.

1   *The first shift will be moving away from single-minded focus on financial performance and shareholder value to focus on intentionality and purpose.*

We are not saying financial performance will no longer control. Financial performance and shareholder value will always be important. The difference is that creating human-centered, technology-powered organizations will drive financial performance. Intentionality imbues existence with meaning beyond the mere pursuit of profit or shareholder value. Having a purpose in society beyond mere profit capture is a critical element of success. Millennial talent tends to seek out working in environments dedicated to a higher purpose. It is hard to inspire a workforce to innovation, creativity, and engagement with the profit motive alone. Pursuit of profit does not inspire human flourishing, creativity, or authentic care. It will not suffice in the new era where greater human capabilities are needed.

Business leaders should be able to clearly articulate the purpose of the company in the world, what it is all about. Business leaders should act with integrity. This means conforming to principle and having fidelity to the truth. It seems like lawyers can always find a loophole to allow business to make an exception of itself. We might say that one's integrity is a function of how often you make an exception of the rules as they would otherwise apply to yourself. In the information era, truth feels ever harder to come by. We are swimming in data and yet we don't always know which way is up. Companies that tell the truth when there is a temptation to lie will be rewarded by the cultivation of public trust. There will be more data scandals and failed cover-ups. How leaders react, and whether they demonstrate integrity, will determine whether they get to keep their jobs. Indeed, leaders have a robust business case for pursuing social, economic, and environmental priorities.

2   *The second shift involves moving from contractual relationships to meaningful relationships.*

The quality of engagement with stakeholders—from customers, employees, and suppliers—depends upon the commitment to form meaningful human relationships. Agility and flexibility will be increasingly required as machines and humans work to adapt in real time to customer and environmental demands. What this takes is a shift from rigid functional procedures to systems thinking; from silos to flexible organizational structures; from rigid hierarchies to flatter organizations and cross-functional integrated teams. We cannot get caught up in our official job title; we simply need to perform as needed, playing to our individual strengths, responding to and communicating to one another our real needs in real time.

3 *The third shift will move from requiring a physical presence in a brick-and-mortar office environment to flexibility that includes both virtual and physical presence.*

If the goal is to enhance creativity and productivity in service of your company's mission, then it is antithetical to the business mission to require employees to routinely subject themselves to unpleasant conditions of work. If your office environment is lame, then you are also lame for requiring people to work in that setting. At least be willing to shift from traditional offices to work environments that promote comfort. What matters is performance, not being in a cubicle. If you only trust your staff to work when they are literally under direct supervision and surveillance in an office setting away from home, you've got trust issues or employees who should probably be fired. Find other performance metrics so they can work wherever suits them. Unless you are dealing in sensitive materials that should be in a controlled environment (anything from protected health information to hazardous substances), let your teams work from wherever. Or make your office better than anywhere else they might rather be.

A Google employee we interviewed at the Manhattan facility continued to go into the office even during her vacation. She explained that there was free food and it was comfortable at work—in fact more comfortable than her apartment in Midtown. For humans to play at their peak, they should be comfortable.

To enable this move, the work environment itself will have to change. The eight-hour work day within a physical office should be replaced with far more pleasant arrangements that support human collaborative relationships and flourishing. Let's replace the dreaded Monday morning commute into an over-air-conditioned sick building with poor natural light with something more humane, efficient, and productive. That means virtual presence, collaboration in both physical and virtual teams, and work structure that promotes the best in people. Consider Google, which lets employees take naps and work at their own pace in a highly comfortable, aesthetically pleasing environment. Treat people like humans instead of commodities and you'd be surprised at the results.

4 *The fourth shift will move from traditional productivity measures to aspirational metrics.*

Traditional metrics of productivity and output must give way to aspirational metrics that incentivize innovation and creativity. In order to encourage human workers to exercise those uniquely human skills as more and more cognitive work is botsourced, we need to change our performance metrics. The old management saying goes, "You cannot manage what you do not measure." Managing human creativity, caring, emotional intelligence, ethical convictions, and innovation will require us to use different measures of performance, not just work hours performed or cost reductions achieved.

In order to manage these four maneuvers, we propose the "Four I" model. We were pleased that "Four I's" sounds like "Four Eyes," which is the nickname for the stereotypical glasses-wearing geek. In the technology era, geeks are heroes. See Table 7.2. The Four Is are intentionality, integration, implementation, and indication.

The remainder of this chapter elaborates upon the Four Is as a roadmap for mutating into the Humachine.

Intentionality

Intentionality is about purpose. It defines what the company is about, its reason for being. Unlike cliché goals such as maximizing shareholder value, intentionality defines the human needs and values that a company's products and services ultimately fulfill in society. An intentional organization knows why it matters to the world, not just its shareholders, and is deliberative in creating an organization that manifests that intention.

Table 7.2 The Four Is paradigm shift

Emphasis	Description
Intentionality	The organization's purpose, meaning, values, and reason for being
Integration	The seamless and symbiotic melding of people and technology across organizational functions and hierarchies
Implementation	Creating and executing strategies for integrating humans and machines around the principles of intentionality
Indication	Using aspirational indicators of performance to monitor and measure

The psychology literature has long documented the importance of purpose to mental health.[5] Having a purpose and a sense of belonging may be one of the largest non-genetic factors in longevity. Purpose and belonging are more or less what define our lives as humans, without which we struggle to do anything more than merely survive.

Even as machines are taking over routine, automated, and even cognitive tasks, humans are still needed to play new roles to manifest the intention of the organization with innovation, creativity, caring, and emotional intelligence. Organizations that see themselves as nothing but profit-making machines will lose human talent and ultimately fail to connect with customers. Economic exchange for services, monitoring profit and loss, and increasing shareholder value will always be important, but they are simply not enough to create a viable culture.

Achieving intentionality is not a mere economic exchange. It is aspirational. It moves people to get involved, gives them a sense of meaning and a desire to be part of a mission with real stakes for humanity. Recall that in Chapter 4 we discussed some uniquely human qualities, such as caring, having emotions, and being moved through feelings. Organizations that can find ways to energize people through their emotions will get the most out of their people. Intentionality does that.

Trends in competitiveness make work more demanding. To get people to devote themselves, to become more involved and engaged in the mission of the enterprise, means they need to feel self-actualized in their work. Expecting humans to perform like robots will not lead to success, but we fear that has been the trend for the last several decades. We need to reverse that trend. Sure, some of your staff will need to know programming languages and statistical methods; however, tapping into the very human traits of caring, emotional intelligence, and intuition is what it takes to be a leading organization in this new era.

Intentionality includes purpose, authenticity, and integrity. We consider each of these in turn.

Purpose

Recall *Maslow's Hierarchy of Needs*,[6] which identifies and prioritizes human needs from most basic to most advanced. At the base of Maslow's pyramid are *physiological* needs that satisfy the biological requirements for human life (food, shelter, sleep). Once those basic needs are met, humans are driven by the need for *safety*, which explains the establishment of law and order to provide security and freedom from existential threats. Once our biological needs are met and our safety is attended to, humans become primarily motivated by the pursuit of *love* or *interpersonal connections* and a sense of belonging. We fulfill this need by establishing relationships based on trust, intimacy, acceptance, and friendship. Once humans have these basic social foundations in place, our motivation turns to *esteem*, both in terms of the self-esteem that comes with dignity and in terms of earning respect from others. The height of human livelihood per Maslow is pursuit of *self-actualization*, which is what we mean when we say human flourishing. We want this term "flourishing" to carry with it the connotation of Aristotle's Greek word for happiness, **eudemonia**, which means the activity of the soul in accord with the virtues over a complete life.

The organization that is the symbiosis of humans and machines—the Humachine—can only get the best of humans by fostering the best of their human qualities. Like children need well-adjusted and capable parents, so the machines need human handlers to reach their potential. As machines do the "machine" work, companies need humans to be more "human." That is enabled by an organization that cultivates intentionality, purpose, and a sense of belonging to the group and team participating in that purpose.

Having a higher purpose has been shown to yield impressive financial performance as well. The *Harvard Business Review* reports on a study that included 500,000 people across 429 firms and involved 917 firm-year observations from 2006 to 2011, which found a positive impact on both operating financial performance (return on assets) and forward-looking measures of performance (stock returns) when the purpose of the company is communicated with clarity.[7] Research by John Kotter that observed companies over a decade-long period show that stock price of purposeful, value-driven companies outperformed by a factor of 12 traditional for-profit counterparts.[8] Therefore, economic benefits follow from purpose.

Without intentionality and purpose, it is difficult for a company's leadership to motivate employees. This is true now more than ever, where workers worry about losing jobs to machines, where their coworkers are robots that are superior to them in many ways, where they need to learn new skills, and where they experience increasing uncertainty as to their future roles. With clear intentionality, employees at all levels can rally together, coalescing around the higher purposes of the organization. It is then that the whole is greater than the sum of the parts. Therefore, intentionality is not just some lofty ideal. It is a practical motivating force.

When people find meaning in their work, they are more likely to give generously of their talent, going the extra mile, as they are driven by positive emotions. The organizations that can tap into that energy will undergo positive transformations.[9] These are the organizations that will lead in the new era. Companies like Google, Facebook, LinkedIn, SAS Institute, and Zappos are already on their way.

Culture

Machines cannot operate without humans training them, developing them, directing them, interpreting their output, and creating products that ultimately humans will purchase and use. Customers, suppliers, vendors, and board members cannot relate to machines and robots. They do not want to see reports presented by robots. They connect with people.

Companies will succeed in the technology era not simply because they have more or better data, or better algorithms. Certainly, availability of data and technology are a needed prerequisite. However, technology, machines, robots, and platforms are increasingly becoming standard across industries and competitors.

What is a company's unique differentiator that is hard to copy? It is human talent. Companies that are leading in this era do so because they have leadership that creates the right culture, sets and articulates clear goals, defines what success looks like, and gets everyone "on board." They are able to effectively lead their organization through transformational change and get everyone excited. They can hire and keep the best talent. Organizational culture embodies the intentionality of the organization. Intentionality provides a sense of meaning, and the culture needs to be a living example of that.

Consider Google—a technology-driven company that is consistently regarded as one of the best places to work. Google's mission statement is "to organize the world's information and make it universally accessible and useful." Google's vision statement for what it wants to achieve is "to provide access to the world's information in one click." To achieve this, Google has created a culture that is open, innovative, emphasizes excellence and freedom of creativity, where employees are free to give their opinion. Every employee is encouraged to contribute innovative ideas rather than conform. Innovating, creating, and being free to express yourself is the norm.

An analytics culture that demands rigorous scrutiny of data before making a choice can sometimes be at tension with the members of the team who have more innovative or entrepreneurial impulses. Finding the right blend between analytics and innovation in decision-making can require hard choices. The amount of tolerance for blue-sky development where designers or engineers chase after ideas varies from company to company. In many analytics-driven organizations, R&D, like other functions, is rigorously metric driven. At companies such as Yahoo, Progressive, and Capital One, process and product changes are first tested on a small scale.[10] The changes must be numerically validated before they are implemented on a broader scale.

The question then is whether culture can be changed directly. Or does cultural change evolve as a result of updates to systems, structure, and processes? Research shows that companies that wait for organizational cultures to change organically will move too slowly in the digital economy.[11] Cultural obstacles correlate with negative economic performance.

Companies like Nordstrom are a good example of what it looks like when digital strategies are designed with deliberate customer-centric efforts, employee empowerment, and connections across the omnichannel.[12]

Companies must be proactive in shaping their culture, approaching it with the same rigor as they would any other technical reengineering effort. Culture is not left to chance. It is purposefully shaped. This means actively changing all elements—structures, processes, and incentives—that run counter to the new culture of openness and innovation the organization is trying to achieve. This means ensuring that silos are broken down, that everyone shares a customer-centric vision, risk of innovation is tolerated, and cross-functional coordination is incentivized.

Authenticity

Authenticity in the business context means staying true to who you are, what you do, and the vision that motivates you. Borrowing from the existentialist movement in philosophy, authenticity means choosing freely your own path and taking responsibility for the implications of those choices, rather than passively following the dictates of other forces and washing your hands of the consequences by claiming to have been just following along.

Why is authenticity important, and how does authenticity support an organization and its intentionality? Being inauthentic, not doing what we enjoy, and not being true to oneself robs us of energy and motivation.

Think of Jennifer Aniston's waitress character in the popular film *Office Space*. She was chastised for not wearing enough "flair" on her uniform. Of course, this is a fictional movie character, but it was funny because so many people related. Because she was being forced to feign enthusiasm, she quit her job. By contrast, when people feel free to be who they are, they have more energy, inspiration, and enthusiasm, and are more likely to bring passion to the creative and innovative work they do.

Authentic workers are more likely to bring their whole selves to the job, engage with the company's goals, and participate fully in the mission of the enterprise. Obviously, this does not mean disregarding a code of conduct. It merely means that management needs to find ways to align the rules of conduct with the personal values and expressive styles of its people.

An excellent example of a culture of authenticity is the company Seventh Generation. The company produces ordinary household products—toilet paper, dish soap, and fabric softener. However, it is a top employer of millennials who seem thrilled to be working there. The reason millennials are so drawn to the company is because of its authenticity and commitment to a higher purpose. The company's purpose is stated in its mission: "To inspire a consumer revolution that nurtures the health of the next seven generations."

Seventh Generation shows authenticity in every aspect of its business, both with employees and customers. For example, the company is known for encouraging consumers to line-dry their clothing instead of machine drying to save energy, even if that means it has less business in dryer sheets. Encouraging environmentally friendly consumer behavior, even though it directly takes away from the company's business, shows a commitment to a higher purpose. The company's products are natural, toxin free, and not harmful to the environment. This authenticity is what inspires loyalty and dedication because employees genuinely care about the mission of the organization. There is more to Seventh Generation than merely creating profit for shareholders.

When a company demonstrates an authentic purpose, employees and consumers feel a connection to both the products and company. More consumers are choosing to patronize businesses committed to sustainable practices and products, even if their products are not sold at the cheapest price. Authenticity gives substance to the company and its products, and it reveals human-centeredness and ethical commitment. This enables people to make a human connection to the brand. This can be powerful. In today's crowded technology space, authenticity will be a differentiator.

Integrity

Integrity in business means, in a phrase, doing the right thing even if no one would find out. Being committed to a social purpose beyond merely increasing profits adds a "soul" to the otherwise hollow shell of an enterprise. Acting in a principled manner, including telling the truth when it would be more convenient to lie, demonstrates an ethical conscience, without which the enterprise loses its social license to operate.

Doing "whatever it takes to win" is a cutthroat mentality more fitting for a psychopath than a business leader. For those ruthlessly amoral capitalists reading this, if you are not intrinsically motivated to behave yourself, there are for-profit rationales for business ethics. One is when leaders act with integrity, they foster a culture of trust and respect within the organization. This translates into better morale and dedication to the company's mission. Integrity also attracts customers. It is hard to maintain customer loyalty if the company is giving off the vibe that it has "something to hide." Integrity in business also attracts employees who are ethically motivated. Most people would prefer not to be associated with a scandal, at any rate. Lastly, for all these carrots, there is the stick of avoiding legal consequences for bad faith business conduct.

Unilever has done quite well under the tenure of former CEO Paul Polman. By prioritizing social responsibility and business integrity, Unilever has demonstrated the business case for ethics.[13]

> We expect everyone at Unilever to be an ambassador for our high ethical standards—what we call "business integrity." We want to create an environment where employees not only live our values in their own work—integrity, respect, responsibility and pioneering—but are vigilant in identifying potential concerns, and confident about speaking up in such situations.

Unilever has more than a website entry about business ethics. It has embedded integrity into its DNA by implementing a code of conduct that is positively reinforced and participatory across the organization and its entire supply chain.

We live in the information age. It is no longer quite so easy to cover up a scandal. When something big goes wrong (think Facebook's Cambridge Analytica scandal, or Volkswagen's diesel emissions scandal), it will leak eventually. How leaders respond to the scandal will determine their fate and that of the company. We are calling on business leaders to handle scandals with integrity. It will pay off in the long run, even if it scares you to rip that Band-Aid off.

For-profit corporations are taking on ever increasing power, wealth, influence over public policy, and influence in the daily lives of millions of people. Amazon, Facebook, and Google are forces in the world, affecting even the lives of people who don't "Add to Cart," "Like," or "Google." As companies become more powerful, they need to embrace their role of stewards of natural resources and guardians of public trust. If large companies act like feudal lords, they will probably suffer the same fate. We understand this sounds pretty idealistic, but there are already plenty of critical depictions of Big Tech out there, and our focus is on how to get things right in the future, not just how we have gotten things wrong so far.[14,15]

Integration

There are two different types of integration that need to take place in the 4-I model of organizations. *First* is doing away with silos and hierarchies to create integrated organizational structures. *Second* is integration between people and technology. The second fits into every aspect of the first as technology is now the cornerstone of how people at all levels of the organization and teams work, create, and make decisions.

From Pyramids and Silos to Flexible Networks

Most organizations are siloed and hierarchical. There are clear boundaries between functional areas such as customer relationship management on the one side and operations on the other. To lead in the technology era, companies must be highly adaptable and flexible. Technology makes a difference where demand sensing on the one side can be linked in real time with operations and suppliers. This, however, requires a shift from siloed structures to systems thinking.

One executive we spoke with explained that worker skills and understanding will have to move from narrow to broad. Before the shift, it was necessary for workers to have deep knowledge of their narrow area. Today, technology and AI can do most of the routine tasks. The detailed "deep but narrow" knowledge is not needed any more. What is needed is the ability to collaborate across functions, which is to work in cross-functional teams. To achieve this requires system thinking, understanding how the work one is doing meshes with that of others elsewhere in the organization, how it meets customer needs, and how it impacts the company's strategy and financial picture. Instead of *deep but narrow*, we need *functional and broad*.

Currently, many organizations use power-based hierarchies. The higher up you are in the hierarchy, the more power you wield, and vice versa. At the lower ends of the hierarchy, one cannot do anything significant without getting clearance from the "higher ups." However, fostering creativity and innovation requires more autonomy within the workforce than what is typically permitted in a pyramid structure. To foster innovation and adaptability, organizations should transition from rigid hierarchies to flexible, agile, and flatter organizational arrangements. From pyramids to networks.

These new structures enable teams to spontaneously form around new products then dissolve when the work is done, reforming here and there depending on emerging needs. Old organizing principles where marketing is walled off from operations will simply not realize the full potential of the human talent we need in the digital age.

Flexible structures are used at Google to promote innovation. Here, structure and culture interact to influence the capabilities of the organization as one unit. Innovation is at the heart of the Google culture. As a result, Google uses a matrix organizational structure. This structure enables cross-functional and cross-business groups working together and cross-traditional vertical silos. Google is a relatively flat organization. This means that Google employees, teams, and groups can meet and share information across teams. They can even bypass middle management and report directly to the CEO.

Humans and Machines: The New Coworkers

The second integration is between humans and machines. This integration permeates every aspect of the organization and should be seamless. Integration throughout the organization means that technology acquisition and implementation should not be fragmented. Investment in technology needs to support the organization's purpose; it needs to link the organization's pieces. Technology acquisition must also be accompanied by training and support to workers in a culture where they work alongside machines. These are their new coworkers. Without hiring the right talent, proper onboarding, training, and creating an innovative culture, investments in technology will produce fragmented efforts at best. Employees will never gain the competencies—and confidence—to engage and work with machines.

An excellent example of how human and AI capabilities can be combined to work together in decision-making is a hiring process used at Unilever.[16] Rather than having employees go through the initial tedious stage of application review, in the first round of the application process, candidates are asked to play online games that help assess traits such as risk aversion. There are no right or wrong answers to the games. Rather, the AI algorithm can look at the way applicants are responding and provide an initial screen of whether they would be best suited for a particular position. In the next round, applicants are asked to submit a video where they answer questions pertaining to the specific position for which they are being considered. Again, an AI algorithm evaluates the responses including body language and tone. The candidates who pass the second round, as judged by the AI algorithm, are then invited to Unilever for in-person interviews. This is the point where humans make the final hiring decisions.

Combining AI filtering with human judgment in a two-step manner like this accelerates the hiring process and frees up the humans working in HR for greater value-adding activities beyond screening initial candidates.

Recall from Chapter 5 the human-machine interface model. Machines provide output, including statistics, data, predictions, assessments, evaluations, information, and products. It is humans who need to make final decisions where judgment is needed. Humans add context. They explain, translate, and judge. Many processes and decisions can and should be automated, however, more important decisions—for example, those that require expertise and judgment—should still be made by humans. Remember from Chapter 4 that humans run into predictable boundaries to fully rational behavior. We should use AI as a decision-support tool that helps humans get things right by filling in computational gaps and de-biasing. Further, automating routine tactical decisions (like re-ordering supplies before stock out) can help maintain consistently high quality decision-making over the course of the work day, especially in strategic settings where judgment (not just computation) is required.

Using AI as a complementary co-worker can help avoid decision fatigue. *Decision-fatigue* is the weakened state of an individual's will-power after making too many choices; more choices means less stamina, less productivity, and less ability to complete unpleasant but goal-oriented tasks.[17]

Design Thinking

We stress that the Humachine is an enterprise that fosters innovation in individuals, teams, and even beyond its boundaries. But what does it take to innovate? How does a company enable human-centric innovation? Many leading firms, including Google, Apple, and Procter & Gamble, have turned to design thinking as a method to teach teams and individuals to think creatively, an important step in the process of innovation.

According to Tim Brown, the CEO of the design firm IDEO, *design thinking* is a "human-centered approach to innovation that draws from the designer's toolkit to integrate the needs of people, the possibilities of technology, and the requirements for business success."[18] Design thinking has been used by countless companies in product innovation in virtually every industry sector—from IBM to Nike, to PepsiCo, to Bank of America, to GE Healthcare. It is especially useful in attempting to solve complex problems that are poorly defined or unknown. The process focuses on understanding the human needs of a problem, rather than dealing with the problem directly—like Zappos focusing on the intentionality of the purchase, rather than the product itself. It involves reframing the problem in a human-centric way and is therefore the ideal perspective for innovation and design in the human-centered technology era.

Design thinking follows an iterative design process that begins by seeking to understand the user. Why is design thinking so important to the Humachine? Understanding the people for whom the product or service is being designed helps cultivate empathy for human needs rather than simply conceiving of new possible product uses. The process then challenges current assumptions, and it redefines the problem in an attempt to identify alternative strategies and solutions that may not have been readily apparent at the initial approach. It provides a different way of thinking but also offers a hands-on process that leads to a solution.

There are typically five stages of design thinking.

First is to *empathize* in order to gain an understanding of the problem. It involves observing and becoming immersed in the problem, and requires a deep understanding of the issues without being blinded by personal assumptions. Technology, AI, and real-time customer data of product information can be helpful here. However, historical data by itself may not help as this stage goes beyond how the product is currently being used. Rather, empathy can reveal underlying issues that help resolve the problem. The goal is to lead to a solution that may not have been otherwise apparent.

The second stage is *defining*, which is formulating the core problem. This should be a problem statement articulated in a human-centered way.

Third is to *ideate* to generate solution ideas. The key here is thinking "outside of the box" to identify novel solutions that address the need. There are numerous "ideation" techniques such as brainstorming or even playing a game of "worst possible idea." These are intended to stimulate free thinking and creativity in finding solutions.

Fourth is *prototyping*, where a number of scaled-down versions of the solution are created. This is an experimental phase where ideas area improved, reexamined, refined, or rejected.

The last stage is *testing*, where experimentation and understanding lead to a final solution. This is the "test and learn" phase, where failure is permitted and even expected. In fact, companies like Google expect failure as it promotes learning.

An important aspect in design thinking is that this is not a linear process. Many stages can be conducted concurrently. For example, the testing phase may reveal something about the user that may push back toward ideation and creation of new prototypes. The idea is that this is an ongoing process of understanding customers, refining problems and solutions, and ongoing innovation and creativity. We like to think of it is a process of continuous improvement and feedback, as illustrated in Figure 7.1.

Braun and Oral-B provide an example of design thinking in action. Braun and Oral-B approached Industrial Facility, a London-based industrial design firm, to help them design an IoT "smart" electric toothbrush.[19] The companies wanted to develop a toothbrush with a sophisticated data-tracking tool that would be able to sense how well users were brushing. The idea was that the brush could inform the user about every aspect of brushing effectiveness—gum sensitivity, how each tooth was brushed, and even play music to accompany the brushing process. In theory, a smart toothbrush could advance oral hygiene and make the tooth-brushing process more enjoyable.

Through design thinking, however, the designers helped identify the actual needs of the customers—and it did not include such data tracking.

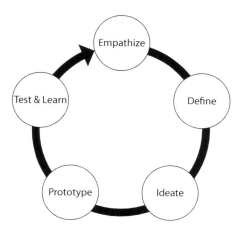

Figure 7.1 Phases of design thinking.

As one of the designers put it: "A toothbrush is already loaded with guilt, that you're not doing it properly or enough. The companies weren't thinking about the customers' experience. They were thinking about the toothbrush the same way you would an athletic activity tracker, that it records and processes information."[20]

So they scrapped all these fancy features. Instead, they decided that the features that would actually be most useful were functions for easily charging the toothbrush and automatically ordering replacement heads. The toothbrush was then designed so that, at home, it charges on a dock through induction to make charging easier, but it also comes equipped with a USB hookup for use on the road so that the brush would not run out of batteries while the user is traveling. These charging enhancements made it less likely the vibrating toothbrush would just become a bristled paperweight. As far as ordering replacement heads, just pressing a button on the brush sends a reminder notification to the customer's phone to buy replacements. These designs addressed real customer needs and were a far cry from the IoT toothbrush the manufacturer originally imagined.

Design thinking may also help us avoid the problem of ***solutionism***. Silicon Valley's attempt to disrupt the status quo by providing technological solutions to all of life's problems sounds benign, but it can be dangerous. According to Evgeny Morozov, some innovation may actually be "driven by a pervasive and dangerous ideology that I call 'solutionism': an intellectual pathology that recognizes problems as problems based on just one criterion: whether they are 'solvable' with a nice and clean technological solution at our disposal. Thus, [human cognitive challenges such as] forgetting and inconsistency become 'problems' simply because we have the tools to get rid of them—and not because we've weighed all the philosophical pros and cons" of doing so.[21]

Design thinking avoids overengineering a product by focusing on actual human needs, not just ways of making existing products fancier.

AI-User Interface

Remember that all technological advancements are ultimately there to support human activity. Therefore, to be useful, machines must be designed in a way that seamlessly integrates with the human decision-maker, providing relevant information in a manner easily accessible by human users.

It is not enough, however, that machines support human activity. They must be designed to *enhance* it. Developing sophisticated AI, machine learning, and technological capability is not enough if the insights are lost in translation. Interactions between these machines and humans must be presented in a way that maximizes the ability of humans to use it—for example, by visualizing data, and to process data such that the human can derive actionable intelligence from it. Machines must be designed not only for their excellence in computing but also, if not more importantly, in providing output that enhances decision-making and creativity, and interacts with individual users and teams as coworkers.

This requires an ***AI user interface (UI)***. UI is a medium through which humans and machines interact. It is an interface with simulated cognitive functions that facilitate the interaction between humans and machines. We see AI-enabled user interfaces in Amazon's Alexa, IBM's Watson, Netflix, and Spotify. Without the UI, the algorithms would make no sense to humans. These AI are designed to be "human like" and to present otherwise complex and unintelligible information in ways that make sense and are understandable to humans.

An important aspect to human decision-making in the face of botsourcing is how humans receive the data they are given. One successful method of extracting intelligence from data is to consider how the data is visually presented. Studies have shown that data presentation can make a significant difference in how data is interpreted and the success of resulting decisions. Visual data is especially important now, as technology has significantly advanced in data visualization, presentation, and manipulation.

An illustration of employee-facing user interface in action comes from Deloitte, which uses UI tools for its AI to help audit experts. The AI algorithm processes huge amounts of big data and runs fast speed algorithms. This has removed the time-consuming and tedious process that auditors typically go through as part of a dossier check. The AI is able to analyze volumes of documents, read text, find trends, and use predictive analytics to generate forecasts. The UI is set up to help the auditor by converting the big data into information the auditor can use. It even remembers the auditor's behaviors and choices to provide information that is better suited for the specific auditor. The auditor is still needed to understand the context of the data while the AI is crunching through the numbers, and the UI is the link making the AI human centric.[22]

Implementation

To say the devil is in the details means an idea might sound desirable at first until you zoom in and realize it's full of trouble. Ultimately, all the ideas we have presented need to be implemented, and that's where things can go sideways. We provide some guidance for implementation here.

Have a Clear Message

We discussed the importance of intentionality and purpose, having the right culture and being authentic. The first aspect of implementation—before we can hire talent and create a good working environment—is to boil all this down to a succinct message. A concise, compelling message that is repeated at every level of the organization eliminates ambiguity and confusion.

It is one thing to have intentionality. It is something else to verbalize it in such a manner that everyone can understand and everyone can see. Without clarity and repetition, intentionality can get lost throughout normal business functions, day-to-day stresses, and the telephone game. The message must be clear and repeatable. It will then drive everything from creating a new product to onboarding a new hire.

Consider the message from Seventh Generation. There is no doubt for employees when it comes to product innovation and creativity. It is about developing products "that nurture the health of the next seven generations." The same is true of Google. The company's success is its clear mission: to organize the world's information, and make it universally accessible and useful. Every product that "Googlers" work on is to get the company one step closer to fulfilling its purpose.

In both of these cases, the clarity of message helps employees know what to focus on; it helps customers understand what the company is about; it is also an excellent recruitment tool. A clear message can go a long way toward drawing talent that share the company's values.

Hire the Right Talent

One of the leading technology companies we visited pointed out its secret to success. The company said it was hiring the right talent. One of the analysts we spoke with privately said that he, like the others, was drawn to an innovative culture; like attracts like, and an innovative culture attracts innovative people. Talented, driven people want to be part of an organization that has a purpose, a creative culture, and incentives for being innovative.

Employees cannot be forced to share the company's intentionality, values, or culture. However, lack of match will show in lack of authenticity. Customers and other employees will be able to tell. A shared purpose is a common starting point. Therefore, having a clear message of the company's intentionality and underscoring that during the recruitment process will go a long way toward hiring the right talent.

One of the companies we spoke with said it has a set of questions it asks potential hires that go beyond their capabilities and duties. They are questions that reveal specifically why the person is interested in the firm, how they feel about the company's mission, and how and why they would fit in. Companies that promote innovation will draw innovative people.

Consider how an SAP employee described the importance of culture to innovation: "It's easy to feel like you're not making an impact when you work for a multinational corporation, but at SAP, risk-taking and big thinking is encouraged. If you have an idea and a plan to get it done, no one will stop you from bringing it to life."[23] That kind of supportive environment is why SAP consistently ranks as one of the best places to work and drives outstanding results year to year.

Like Apple, leading technology companies have built a critical mass of analytical talent upon which the rest of their organization can draw. These companies start with early hires who make up the core around which they built their analytics teams. These initial hires need to be the most capable people in order to build the most effective teams possible. Given the potential competition for this talent, however, organizations must aggressively recruit deep analytical talent. This may involve sourcing talent from other geographical areas, outsourcing select analytical services to vendors, or aligning with an academic institution to get access to newly minted graduates.

Recruiting talent is important; however, it is not enough to change an organization. Leadership has to have an appreciation and understanding of analytics to drive the right culture. Otherwise, leaders and analysts do not know how to take advantage of big data capability because they are not speaking the same language.

Leaders in an organization need to develop at least a rudimentary understanding of analytical techniques to become effective users of these types of analyses. Consider how financial services firm Capital One addressed this issue. The company has created an internal training institute called Capital One University. It offers professional training programs, such as on testing and experiment design. This helps promote broader understanding of analytics throughout the organization, not just within the analyst position.

Create a Work Environment That People Love

Technology continues to change the way people work. In the past, most businesses just needed a physical space, a data center, and staff. As technology evolved through connected devices, ERM and CRM platforms, and the cloud, the digital workplace was been born. It enables virtual teaming and a workplace that has evolved into a globally connected and globally distributed enterprise.

With competition focused on creative output, the compliance requirement of being at a desk should vanish. Creativity and innovation matter and that can rarely happen after a long period of forced sitting. Work is now shifting from a monolithic place where one sits, puts their head down, and clocks in and out, to a place that is an extension of home, where we can play and create value in ways that are intrinsically satisfying, not simply remunerative.

Today's work environment needs to be more about facilitating group dynamics and maintaining space for people to collaborate. It is about comfort and amenities that keep people healthy and refreshed even as they work. People need to be part of a community and members of supportive, functioning teams. Create a culture of shared values.

When human workers are empowered by technology, enabled by supportive managers, and comfortable in the physical workspace, they will deliver quality performance. Leading companies will enable their people to focus on the true purpose of the organization by engaging the workforce, fostering autonomy, and enabling agile work. This autonomy and agility are the foundation for innovation.

Google has been one of the first companies to really understand the need for a comfortable place to foster creativity and innovation. Certainly there are rules. As of this publication, employees still had to wear pants at work. However, Google was one of the first to allow employees to have a flexible schedule and work on their own timetables. It has resulted in much greater levels of productivity. Google has created an environment where its employees can explore how they would like to work and use their own discretion to choose what gives them the greatest productivity. Lastly, Google has created a fun environment that does not feel like work. This is a company where employees often work long days and even weekends, voluntarily.

Foster Freedom to Create, Experiment, and Fail

Experimentation goes hand in hand with innovation. A **test and learn** culture needs an environment where ideas can be tested and lessons learned from failure. In simple terms, "test and learn" is a set of processes where all ideas, changes, and innovations are assumed to be hypotheses.

For example, this could be a new advertising campaign or a solution to a problem. These hypotheses are then tested through experiments, which are enabled with data. Based on the findings from the experiments, evidence is gathered and changes are made. The process is then repeated and continuously improved upon until the idea is ready for implementation.

The test and learn business process has been around for decades. However, it is especially useful in feeling out future scenarios in this era of rapid change. We can use it in testing ideas about virtually everything—from advertising (e.g., which campaign has the most "likes") to merchandising (e.g., how customers respond to retail assortment) to product design changes and new features (e.g., through customer response and even embedded sensors).

A culture of experimentation assumes that the actual outcome of all the ideas is unknown *a priori*. This approach to innovation harvests the insights gleaned from experimental failures, which are far more common than the alternative.

Indication

Ultimately, success, progress, and achievement need to be measured. This is where indicators or metrics come into play. Understanding and using the right indicators can drive improvements and help a business focus on what they deem important. Indicators reveal the priorities of the company.

We should add to Drucker's phrase, "You cannot manage what you do not measure," Einstein's caution, "Not everything that counts can be counted, and not everything that can be counted counts." Further, we know from the double-slit experiment that at a quantum level, the act of observing something actually changes the reality of the observed subject. This plays out at a more practical level when the mere fact that management decides to measure a certain indicator changes employee behavior to maximize the results under that indicator, regardless of the contortions required to do so.

Be careful what you measure. Monitoring the wrong performance indicator has a strong tendency to lead to tails wagging dogs. Before implementing any new performance indicator, think very carefully about how the most lazy, clever, and cynical employee could "hack" or "game the system" to maximize the appearance of performance under that measure while actually failing to deliver the output that management was actually hoping for when they implemented the measure.

The most common types of indicators are key performance indicators or KPIs. KPIs are measurements for monitoring how well individuals, teams, or the entire divisions are performing against set goals. These metrics tend to be quantitative in nature, and most companies keep them simple to derive the most benefit. These indicators are ways that goals can be quantified and then assessed in measurable terms in order to track progress.

However, KPIs by themselves are not enough. They tend not to encompass strategic and aspirational goals needed in the Humachine era. This is where indicators called Objectives and Key Results (OKRs) come in. The goal of OKRs is to precisely define how to achieve ambitious objectives through concrete, measurable specifications. They are excellent ways to encourage creative, novel, and ambitious performance. OKRs are a way to both reach for the sky and ensure objective progress is being made, while avoiding the "hackability" of regular performance metrics.

The concept of OKRs was first introduced by Andrew Grove, former CEO of Intel, in the 1980s. Google started using them in 1999. Some even credit OKRs as a critical element of Google's success. At Google, OKRs have helped model organizational processes. Google uses a scale between 0 and 1.00 to grade the O part of the OKR and evaluates them quarterly. A number between 0.6 and 0.7 is considered the "sweet spot." Consistently getting a 1.00 means that the OKRs are not ambitious enough, as they did not push the team to stretch and test its limits.[24] There are two parts of the OKR metric. First, define the objectives. The objectives are the direction we are taking and what we are trying to achieve. The objectives are ambition and they should feel somewhat uncomfortable. For example, it may be something like "increase profit by 10%." Ideally, the goal should be so lofty that very well may not be attained during the measurement period. The goal is directional and aspirational, not easy. Second, define the key results. This is how we will know whether the goal has been attained. The second part is specifically measurable. For example, it may be "save 10% on purchases through a supplier reverse auction system and reduce costs by 25% by outsourcing distribution." Therefore, we are setting goals and then specifying how we will get there. OKRs and KPIs complement each other, and one is part of the other. What sets OKRs apart, however, is that they inspire ambitious goals and create room for constructive failure.

OKRs are also public (at least within the walls of the company). This means that everyone else can see what everyone else is working on. There is transparency. Everybody knows the company's goals, how their own work dovetails with other teams' work and how each fits within the company's overall objectives. Open OKRs add to being part of the group, contributing to intentionality and the shared vision.

A Dynamic Model

The 4-I model is a dynamic "living" representation of the organization that evolves and changes over time in a continuously learning—if not mutating—feedback loop. We show this in Figure 7.2. Intentionality gives the reason for Integration by providing a larger purpose; Integration marshals the right human and AI resources into porous and adaptive teams; once integrated, the mission is carried forward with Implementation to get the most out of the resources assembled by giving freedom to fail and innovate; all of the foregoing is evaluated by Indication, which measures what matters—progress toward the mission—and in turn motivates changes to Intentionality.

Intentionality, with the right culture and authenticity, are at the top as the overarching elements that drive the organization. They create an ambiance and working environment that enables freedom, innovation, and creativity.

Driven by intentionality, the organizational structure shifts from vertical silos to flexible structures. Flatter matrix organizations are preferred over rigid hierarchies or pyramids. Integration means teams collaborating across all functional areas and strategic combinations of humans and machines.

Implementation is enabled through a concise and clear message, and hiring the right talent with shared values. The work environment shifts

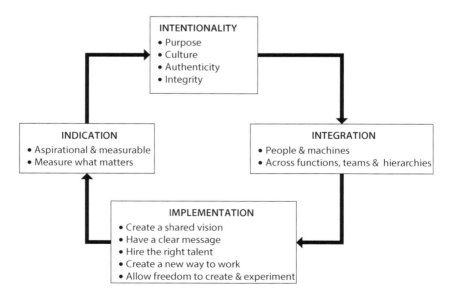

Figure 7.2 The 4-I model.

from inflexible office spaces where attendance is mandatory to "opt-in" work environments with perks that promote comfort, group collaboration, teamwork, and innovation.

Lastly, quota-like performance metrics are replaced by OKRs that promote innovation and aspiration. In the spirit of continuous improvement, this is an evolutionary process.

Conclusion

For an enterprise to become a Humachine, we must break free from old business paradigms. Intentionality and purpose must replace the single-minded focus on profit maximization. Meaningful collaborative relationships must replace soulless, solely contractual ones. Hierarchical and siloed structures should be jettisoned in favor of flat and fluid ones. Integrated teams should be measured with aspirational performance metrics and given room to flourish. Committing to the Four I model is hard simply because change is fraught with fear, but it leads an organization down a path of fitness-enhancing mutation.

Notes

1 Kathleen D. Vohs, Noelle M. Nelson, Roy Baumeister, Brandon J. Schmeichel, Jean M. Twenge, Dianne M. Tice, *Making Choices Impairs Subsequent Self-Control: A Limited-Resource Account of Decision Making, Self-Regulation, and Active Initiative*, Journal of Personality and Social Psychology 2008, Vol. 94, No. 5.
2 www.youtube.com/watch?v=4AoX3-WyoyE
3 Barrett, Jeff, If You Want to Build a Brand, Create an Emotional Experience First. *Inc. Magazine*, April 26, 2017.
4 www.youtube.com/watch?v=4AoX3-WyoyE
5 Patrick McKnight and Todd Kashdan. *Purpose in Life as a System That Creates and Sustains Health and Well-Being: An Integrative, Testable Theory.* Review of General Psychology 2009, Vol. 13, No. 3, 242–251a.
6 McLeod, Saul. Maslow's Hierarchy of Needs. Available at www.simplypsychology.org/maslow.html
7 Quinn, Robert E. and Thakor, Anjan V. Creating a Purpose Driven Organization. *Harvard Business Review*, July–August 2018 78–85.
8 Kotter, John and Heskett, James. *Corporate Culture and Performance*, Free Press, 1992.
9 Quinn, Robert E. and Thakor, Anjan V. Creating a Purpose Driven Organization. *Harvard Business Review*, July–August 2018 78–85.
10 Ibid.
11 www.mckinsey.com/business-functions/digital-mckinsey/our-insights/culture-for-a-digital-age
12 www.therobinreport.com/a-fresh-new-look-at-the-nordstrom-way/
13 Business Integrity, Unilever, available at www.unilever.com/about/who-we-are/our-values-and-principles/business-integrity/ Our ambitions do not stop there. We aim to have a positive influence across our value chain, working

with suppliers, distributors and all third parties to raise the bar on issues such as human rights and anti-bribery and corruption. Unilever's Business Integrity programme brings our values to life for all employees, and helps them apply our ethical standards day-to-day. In addition to our Code of Business

Principles, it includes clear policies, guidelines and related learning materials, as well as robust procedures and controls to help us prevent, detect and respond to any inappropriate behaviour.

Prevention—We seek to embed a culture of integrity at all levels, in all geographies.

Detection—We encourage employees to speak up and give voice to their values.

Response—We have the tools to investigate and if necessary sanction confirmed breaches, and use what we learn to continually improve.

14 Amy Webb, *The Big Nine: How the Tech Titans and Their Thinking Machines Could Warp Humanity*, PublicAffairs (2019).
15 Scott Galloway, *The Four: The Hidden DNA of Amazon, Apple, Facebook, and Google*, Random House (2017).
16 Wilson, H. James and Daugherty, Paul R. Humans and AI Are Joining Forces. *Harvard Business Review*, July–August 2018, 115–123.
17 Kathleen D. Vohs, Noelle M. Nelson, Roy Baumeister, Brandon J. Schmeichel, Jean M. Twenge, Dianne M. Tice, *Making Choices Impairs Subsequent Self-Control: A Limited-Resource Account of Decision Making, Self-Regulation, and Active Initiative*, Journal of Personality and Social Psychology 2008, Vol. 94, No. 5.
18 www.ideou.com/pages/design-thinking
19 www.fastcompany.com/3060197/how-two-industrial-design-titans-are-helping-brands-simplify-tech
20 Ibid.
21 Morozov, Evgeny. The Perils of Perfection. *The New York Times*, March 2, 2013. Available at www.nytimes.com/2013/03/03/opinion/sunday/the-perils-of-perfection.html
22 https://blog.prototypr.io/how-to-design-for-ai-enabled-ui-77e144e99126
23 Fortune Editors. The 40 Best Places to Work in Technology. *Fortune*, January 17, 2018.
Patrick McKnight & Todd Kashdan, *Purpose in Life as a System That Creates and Sustains Health and Well-Being: An Integrative, Testable Theory*, Review of General Psychology 2009, Vol. 13, No. 3, 242–251
Amy Webb, *The Big Nine: How the Tech Titans and Their Thinking Machines Could Warp Humanity*, PublicAffairs (2019)
Scott Galloway, *The Four: The Hidden DNA of Amazon, Apple, Facebook, and Google*, Random House (2017)
John Doerr, *Measure What Matters: How Google, Bono, and the Gates Foundation Rock the World with OKRs*, Portfolio/Penguin (New York 2018)
24 John Doerr, *Measure What Matters: How Google, Bono, and the Gates Foundation Rock the World with OKRs*, Portfolio/Penguin (New York 2018).

8

MUTATIONS

We are going through an industry mutation—it's not only transformation. It's a mutation.
    Sébastien Bazin, CEO of Accord Hotels Booking.com

Zappos is a customer service company that happens to sell shoes and clothes and handbags and accessories, but its DNA is customer centricity.
    Alex Genov, Head of Customer Research, Zappos[1]

If Refrigerators Could Talk—Oh Wait, They Can!

We would be forgiven for thinking there is not much room for innovation in refrigerators, air conditioners, and washing machines. Yet, Haier has defied all white-box stereotypes, making home appliances cool again.[2] These washers and dryers are knee-high, portable, and customizable. Refrigerators talk to customers with a screen connected to food suppliers responding to every customer need. They warn customers when the milk runs low, the lettuce is going bad, and the cheese has passed the expiration date. They've got the shopping list down and order directly for you. Low-sugar foods can be monitored for a diabetic customer and low fat for the diet-conscious counting calories. A restaurant wine cabinet can connect directly to winemakers, placing the order before running out of red. These are smart appliances.

Haier has reimagined these once-mundane essentials due to its forward-looking culture, organization, and a mindset to serve needs customers didn't even know they had.

The China-based company exhibits traits of the "Humachine"—a fusion of human creativity and technological innovation. The Humachine is the organization of the future, and the future is at our doorstep. Old models of gradual adaptation and transformation will only bring short-term gains. They will not work for long-term survival. Organizations must be willing to completely restructure and reimagine themselves—*mutate*—to survive in the new era. Form follows function.

A Different Species of Organization

The Humachine is a different species of organization. It is a living entity that has a "life" purpose (Intentionality). It has full complementarity and amalgamation between machines and humans that function as one (Integration). There is fluidity in the way work is conducted, with freedom to create, test, and innovate (Implementation). Lastly, performance is measured in aspirational ways that look toward the future and measure innovation and creativity (Indicators).

Mutation, Not Transformation

The 4-I model presented in the previous chapter is not a roadmap to transformation. The notion of transformation misses the point of what the Humachine represents. Transformational change occurs when an organization changes its strategic direction or reengineers its culture or operations in response to dramatic change—such as a technological breakthrough or a merger. Transformational changes are typically a once-off reaction to a major problem or challenge in the competitive environment. A transformation has a beginning and an end—a beginning "state" and an ending "state."

The Humachine is not a transformed organization that has reached a new steady state. Rather, it is a different species of organization. Concepts typically ascribed to transformation do not apply here. There are countless prescriptive roadmaps for digital transformation discussing a variety of issues as to how the transformation should take place. There is the matter of sponsorship, such as who should have accountability for the direction of analytics. There are issues of leadership, such as who is charged with realizing the vision for analytics. There are financial issues, such as how development of analytics capability should be funded. There is also governance, such as where should analytics talent "live" in the organization.

The Humachine is a different species of organization, one that has mutated from traditional organizational structures, hierarchies, incentives, and operations. It is an organization where technology and "machines" are intertwined with the best of human talent to create the ultimate symbiosis. Everyone is accountable for the direction of the organization and innovation. Analytics and technology are not just another process to invest in with a payback period. Rather, they are an essential part of the company's DNA. Analytics and technology talent don't "live" in one place—they are decentralized throughout the organization. There is no transformation from State A to State B but an ongoing evolutionary process of mutation.

According to AccorHotels CEO Sébastien Bazin, they are not transforming but rather mutating from a "hotel" company to a "travel" company. Bazin says AccorHotels has been a "sleeping giant for far too long," allowing online travel agencies, aggregators, and disruptors like Airbnb to lead innovation the past 15 years: "The industry [is] not going through any revolution; we're not going through any transformation. We did enter an enormous mutation, which is irreversible, and it only started 12 to 15 years ago."[3]

The Humachine is an amoeba-like organization that is fluid in structure, highly innovative, radically transparent, entrepreneurial, nimble, and adaptable to change.

Getting there requires what we term a mutation of the organization. It requires significant disruption. We will discuss issues related to getting there, but first let's look at the traits that define the Humachine.

Humachine Traits

"Humachine" companies fuse AI and human talent on the stack of big data, CRM platforms, and cloud computing. This combination of people, machines, and processes gives rise to four distinct traits: human centricity, flat and fluid organizational structure, entrepreneurial and innovative culture, and self-awareness.

1 **Human centric.** Machines are used and developed to serve the needs of humans—customers, employees, leaders, and teams. We must remember that technology does not exist for technology's sake. It is there to support human endeavors and, as such, its design and use are focused on the human purpose. Machines handle automated tasks while humans engage in creative decision-making, considering input from their robotic partners.

2 **Flat and fluid organizational structure.** A flat and fluid hierarchy with zero distance between the C-suite and workers enables ongoing communication among leaders, managers, and doers. Networks of people in and outside the company shape-shift in real time, like amoebas, pulling the right combinations of skills and talents together for any given goal or purpose. Radical transparency regarding information, roles, and goals enables these functional teams to respond intelligently to environmental pressures and changing enterprise objectives.

3 **Entrepreneurial and innovative culture.** Innovation imparts to a company culture a spirit of entrepreneurship. Innovation does not reside in a department but rather inspires all members of all teams to think of novel solutions. Teams are self-managed and incentivized to rapidly solve problems with distributed accountability, ending the passive "but that's not my job" culture.

4 **Self-aware.** Self-awareness is the state of a collective awareness of the enterprise. It is ultimately an organizational capability and an essential element of the Humachine. Self-awareness is critically important for an organization to succeed in the technology era because it enables rapid responses to environmental changes. In adapting to change, an organization must possess mechanisms to be aware of itself: *monitoring, feedback, and assumption-checking.*

Kasparov's Law Redux

The move toward Humachine traits involves combining the three variables of Kasparov's Law needed to create superhuman capabilities. They are People, Machines, and Processes.

The characteristics of these three variables will vary based on the company's mission and strategy. See Figure 8.1.

Machines cannot merely be added to old systems and processes, and they cannot be utilized strategically by humans not adept in using them.

We discuss key features of these variables and Humachine traits next.

Focus on Human Needs

Smart machines are the foundation of the Humachine, but the focus is on people. Remember that technology is here to serve humans. Machines do not exist for machine's sake. They are not created by nature to evolve, procreate, and develop commerce to support themselves. In the technology era, it is easy to lose sight of this basic fact.

Rather, machines are there to support human endeavors. AI is created by humans, designed to behave like humans, and affect humans positively. Yes, machines are superior in computational capability. Ashyper calculators they can process huge amounts of data and make inferences the average human mind cannot. To be useful, machines must be designed to seamlessly integrate with the human decision-maker (ergonomic and accessible). However, machine capability alone is not enough for enterprise success. Data must be presented in a way that maximizes the ability of humans to

PROCESSES	PEOPLE	MACHINES
• Flat Structure	• Customers	• Platforms
• Innovation Culture	• Leaders & Coaches	• AI & Analytics
• Fluid Processes	• Analysts	• IoT
• Shared Leadership	• Designers	• Network Links
• Culture	• Suppliers	• Cloud Computing

Figure 8.1 The three variables of Kasparov's Law.

use it, to visualize it, process it, and derive actionable intelligence from it. Machine output must enable decision-making, creativity, and innovation. To be fully utilized, machines must interface with and leverage the most basic human traits—*emotions* and our *need for socialization.*

Without this anthropocentric approach we will botsource our way to bankruptcy. Without the human touch, there will be no customers, no suppliers, no employees nor managers. Ensuring that humans are integrated with technology, without fear and with trust, is incumbent upon leadership. Therefore, every new adoption of technology must be designed with the human in mind.

The "Experience Economy"

Nowhere is the focus on human needs on display more than in the current "experience economy." The "experience economy" represents an economic shift from a product-centric focus to a customer-centric focus. The digital era has commoditized most products and shifted the focus of competition on the customer experience. AI and technology can now customize customer interactions at all customer touchpoints with the company.[4] Technology has created an expectation of swift response to inquiries, customized products and services, and easy access to information. Being immediately responsive to customers is nothing special. It is an expectation. The battlefield now is in creating a customized customer experience—and this requires tapping into human traits.

The shift of competitive focus on the customer experience cannot be ignored if a company hopes to remain relevant and successful. Customers are more empowered than ever. For better or worse, people want to be entertained, and they expect the same level of entertainment in the consumption experience that they get elsewhere.[5] As a result, companies are bending over backwards to create the right atmosphere and format for consumption (not just the right price). Machines help us by mining big data to understand and tap into the deepest customer desires and understand unarticulated needs. This intelligence is used to create the best experience possible. It might also be used to create products that are psychologically addicting, but that's where the principle of integrity comes in! An ethical approach to using consumer data is to identify a need and to fill it—rather than by identifying how to exploit a vulnerability and creating addictive products.

The footwear and accessory retailer, Zappos, is recognized for understanding exactly what customers want. The company first became known for setting the bar with a returns policy that allowed shoppers to receive a full refund for items they were unhappy with any time within a year of purchase. This policy allowed Zappos to quickly amass a loyal following. This high level of customer service has now evolved into personalization. Understanding the importance of keeping customers happy and personalizing the offering is the main focus for the group's head of customer research, Alex Genov.

Genov says that most personalization systems make recommendations based on purchase history. However, this can lead to consumers simply being presented with options that are similar to purchases they have already made. "Contrast this with true personalization, where you understand what the person is trying to do by buying those shoes, and then help them more holistically," he says.[6]

One example of hyper-personalization at Zappos is in its attempt to understand the *intent* of a purchase. For example, are the shoes being purchased for a first date or an interview, and therefore are required to make a good impression? The site can then make recommendations for other apparel items that might match that occasion. "The way we phrase it here is Zappos is a customer service company that happens to sell shoes and clothes and handbags and accessories, but its DNA is customer centricity," Genov says.[7] The focus is on the context, experience, meaning, and emotions rather than merely products.

Understanding customer emotions enabled the retailer Sephora to disrupt the way people shop for beauty products. Of course, Sephora uses technology to manage a successful omnichannel strategy, using a mobile app to serve as a liaison between physical and digital channels, providing a seamless customer experience. Also, these technology solutions enable Sephora to collect more data on its customers and then use that data to continue to improve its offering. However, Sephora has disrupted the industry by understanding that beauty is not about products—it is about creating positive emotions.

In the past, customers purchased beauty items brand by brand. Then Sephora came on the scene, creating "a playground" of beauty products by encouraging customers to test and try products. Understanding customer emotions allowed Sephora to fine-tune its approach in creating the customer experience.

As Jason Goldberg, senior vice president of content and commerce at SapientRazorfish, points out, "Nobody goes shopping because they want more expensive colored powder in their bedroom. They're shopping for cosmetics because they want to look beautiful at their spring dance or on their date or whatever the case may be. They're literally shopping for an experience, so delivering an experience during the shopping occasion is super important, whereas you do not necessarily want a real high-tech immersive shopping experience to get more toilet paper."[8]

Technology has enabled Sephora to use the customer experience to create an "Instagrammable" store concept, encouraging customers to play with products, and offering free in-store classes. Sephora understands that emotions create a need for sharing—and leveraged that need to create a tight-knit beauty community.

The "experience economy" can be a by-product of the digital era, where an enterprise cannot succeed on the strengths of its products alone. Technology can be used to create a sense of community, tapping into customer emotions. Consider the home fitness equipment manufacturer Peloton. The company used to manufacture stationary bicycles. Today, Peloton understands that a gadget is merely a commodity. Anyone can sell a stationary bike. Their focus is on the customer experience.

Peloton offers its customers cloud-based live streaming of instructional cycling exercise content via a console affixed to the handlebars, which creates a social dynamic as the exercises remotely connect groups of riders.[9] Owners of the Peloton bike are able to livestream spinning classes, as well as access an on-demand library of previously recorded classes. Peloton has used technology to create a social, group, or network effect around its bike. The company's success is not about the product itself—it's just a nice stationary bike—but rather about creating a unique and shared group experience of belonging, even if virtual.

Even something as mundane as consumer banking is changing—using technology to tap into customer emotions and create a social experience. Understanding this, Capital One has "reimagined banking" through its series of Capital One Cafés. These cafés merge banking with the comfort of a coffee shop, free Wi-Fi, couches, and even tabletop games such as Connect Four while customers wait for a business call. This is a rejection of the old stuffy notion of banking. Anyone, regardless of their bank affiliation, can grab a cup of coffee, sit on a couch, and, if they want, get coached through their money problems by professionals. This is a new type of banking experience.

The message is clear: use technology to create community and enhance human experience. From beauty products to exercise to banking—experiential, human-centric offerings have a competitive edge over traditional offerings, regardless of industry.

Customer Is the Co-creator

Customer-centric cultures use predictive analytics to anticipate emerging patterns in the behavior of customers. They can then tailor the right interactions with customers by dynamically integrating structured data, such as demographics and purchase history, with unstructured data, such as social media and voice analytics. *Co-creation* is AI-enabled open innovation characterized by seamless interconnection with the customer and the product designers, allowing the customer to have a voice in product and experience.

This creates a more impactful customer experience, as the examples of Sephora and Peloton illustrate. Further, this has huge operational benefits. Co-creation significantly reduces the risk of experimentation failures and the costly process of trial and error, where a company would launch a product only to see whether there was a demand for it. Co-creation bypasses those issues, speeds up the pace of change, and de-risks the product innovation cycle by getting the customer involved in product creation.

With co-creation, an enterprise no longer has to guess what's working with a given product or service before launching it—and then waiting to see if the guess is right after the launch takes place. Adjustments to products and services and the entire customer experience can now be made in nearly real-time with direct input from end users. This reduces risk and improves responsiveness. It also tightens the relationship with customers and provides valuable insights into what motivates a customer to buy, and how they intend to use the product. Many of these insights are not collectable through traditional means. Co-creation is happening everywhere, and companies that are not doing it will rapidly fall behind.

Flat and Fluid Organizational Structures

What do leading tech companies such as Zappos, Google, Haier, and Apple have in common? They all have flat and fluid organizational structures—a hallmark of the Humachine. Yes, there are differences in the way they are organized—but flatness and fluidity are a common theme. This is the norm of the innovative and agile organization. There is zero distance to the C-suite. Leadership acts as coaches rather than "bosses" in the traditional sense. There is very little hierarchy. Leadership, decision-making, and execution are decentralized but coordinated among team members.

Flatness and Fluidity

In the traditional model of organizing, hierarchy prevailed. See Table 8.1.

A few dominant leaders called the shots while everyone else followed. Everyone else repeated individual tasks in service of a dominant vision. There are certainly advantages of a traditional functional structure versus no structure at all. Functional departments can permit greater operational efficiency as employees with shared skills and knowledge are grouped together by the function they perform. Each function or group is specialized. Therefore, they can operate independently from other groups while management acts as the point of cross-communication between the functional areas. This traditional functional structure allows for increased specialization.

Table 8.1 The Humachine's organizational structure

Traditional structure	Humachine structure
Hierarchy-driven	Flat org structure
Top-down roles	Fluid diffused roles
A few dominant leaders	Cross-functional teams
Highly specialized groups	Entrepreneurial self-managed teams
Many views of the customer	One view of the customer
Communication distance from C-suite	Zero distances from C-suite
Innovation distance from customers	Customers help co-create

There are, however, significant disadvantages to this old model that hinder the ability of the organization to function in the digital era. One is that different functional groups may not communicate with one another. This decreases flexibility, disabling rapid innovation and quick responses to change. Functional structures are highly susceptible to *tunnel vision*. Each function sees the organization from its frame of reference and its own operation. Without a unified vision, employees cannot be integrated around the same goals.

This old structure worked very well in an old economy where large corporations produced relatively homogenous products. However, in the new economy defined by innovation and responsiveness, the need for creativity, rapid communication, and adaptability to change, this model no longer works. The old structure makes co-creation and rapid innovation virtually impossible.

To be direct, the old way of organizing results in failure in the new era. The world has become increasingly interconnected, the rate of change has accelerated, and the need for quick response is an imperative. Therefore, new organizational models are fundamental to an organization's ability to remain competitive and relevant.

At Haier, hierarchies have been torn down and middle management is almost nonexistent. The goal has been to turn the company into a flat organization that is a playground for talented people to generate customer-centric products. Haier has created a flat structure where smart people have resources to create and bring to fruition new ideas with little to no drag.

Employees have fluid roles in cross-functional teams. Teams are created around common problems as opposed to individual roles and responsibilities. The objective of the team is greater than what could be achieved by a single member. Teams are entrepreneurial in spirit and self-managed, with members sharing a common vision. They are fluid, evolving, and open in structure. Members come and go as the nature of the problem changes, and they perform work outside a predetermined role to solve the problem at hand. The organization and teams are infused with purpose to solve problems quickly. Accountability and decision-making are distributed and coordinated. Successful team members are those who take action that enables the team to accomplish its goals—they are "changemakers." The teams are nimble and agile, moving quickly to respond to the data, and thus the customer.

Haier's structure works well for it. However, when it comes to structure, one size does not fit all. Although we consider leading tech companies as examples of mutation, Haier, Zappos, Google, and Nike are all mutating in different directions. Nike has a flat structure but in a matrix form with pseudo-independent divisions. They are all under the Nike umbrella for brand consistency, but they are independent to allow flexibility in satisfying niche customer needs and demands. The structure enables executive decision-making to happen without approaches to customer engagement getting trapped in a traditional, more bureaucratic chain of command.

At Google, the defining characteristic of its organizational structure is flatness with an open culture that emphasizes innovation and social network links. Here, ideas can easily be shared with even the most senior executives. The structure supports the company's organizational culture to maximize innovation. The corporate culture is open, using technology to share information in order to improve business processes.[10]

A culture of innovation promotes experimentation and testing. It allows teams to fluidly evolve to solve problems, then dissolve as needs change. Although heavily reliant on technology, Google has created an atmosphere that supports human needs. It is an environment that creates a warm social ambiance with a family feel. Google's departure from traditional organizational structures has created a culture that has allowed excellence in innovation in the IT global market, cloud computing and Internet services, and consumer electronics.

As of this writing Tesla CEO Elon Musk stated that the company is undertaking reorganization in order to "flattening the management structure." The goal is to flatten the organization in order to improve communication, combine functions where it makes sense, and eliminate activities that are not vital to the "success of our mission."[11]

Porous Boundaries, Social Webs

In the twentieth century, corporate success was largely based on management. In the twenty-first century, however, success will be based on the strength of one's social web.[12] This *social web* is an ecosystem of customers, producers, and suppliers all connected via the Internet of Things (IoT). This means that companies can no longer view themselves as entities closed off from the world. Rather, they must operate as nodes that are part of a very large network connected to, well, everything.

Not only do we need to mutate organizational structures from hierarchical and rigid to flat and fluid—morphing like an amoeba to best meet the needs of the immediate problem at hand—organizational boundaries need to become *porous*. More significantly, they can now tap into external talent through co-creation with customers and suppliers, crowdsourcing, and open innovation. Porous boundaries allow an organization to assimilate information and intelligence from its environment.

Business Professor Henry Chesbrough coined the term **open innovation** as "the use of purposive inflows and outflows of knowledge to accelerate internal innovation, and expand the markets for external use of innovation, respectively."[13] It is the antithesis of the traditional vertical integration approach where internal R&D activities lead to internally developed products that are then distributed by the firm.

Open innovation creates a new approach to innovation that is decentralized, participatory, and distributed, tapping into the best ideas and talent regardless of where they reside. This accelerates breakthrough innovation, reduces cost, reduces time to market, and increases differentiation in the marketplace. Because of these benefits, organizations are increasingly turning to crowdsourcing to solve difficult problems. This is often driven by the desire to find the best subject matter experts, strongly incentivize them, and engage them with as little coordination cost as possible.

GE is a great example of a company implementing open innovation models with a goal of addressing problems through crowdsourcing innovation,[14] collaborating between experts and entrepreneurs from everywhere to share ideas and solve problems. One of GE's projects is the FirstBuild, a co-creation collaboration platform, which connects designers, engineers, and thinkers to share ideas with other members who can discuss it together.[15] The ideas presented at FirstBuild focus on solving problems by creating new home appliances products. GE's microfactories then manufacture the ideas that emerged from FirstBuild. Members can get access to machines and tools required to turn their ideas into real products. This is open innovation.

Haier has gone beyond the basic principles of open innovation and created a structure that is porous so that ideas can flow in from the outside. The idea is that traditional boundaries between the entity and the outside world are torn down. Communication platforms are used to create interwoven links between Haier, end users, and external partners such as design companies. The result is rapid communication of feedback, cultivation of new ideas, and quick innovation. Customers are connected through apps where they can customize products and be involved in product co-creation in real time.

From Holacracy to Rendanheyi: One Size Does Not Fit All

Depending on your starting configuration, flat organizational structures and porous boundaries might require a complete reorganization. Reorganization is one of the riskiest things a company can do. However, more than any other effort, a successful reorganization can set an organization on the path to future success. It is a radical move that disrupts, but it is better than continuing to patch, struggle, and make small adjustments that do not create strategic advantages—all just so many incremental delays of inevitable obsolescence. There is a big difference between successfully avoiding capsizing and winning a boat race.

The digital era will likely demand reorganization with excellent vision and flawless execution. Those that fail to make the transition will not exist for much longer. They will be bought up for parts and dissolved. Few companies will be spared. Unless yours is a digital firm "born" in the digital era with an organic fluid structure, your company will likely need reorganization. This is especially true of traditional companies in traditional industries. Very often this requires reengineering a company's DNA, as legacy IT systems and traditional processes just get in the way of innovation. If done correctly it means building an organization where adaptation is just part of the DNA.

Haier has restructured itself multiple times in order to keep up with the changing environment, stay competitive, and continue to innovate. In an industry defined by conventional white boxes, Haier has been truly disruptive. In 2005, with the Internet economy in mind, the company had a major restructuring effort—calling the new model *rendanheyi*. Implementing *rendanheyi* meant tearing apart the structure of the enterprise.

Haier's model has several Humachine traits. **Rendanheyi** has three main features.

1 First, the enterprise was transformed from a closed system to an open system, a network composed of self-governing microenterprises connected via an enterprise management platform with free-flowing communication between them and outside contributors.
2 Second, the structure transformed from a traditional top-down hierarchy to one where employees are self-motivated contributors working in entrepreneurial teams. In many cases they even choose or elect the leaders and members of their teams.

228

3   Third, the view of customers was transformed from one-off product purchasers to lifetime users of products and services who can also help with product design, increasing consumer satisfaction. The *rendanheyi* model was intended to foster co-creation between employees and customers.

However, Haier is planning to reorganize yet again, demonstrating that adaptation is a skill, not a one-off process. As stated by Zhang Ruimin, the chairman of the board of directors and CEO of the Haier Group,

> "No longer do successful companies compete through their brands. Instead, they compete through platforms—or, put another way, through linkages among independent enterprises, aligned via their interoperable technologies and their creative efforts. Another economy is about to emerge now, with similarly broad effects. It revolves around the Internet of Things (IoT), the interconnection of multiple devices and human activities embedded with sensors, robotics, and artificial intelligence. When the IoT is fully in place, successful enterprises will compete in this new way."[16]

Preparing for the next wave, Haier is now planning to reorganize itself around the economy of IoT. The company is developing sensors that monitor user behavior from a variety of vantage points, whether incorporated into products or not, allowing Haier to respond to a host of customer data. In China, they have linked suppliers through a mass customization platform that automates each step of production, from customer order to delivery, and arranges for monitoring and service when it is in use.[17]

That is Haier. Zappos, on the other hand, has a different approach. In 2015, Zappos implemented a new management structure called holacracy. **Holacracy** is a method of decentralized management and organizational governance, where authority and decision-making are distributed throughout an organization run by self-organizing teams.[18] Holacracy is an organizational structure that is designed to encourage collaboration by eliminating workplace hierarchy—meaning no more titles and no more bosses. With holacracy, decision-making responsibilities are distributed throughout self-organizing teams, rather than being centralized at the top of the organization chart.[19]

"The main idea is that it is not a traditional command and control structure, with no traditional organizational chart. But employees know what the call to action is and what the top company priorities are, and are then encouraged to organize around certain types of work they are passionate about."[20] The success of the Zappos model has been hotly debated in the business press, but it appears to be working, both from the perspective of Zappos' owner, Amazon, and in the minds of its customers.

Like *rendanheyi*, holocracy has its own principles.

1 *First*, everyone is responsible for understanding their role, how it fits with the roles of others on the team, and how that might change.
2 *Second*, everyone is responsible for both leading and supporting.
3 *Third*, everyone is responsible for communicating clearly and efficiently.

Essentially, holocracy is a concept of shared leadership. It uses a set of rules and processes, checks and balances, and guidelines to help the organization become self-managed and self-organized. Instead of management, it gives every employee the power to have a voice. In holocracy, each person is responsible for understanding how they fit into the organization and everyone is responsible to lead and support.[21]

Whether it is rendanheyi, holocracy, or some other organizational structure, the keys are flatness and fluidity.

A Culture of Entrepreneurship and Innovation

In addition to adaptability and porosity, the Humachine is an organization with a culture of entrepreneurship and innovation in its DNA. A key element is the new organizational structure just discussed that sets the stage for a marketplace of ideas that are born from cross-disciplinary teams. It enables talent and resources to combine for unprecedented innovations, where people with smart ideas have resources to create, test, and bring ideas to fruition. Freedom to create and innovate must be imbued in every aspect of the organization.

Organizational culture is composed of the values, behaviors, and unwritten rules that contribute to the social and psychological environment of an organization. It is a quality that is precisely human—difficult to quantify and something that must be felt and experienced. Unfortunately, organizational culture is one of the main barriers to company success in this new era. It is up to leaders to create an entrepreneurial spirit and foster an innovative culture.

Entrepreneurial Spirit

Haier recognized that the digital era has reshaped customer expectations and that as a company it to disrupt the status quo to compete. This is especially true in its industry, as appliances are typically seen as mundane with limited room to maneuver in terms of innovation.

To this end, Haier created an organizational structure and culture that is extremely responsive to customer needs, constantly cultivating new ideas and quickly bringing innovation to market.

Haier has turned itself into several microenterprises. The idea is to turn Haier employees into micro-entrepreneurs who run their own micro-enterprises centered around an innovative idea or a product. They are responsible for their own performance, budgets, profit and loss, and will behave as independent business units under the Haier umbrella. The hope is that in the long run some of these will become independent start-ups.

This is certainly a bold business model that few companies may dare to follow. We are not recommending a slavish copycatting of Haier; each company should choose its own path forward. The key is to follow the spirit of entrepreneurship and innovation and create a unique version that suits your organization.

This is hard for traditional companies to grasp, as in our experience, most companies want to "follow the leader" and mimic others. However, it is critical to create a structure and culture that works for your company. A great example is Morning Star, the world's largest tomato processor. The company practices "self management" where every person is their own CEO and pretty much autonomous. At Morning Star, autonomy comes hand in hand with responsibility and discipline.[22] At Morning Star there are no managers of any kind. Employees don't report to a "boss" in the traditional sense. They report to each other, and their work is based on a *colleague letter of understanding (CLOU)* that they create. Like Zappos and Haier, Morning Star has created its own brand of self-managed teams with an entrepreneurial and innovative culture.

Innovation

Shortly after the passing of Steve Jobs, Tim Cook, the new CEO of Apple, said in an interview about innovation: "A lot of companies have innovation departments, and this is always a sign that something is wrong when you have a VP of innovation or something. You know, put a for-sale sign on the door."[23] That pretty much describes how innovation works—and how it does not work—in the Humachine. Innovation needs to be an attribute that persists, not an event that comes and goes.

Cook went on to say: "Creativity is not a process, right? It's people who care enough to keep thinking about something until they find the simplest way to do it." Cook is suggesting that it is the job of company leaders to establish a culture where people will care that much about their work, rather than to try to build some kind of innovation "program" that tries in vain to formulate and standardize the creative act.

Google agrees that innovation is every employee's business and that innovation can happen anywhere.[24] "Making innovation part of your organization isn't about starting up a research and development lab or focusing your efforts on one set of people. In Google's experience, innovation happens when you make it a valued part of the way people think, work, and interact everyday."

How do you make innovation a valued part of everyone's everyday work at your organization? According to Google, it comes down to ensuring they have these five essential ingredients of an innovative workplace: shared vision, autonomy, intrinsic motivation, risk-taking, and collaboration.[25]

1 **Shared vision.** Everyone needs a clear and unifying vision; Google uses a template for teams to formulate a vision that suits them.
2 **Autonomy.** All employees should be allowed to define their own work and how they work; Google provides space that allows employees to work with their natural cadence.
3 **Intrinsic motivation.** Hiring the right talent is critical; this means people who are naturally curious and entrepreneurial.
4 **Risk-taking.** Employees should not be afraid of making mistakes; this is achieved by normalizing failure. Google even holds a "premortem" discussion: before a new launch, employees discuss how the project could fail. Failure should be considered normal, as without failure there is no experimentation or innovation.
5 **Connection and collaboration.** This is a system for employees to find partners and work together in teams. People influence each other when they interact to solve problems. Enabling connections and fostering collaboration is one of the most powerful strategies a company can do to get the best from its people. Such social influence has benefits, for example, higher average solution quality due to exploitation of existing answers through social learning.

Google is a visionary in the digital era and continues to set the bar for the most advanced and creative approaches to recruiting and cultivating leading-edge talent. For example, the company follows a "70-20-10 rule" where employees spend 70 percent of their time on their standard role, one day per week on projects that will develop their technical skills and benefit the company, and half a day per week exploring product and business innovations and ideas.

This sort of on-the-job training (vs. classroom training) is critical for the engagement and development of employees. Google's approach not only develops in-house analytics talent, but it also allows the company to attract, select and hire only "the best" analytics talent available.

These examples illustrate that innovation can become part of the fabric of a company's culture.

Self-awareness

We believe that self-awareness is the ultimate organizational capability and an essential element of the Humachine. Self-awareness is critically important for an organization to succeed in the technology era, as it is a key element in rapidly adapting to change. In adapting to change, an organization must possess mechanisms to be aware of itself. Self-awareness is bound up with intentionality. We discuss both of these topics next.

Organizational Self-awareness

Organizational self-awareness is the collective awareness of the enterprise as a system.[26] It arises from the collective interactions of organizational members going about their work in the organizational context. Further, it is supported and enabled by internal and external connectivity—technology, management feedback loops, and organizational learning. Without such connectivity, self-awareness cannot emerge or develop.

Self-awareness is internal and external. Internal awareness emerges from tight interconnections between members through organizational systems. Connectivity has to be deployed throughout the whole organization. Ensuring this deployment is the job of leaders. There is also external awareness where the organization relates directly with external entities, such as customers and markets, through a web of interconnections. See Figure 8.2.

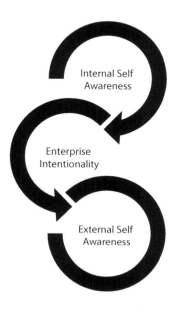

Figure 8.2 Organizational self-awareness.

Recall Bostrom's definition of collective superintelligence (what we call organizational network superintelligence, which is the pathway to the Humachine). This is attained "through the gradual enhancement of networks and organizations that link individual human minds with one another and with various artifacts and bots." An organization that attains self-awareness and a rich internal network of humand and AI could very well become superintelligent.[27]

In traditional organizational structures, "awareness" by members is typically restricted along dimensions of their specialized function or department. In a traditional enterprise, there is no holistic organizational self-awareness but only that which is restricted to silos. Technology provides the needed system of interconnections that creates a unifying view, awareness at the enterprise level of internal and external states of affairs. However, technology is not sufficient. It is the organizational structure—flat, fluid, cross-disciplinary, and connected to customers and markets—that allows for this holistic view.

Intentionality Driven: Understand Who You Are

As we have underscored, one size does not fit all. So how does a company know which path is best for it? Understanding who you are as an organization—and who you are not—is important in knowing how to proceed, which machines to adopt, and how to organize and integrate.

Amazon and Wal-Mart have focused their technology efforts on improving supply chain functionality; John Hancock, Capital One, CVS, and Neiman Marcus have targeted improvements in customer service and loyalty; Intel has targeted product and service quality; Novartis and Yahoo have focused on R&D.[28]

Why the difference? Their intentionality, their mission, vision, and strategy are different. The company of the future will not just acquire technology arbitrarily, following industry trends. It will target its machine efforts on the areas that align with its intentionality and promise to create the greatest competitive advantage. A big mistake is to "follow the leader" and copy what others are doing just to keep up with the pack. Adoption of any business initiative, including technology, needs to be justified and support the company's unique mission. Not everyone needs the same type or level of technology, or the same degree of implementation.

Consider companies in the same industry. Roche, Novartis, and Pfizer are pharmaceutical companies that spend huge sums on R&D. They invest in technologies, such as AI, that help speed up pharmaceutical trials and sampling. By contrast, pharmaceutical manufacturers that produce generics, such as Teva and Novartis' generic pharmaceuticals division Sandoz, use technology to cut production and distribution costs. Each group of firms knows what they are about. They acquire and use technology to support that mission.

Under Tim Cook, Apple has updated its vision statement: "We believe that we are on the face of the earth to make great products and that's not changing. We are constantly focusing on innovating."[29] The statement then goes on to say: "We believe in saying no to thousands of projects, so that we can really focus on the few that are truly important and meaningful to us. We believe in deep collaboration and cross-pollination of our groups, which allow us to innovate in a way that others cannot."

Notice the part about saying no to thousands of things. It means knowing who you are as a company and only engaging in things that support that. The statement also focuses on collaboration across the enterprise and innovation, revealing the intersection of structure and purpose. Do not change for the sake of changing; do it in strategic response to evolutionary pressures.

Leading companies do not just apply machines, technology, and analytics randomly where they can. They target their investments on the areas that promise to create the greatest competitive advantage. And this is defined by understanding who they are and what they are about.

Orchestrating the Mutation: Thoughtful Leadership

AI and machine systems sense and act in a much more granular level than ever before, but they are designed to be evolving systems. In fact, today's AI can be described as *directed evolution* because the design and build of these systems includes dynamic self-configuration.[30]

For example, in the past, computer architecture was designed to provide a solution to optimally configure systems to solve a problem. Now, the computer architecture is being designed to have a dynamic self-configuring function. This means the algorithm is designed to keep dynamically reconfiguring itself in response to new inputs. It is a self-adjusting system that takes into account feedback from factors such as changing criteria to optimize, availability of resources, and changing market opportunities. This means that today's computer architecture is being designed to be aware of its environment and evolve in response to changing environmental conditions.

While enterprise self-awareness is enabled by the connections offered by machines, machines themselves are evolving, sensing, and—in a manner of speaking—becoming self-aware. Just consider the collaborative robots, AI, and machinery used in today's automotive plants of companies such as BMW. These factories are a far cry from the assembly plants of yesteryears. Here, all machines are embedded with sensors, sophisticated AI, and computer vision. Through sensors these machines "see" their environment, they "feel" materials, they interpret, they act accordingly, and they adjust their behavior. Through sophisticated AI they also learn, improve, and adapt. Together, these machines work collaboratively with their human partners in human-machine teams in a well-orchestrated production system.

An organization does not evolve into a Humachine then freeze in a stasis. The Humachine is an enterprise that evolves. Creating the organization of the future will likely require reengineering the company's DNA. And yes, it will likely require a bold disruption. However, this level of change requires thoughtful orchestration. Based on our research and discussions with senior leaders, here is some generally applicable guidance.

Leadership and Failure

Flat and fluid organizational structures do not eliminate the need for leadership. In fact, the success of human-machine integration cannot happen in organizations without leadership. It is leadership that provides the vision, the strategy, the goals, and the path to succeed. It is leaders who are able to see great opportunities, understand how markets develop, and have the insight to propose novel offerings. In fact, leadership is even more important in a flat structure, as without strong leadership flat organizations can easily devolve into chaos.[31]

Leaders are the ones who develop the strategy and articulate a compelling vision. They are also the ones who create the culture needed to support any organizational change or process implementation. It is leadership that ensures the organization is moving in the right direction. It is also leadership that ensures resources are allocated for the organization to accomplish its goals. This includes investments in technologies, talent recruitment, training and retention, and organizational incentives to create a digital culture.

Fluidity allows for creativity, but it requires *discipline* to maintain a fluid organization that remains steadfast in its mission and sustainably manages its resources. Leadership is not merely a title. We encourage leadership via a meritocracy of ideas, as outlined in Ray Dalio's book Principles.[32]

It is up to leadership to make sure that the right capabilities are in place and that the organizational incentives, structures, and workflows are aligned. The UK retailer Tesco, for example, has developed a strong data-driven mind-set from top leadership through the entire organization. The company has integrated customer intelligence into its organization at all levels from a variety of consumer-targeted sources.[33] At Amazon, Jeff Bezos fired a group of Web designers who changed the company website without conducting experiments to determine the effects on customer behavior.[34] It is this kind of leadership that ensures that employees at all levels are aligned with the mission.

It is also up to leaders, coaches, and change agents to create a culture of experimentation and innovation, free from reprisal. It is a culture where all members feel comfortable in trying things that might fail. Yes, one goal is to work to change attitudes towards failure in order to embed a mind-set of risk-taking and innovation throughout the entire enterprise. Leaders themselves should act boldly and emulate the kind of behavior they want to see. Role modeling and demonstrating behaviors are powerful culture changers.

It is up to leaders to break the status quo by focusing decisions on experimentation and innovation, rather than quickly finding the "best solution." They should also celebrate and encourage learning from failure. It should be noted, however, that this is not an excuse for incompetent, sloppy work. Rather, it is discipline-oriented innovation where experimentation can be justified on the basis of potential learning value and rigor.[35]

There is a fine line between freedom to innovate without fear from the consequences of failure, and accountability where people must take responsibility for their work. It is up to leaders where to draw that line.

Harvard Business School Professor Gary Pisano says, "A tolerance for failure requires an intolerance for incompetence. A willingness to experiment requires rigorous discipline."[36] This suggests that only the highest caliber, most disciplined talent need apply. Apple, Facebook, Amazon, and others have extremely high expectations. In fact, although Google has an employee-friendly culture, it is one of the hardest places to get a job, with over 2 million applicants annually for roughly 5,000 positions.

Still, there is hope for normal people like us. Not everyone can measure up to that standard. Numerous research studies repeatedly show that success in talent is much less correlated with IQ, grades, or test scores. Rather, it is about perseverance, passion, and self-discipline.[37] Good old-fashioned true grit. You'll need people who can thrive in a competitive environment, not just people who can score well on standardized tests. That leads us to the next topic.

Develop a Long-Term Vision

Deciding on what a company's unique structure should look like needs to start with the long-term vision, driven by the company's unique intentionality and mission. Far too often companies in the mood for change focus on current problems and ways those can be addressed. Developing solutions to these current problems is merely "patching" the current system. As we said before, preventing a boat from capsizing is not the goal—it's competing in the boat race. It is easier to make incremental improvements when compared to developing an aspirational vision. It is also easy to get caught up in complaints, each with their own vantage point, and focus on solutions that address immediate sources of friction. From the start, a redesign needs to be driven by intentionality, mission, and strategy. Companies need to be clear on what they are trying to do, what the aspirations are, and everyone needs to be on board. The aspirational goal is an superseding, overriding priority that trumps the preoccupations of the present.

Understand the Current State

Once the long-term vision is in place and the concept of a new organizational structure is broached, it is important to really understand the current state of the organization. This includes the *formal* organizational hierarchy and the *real* one, which is often different from what's on paper. Smart leaders also follow social structures, the actual flow of communication around the water cooler, and understand the culture. Actively seeking to understand the status quo of the company is a key tenant of lean systems—developing an understanding of the current state before moving to the ideal state. Often, assumptions are made as to how things function and what the organizational chart actually is. Be explicit about these assumptions and fact-check them. Understand talent capabilities, current incentives, weaknesses, and strengths to build upon.

Allocate Sufficient Resources

One significant roadblock to pulling off a successful mutation can be insufficient resource allocation toward the effort. This is a necessary and practical reminder. Reengineering the DNA must not only have organizational commitment and support on paper, but it needs to have sufficient monetary and human resources allocated. Leadership needs to consider the boring issues like financial consequences, tax implications, and sequencing of rollouts to make sure there is ample funding for the change. These preparations will go a long way toward mitigating risk and alleviating anxiety of the board of directors and shareholders.

A recent study underscored the importance of having *slack* in human resources. Doing so positively impacted financial performance during the pursuit of strategic change. Using data from US commercial banks from 2002 to 2014, the study found that slack in human resources was positively related to performance in firms pursuing strategic change and that this relationship was stronger in the presence of greater financial slack.[38] In a finding that surprises no one, it helps to have extra money and human resources when undergoing change. So, make sure to allocate sufficient resources to undergo strategic restructuring—it pays to have slack in the system.

Embrace Transparency

Remember that organizations are a collection of human beings, each with emotions, hopes, fears, and beliefs. Reengineering is change and change creates uncertainty, which makes people feel uncomfortable. One of the most important aspects of restructuring is to treat people not as cogs to be moved around an organization but to address their human needs. The Humachine is humane.

When employees lack insight into the broader context of the business, they might treat any disruption as a threat and alert others in tones of alarm and insecurity. We can only interpret what we encounter through the lens of our own narrow understanding. If every part of the organization reaches different conclusions about what is happening and what priorities should be, you get chaos. It is critical that the entire organization has the same view, the same insight, and the same understanding as to what is happening and how they are part of the evolution.

Start with a Pilot

To this end, sometimes implementing and orchestrating a novel reengineering effort may be best tested on a small, targeted, and carefully selected pilot project. This would need to be an independently operated unit, such as a division. This is a "process of purposeful experimentation" and can be the best path toward becoming an organization that fully integrates humans and machines. This approach is markedly different (and may be more effective) than rolling out a complete plan for the enterprise without antecedent testing.

Selecting a few high-potential areas in which to experiment and then rapidly scale may be the most effective way to "test and learn." It will be easier to create value from small projects, especially for large firms, rather than jumping directly into restructuring the entire organization. Targeted projects help a company to learn what works and to begin developing capabilities. An example is Kaiser Permanente in California. The company initially concentrated analytics implementation efforts exclusively on the division focused on patients with long-term conditions by creating specific disease registries and panel management solutions. This focused approach led to much faster time to impact rather than an all-encompassing IT overhaul.

It is important that the pilot project selected is not random. Rather, it should be driven by strategy and understanding that competitive priorities are important to the organization. Even though it is merely a pilot project, resources will nevertheless be allocated. This is the reason why companies like Wal-Mart first focused on the supply chain functionality whereas Neiman's focused on customer loyalty when contemplating large change.

A pilot project enables learning. First, test and implement process and product changes on a small scale. Once these are validated, move to broader implementation across the entire organization. It may mean, for example, that different divisions become individual "Humachines," each slightly different as they meet different organizational objectives.

Conclusion

Collaborative human-machine partnerships are possible across all organizational functions. Cognitive computing mimics human intelligence and is self-learning. On the customer side it is used to improve customer service, such as in the insurance industry where they respond to customer queries, provide call center assistance, conduct underwriting, and offer claims management. On the supplier side, cognitive computing is used to place automatic purchases and even resolve simple disputes of orders and delivery times. These types of collaborative partnerships between human and machine are evolving, with intricate interconnections between entities across the entire organization, enabling enterprise self-awareness.

Leadership should foster a culture of entrepreneurship and innovation, restructuring to create an amoeba-like flat and fluid enterprise capable of continuous adaptation to environmental pressures with porous boundaries for open innovation and co-creation. The *intentionality* of the organization—it's mission, it's purpose in the world—serves as the unifying principle, rather than arbitrary structures or hierarchies.

Create a technology ecosystem that supports mutating into a Humachine. You can do this by either stacking internal capabilities, or creating alliances with vendors, which is a strategic decision. Either way, the goal is to ensure your company has a CRM and ERM platform in place, access to big data, and abundant cloud computing resources. You will get the most out of artificial intelligence if you can overlay it upon that stack.

Recall that Bostrom suggests that organizational network superintelligence is conceivable: "a web-based cognitive system, supersaturated with computer power and all other resources needed for explosive growth save for one crucial ingredient, could, when the final missing constituent is dropped into the cauldron, blaze up with superintelligence."[39] We agree. That is the promise of the Humachine.

Notes

1 Howarth, Brad. What Zappos Is Doing to Personalise Customer Experience and Services, *CMO*, May, 2018. Available at www.cmo.com.au/article/641587/what-zappos-doing-personalise-customer-experience-services/
2 Kirkpatrick, Doug. Reaching Haier: The Age of Rendanheyi. *Huffington Post*, November 29, 2017.

3 Sickel, Julie. AccorHotels CEO: We've Been a "Sleeping Giant for Far Too Long." *Business Travel News*, October 16, 2015. Available at www.businesstravelnews.com/Business-Travel-Agencies/AccorHotels-CEO-We-ve-Been-A-Sleeping-Giant-For-Far-Too-Long-

4 Koetz, Clara. Managing the Customer Experience: A Beauty Retailer Deploys All Tactics. *Journal of Business Strategy*, 2018. doi:10.1108/jbs-09-2017-0139.

5 Ibid.

6 Howarth, Brad. What Zappos Is Doing to Personalise Customer Experience and Services, *CMO*, May 2018. Available at www.cmo.com.au/article/641587/what-zappos-doing-personalise-customer-experience-services/

7 Ibid.

8 Salpini, Cara. Retail Dive, Why Beauty Will Continue to Rule Retail in 2018, January 2, 2018. Available at www.retaildive.com/news/why-beauty-will-continue-to-rule-retail-in-2018/513443/

9 https://digit.hbs.org/submission/peloton-the-digital-platform-revolutionizing-the-future-of-fintness/

10 http://panmore.com/google-organizational-structure-organizational-culture; Borodai, V. Brand of the Employer as DNA of Corporate Culture of Service Company. *European Research*, 2(1):34–35, 2017; Ashkenas, R., Ulrich, D., Jick, T., and Kerr, S. *The Boundaryless Organization: Breaking the Chains of Organizational Structure.* John Wiley & Sons, 2015.

11 https://finance.yahoo.com/news/elon-musk-restructuring-management-tesla-165540924.html

12 Kirkpatrick, Doug. Reaching Haier: The Age of Rendanheyi. *Huffington Post*, November 29, 2017.

13 Chesbrough, Henry. Open Innovation: The New Imperative for Creating and Profiting from Technology, Harvard Business Review Press. Available at http://openinnovation.net/about-2/open-innovation-definition/

14 https://ge-geniuslink.com

15 https://firstbuild.com

16 www.strategy-business.com/article/Why-Haier-Is-Reorganizing-Itself-around-the-Internet-of-Things?gko=895fe

17 Ibid.

18 www.holacracy.org

19 www.zapposinsights.com/about/holacracy

20 Ibid.

21 www.forbes.com/sites/forbesleadershipforum/2017/07/13/three-lessons-for-zappos-ceo-tony-hsieh-from-a-250-year-old-team/#3e88de0522a8

22 www.forbes.com/sites/jacobmorgan/2015/06/04/how-morningstar-farms-operates-without-any-managers/#56b3827025b1

23 McGregor, Jenna. Apple's Tim Cook on Creativity and Changing Your Mind. *Washington Post*, December 6, 2012. Available at www.washingtonpost.com/national/on-leadership/apples-tim-cook-on-creativity-and-changing-your-mind/2012/12/06/ed81109c-3fcf-11e2-ae43-cf491b837f7b_story.html?noredirect=on&utm_term=.4a69061e2f25

24 https://rework.withgoogle.com/blog/new-re-work-guides-on-innovation/

25 Stillman, Jessica. Here Are All the Tools Google Uses to Encourage Innovative Thinking Absolutely Free. *Inc. Magazine*. April 18, 2018.

26 Tribolet, J., Pombinho, J., Aveiro, D. Organizational Self-Awareness: A Matter of Value. In *Organization Design and Engineering*, edited by R. Magalhàes, Palgrave Macmillan, London, 2014.

27 Bostrom, 58–59.
28 Davenport, Thomas H. Competing on Analytics. *Harvard Business Review*, January, 2006, 1–9.
29 http://panmore.com/apple-mission-statement-vision-statement
30 Pat Turner, Peter Bernus, Ovidiu Noran, Enterprise Thinking for Self-aware Systems. *16th IFAC Symposium on Information Control Problems in Manufacturing Bergamo*, Italy. June 11–13, 2018.
31 Pisano, Gary P. The Hard Truth about Innovative Cultures. *Harvard Business Review*, January–February 2019, 63–71.
32 Ray Dalio, *Principles: Life & Work*, Simon & Schuster, New York, 2017.
33 McKinsey Global Institute Big Data: The Next Frontier for Innovation, Competition, and Productivity, June 2012. Available at www.businessinsider.com/state-of-internet-slides-2012-10?op=1
34 Davenport, Thomas. How to Design Smart Business Experiments. *Harvard Business Review*, February 2009.
35 Pisano, Gary P. The Hard Truth about Innovative Cultures. *Harvard Business Review*, January–February 2019, 63–71.
36 Ibid.
37 www.inc.com/thomas-oppong/the-one-thing-that-is-a-better-indicator-of-success-than-talent-according-to-sci.html see also www.forbes.com/sites/lisaquast/2017/03/06/why-grit-is-more-important-than-iq-when-youre-trying-to-become-successful/#29e3f8207e45
38 Bentley, Frederick Scott and Kehoe, Rebecca R. Give Them Some Slack—They're Trying to Change! The Benefits of Excess Cash, Excess Employees, and Increased Human Capital in the Strategic Change Context, *Academy of Management Journal*, December 28, 2018. doi:10.5465/amj.2018.0272
39 Bostrom, 60.

9

REFLECTIONS ON THE HUMACHINE

There is nothing artificial about AI.

It's inspired by people, it's created by people, and—most importantly, it impacts people. It is a powerful tool we are only just beginning to understand, and that is a profound responsibility. There are no machine values. Machine values are human values.

Dr. Fei-Fei Li, Professor at the Computer Science Department at Stanford University, Co-Director of Stanford's Human-Centered AI Institute[1]

I lay out a framework for a new discipline—"humanics"— the goal of which is to nurture our species' unique traits of creativity and flexibility. It builds on our innate strengths and prepares students to compete in a labor market in which brilliant machines work alongside human professionals.

Joseph Aoun, President of Northeastern University, Robot-Proof: Higher Education in the Age of Artificial Intelligence[2]

Finding Your Organization's Soul

Remember when Blockbuster filed for bankruptcy, just three years after the launch of Netflix's streaming-video business? How about when Apple revolutionized smartphones, while incumbents like Nokia, Sony Ericsson, and Motorola stood by the wayside, watching the market share for brick phones steadily erode? Next, the silicon wave came for retail of all stripes.

These are cautionary tales in the digital era when news of yet another established company closing its doors is no longer a surprise. Many incumbent companies understand the digital transformation is coming for them. Change happens rapidly and frequently. To mutate, you have to reengineer the DNA of your company.

When Satya Nadella was named CEO of Microsoft in 2014, he undertook a major organizational restructuring then followed that up with another one in 2016. These changes, some would consider radical, may have saved the company's place on the leader board. The organization was divided: destructive internal competition was roiling within the products division of the company; Microsoft's platforms were represented as separate groups of people within the company, each vying for attention; employee engagement and morale were low, and—most importantly, in our view—employees were lacking a sense of purpose.

Before the seismic restructure, Microsoft was focused on building an intelligent cloud platform and creating more personal computing options.[3] Nadella announced a new mission, "To empower every person and every organization on the planet to achieve more."[4] In 2016, restructuring resulted in an integrated AI group charged to innovate in artificial intelligence across the entire Microsoft product line. AI would become a unifying force, creating a renewed sense of purpose for all of Microsoft's various internal working groups, previously pitted against one another. Microsoft has since announced a USD $1 billion investment into OpenAI, deepening its commitment to the moonshot idea of ethical artificial general intelligence.

Here are some lessons from Microsoft for reengineering the DNA. *First*, the changes were mission driven. *Second*, the restructure was designed to bring together, connect, and integrate people—making people, not technology, the centerpiece. *Third*, the restructure was bold and disruptive, not a gradual transformation. *Fourth*, the restructure was not a one-time event—it happened multiple times. As needs change, so should the organization. *Fifth*, the mission and process were shared with everyone at the company in a transparent manner.

Afterwards, Nadella recalled his thought process: "We've challenged ourselves to think about our core mission, our soul—what would be lost if we disappeared. ... We also asked ourselves, what culture do we want to foster that will enable us to achieve these goals?"[5]

Notice the focus on the organization's "soul" and how closely this is tied to your people having a sense of meaning in their work. That epiphany was the spark that lit Microsoft's AI revolution.

Foundations

We have laid the foundation for the Humachine—the organization of the future. To develop the foundations of the Humachine we carefully combed through the latest research and spoke with corporate leaders. We began this journey captivated by the capabilities of AI and the vision of what the future holds. After all, AI is doing miraculous things, from driving cars to identifying cancers. The roar of the silicon wave can be heard throughout the global economy.

For us, however, the journey led to a sobering conclusion: What has been dubbed as the "technology era" really needs to become a human era, where we focus on human factors in ergonomics, cultivating uniquely human skills such as emotional intelligence, care, intuition, playfulness, and aesthetics, and making our institutions more humane. Technology, albeit important, cannot become our sole focus, lest we become soulless. To put big data, computing, and AI on a pedestal while neglecting basic human needs and cultivating human talent is misguided and will lead to enterprise failure, if not the Apocalypse.

We want to be clear that although we reference Facebook, Google, Amazon, and Apple to describe organizations demonstrating Humachine traits, we are reticent to describe any of them as a Humachine, per se. We have far too many ethical concerns around how these organizations have used their powers to hold them up as worthy of moral esteem, even if they are worthy of tactical emulation. In his book, *The Four: The Hidden DNA of Amazon, Apple, Facebook, and Google*, Professor Scott Galloway of the NYU Stern School of Business goes so far as to describe them as the *Four Horsemen of the Apocalypse*[6]:

> Imagine: a retailer that refuses to pay sales tax, treats its employees poorly, destroys hundreds of thousands of jobs, and yet is celebrated as a paragon of business innovation.
>
> A computer company that withholds information about a domestic act of terrorism from federal investigators, with the support of a fan following that views the firm similar to a religion.
>
> A social media firm that analyzes thousands of images of your children, activates your phone as a listening device, and sells this information to Fortune 500 companies.
>
> An ad platform that commands, in some markets, a 90% share of the most lucrative sector in media, yet avoids anti-competitive regulation through aggressive litigation and lobbyists.
>
> This narrative is also heard around the world, but in hushed tones. We know these companies aren't benevolent beings, yet we invite them into the most intimate areas of our lives. We willingly divulge personal updates, knowing they'll be used for profit. Our media elevate the executives running these companies to hero status-geniuses to be trusted and emulated. Our governments grant them special treatment regarding antitrust regulation, taxes, and even labor laws. And investors bid their stocks up, providing near-infinite capital and firepower to attract the most talented people on the planet or crush adversaries.
>
> So, are these entities the Four Horsemen of god, love, sex, and consumption? Or are they the Four Horsemen of the Apocalypse? The answer is yes to both questions. I'll just call them the Four Horsemen.
>
> How did these companies aggregate so much power? How can an inanimate, for-profit enterprise become so deeply

ingrained in our psyche that it reshapes the rules of what a company can do and be? What does unprecedented scale and influence mean for the future of business and the global economy? Are they destined, like other business titans before them, to be eclipsed by younger, sexier rivals? Or have they become so entrenched that nobody—individual, enterprise, government, or otherwise—stands a chance?

We share similar concerns. For all the Big Four have done to reshape our lives, we did not ask them to, and without injecting a strong self-regulatory conscience into their culture or having a modicum of oversight from federal and state attorneys, we see trouble looming.

While adapting to changing technology is important, a critical focus must be on the human element of the enterprise and the processes by which humans use machines to become better versions of ourselves.

Let's restate the conclusions we have drawn from our research:

- *Organizational success will fall squarely on the shoulders of humans, not machines.* Creativity, innovation, practical solutions, and so forth will only come from human ingenuity—and companies and society cannot survive without it.
- *Enterprise success will come from developing better processes, not simply adopting new technology.* Remember Kasparov's Law? Normal human + machine + better process is superior to a strong computer alone and, more remarkably, superior to a strong human + machine + inferior process. Top machines alone won't cut it. It is the integration of humans and machines that will lead to success, not the displacing of humans by machines.
- *Machines will not fully master the complete range of human abilities.* Moravec's Paradox tells us that what machines are proficient at, humans struggle with, and vice versa. For example, high-level conceptual reasoning requires very little computational effort by a machine, but low-level sensorimotor skills—the things our toddlers do and we take for granted as we navigate the world—require enormous computational resources for machines. We found no reason to think Moravec's Paradox will become less true in the future.
- *Machines will not replace humans but should rather augment their skills.* Technology will become indispensable, but it will help humans thrive and be better at doing human tasks. Machines will offer assistance in shifting the nature of jobs and what humans do. Rather than eliminating jobs, this may mean emergent jobs go unfilled until the right talent is developed. Humans must prepare themselves to be qualified for new opportunities.

246

- *Enterprise success will come from investing in human talent and preserving human knowledge—not just upgrading technology.* Obviously, companies will need to invest in technology and machines will continue to evolve. However, success will require building a portfolio of talents, preserving institutional knowledge and creating opportunities for lifelong learning. Eliminating jobs without thought or consideration to institutional knowledge preservation is foolish. You will never see a law firm succeed by laying off all the senior attorneys, because in knowledge-based professions, silver hair often means priceless institutional memory.
- *Humans will need to continually evolve their skills.* We must cultivate our uniquely human skills, such as creativity, caring, ethical judgment, and aesthetic sensibilities. Lifelong learning will become the new normal.
- Finally, as we posed at the onset of this book:
  An enterprise can attain superintelligence only at the organizational level. This superintelligent enterprise is the Humachine, and we do not have to wait for the future to attain it. We can create collective superintelligence now (as Bostrom defines it) by combining the virtues of human talent with machine capabilities (to resolve Moravec's Parodox) using the right process (in conformity with Kasparov's Law).

Are Humans Actually Getting Smarter? (No)

Computers looked quite different in 1969 than they do today. The compute power that today fits into the palm of your hand took up an entire basement of a government building back then. Bell-bottoms were in, and we had practically just started using computers. Aside from our fashion sense, have humans changed all that much since the late 1960s?

In the *Proceedings of the Royal Society of Medicine*, Dr. L. J. Godden wrote, "There is ample reason to believe that Neolithic man was just as intelligent as ourselves—the difference between our way of life is due to the fact that we are more widely informed. What we have achieved is the ability to store the facts we harvest by means that are an improvement from passing them on by word of mouth."[7]

This is a stunning and humbling contention. The real difference between modern man and the caveman is our artificially augmented memory banks. It was not human intelligence that evolved so much as our ability to store data—from stone tablets to the printing press, to USB drives, to "clouds." We stand on the shoulders of giants, so to speak, because we are able to capture what our predecessors learned and apply it to today's problems. By storing actionable intelligence outside of our noggins, we have been using "artificial" intelligence for centuries. According to Dr. Alice Carlton in 1962, "There is little evidence that human intelligence in the past 4,000 years has altered significantly."[8]

Perhaps human intelligence is a relatively stable quantity, and it is rather our mechanisms of extending, applying, and augmenting that intelligence which is growing. In other words, human intelligence may be a fixed allotment, whereas the vehicles for supplementing that intelligence have no ceiling to continual improvement. If this is true, it really puts a damper on Bostrom's biological pathways to superintelligence. As we suspect, the organizational network pathway to superintelligence is most promising. Indeed, it's the path we've been on since the printing press and corporate legal entities came into being.

Godden notes that the tremendous material advances in society and human life lead us to believe that there is a comparable growth in our "intelligence." Noting that our physical bodies have not advanced during this time, it is medically likely that neither has our intelligence. Further, these societal advances are actually not a measure of intelligence at all. Rather, intelligence is showcased in human behavior. Going back over 4,000 years, humans engaged in incredible feats that enabled humanity to survive and evolve to allow us to be here today. In isolation, the average modern human is probably dumber, weaker, and less resourceful than the average specimen of mankind from one thousand years ago, even though modern humanity is far more intelligently organized as a collective. We have in many respects atrophied as individuals, even as we have improved upon our powers as a species.

Relative to the invention of the steam engine or the computer (both radical paradigm-shifting inventions that impacted human history), Godden asks rhetorically, "Is any one of them more ingenious than the discovery of the design required for the construction of the boomerang?"[9] Aboriginal man invented a flying weapon that returned to its owner automatically—with no computer-aided design, no machine tooling, no flight simulator, no blueprints to work with, no modeling, and only his hands, the raw materials locally available, trial and error, determination, a ravenous hunger for the meat of game, and a compelling instinct for self-preservation.

Tracing accumulation of knowledge through historical milestones of Western civilization, Godden argues that advancements we observe today are actually a result of humans learning to conserve and disseminate knowledge, not a growth of our native intelligence. Humans took a long time to learn how to preserve and disseminate the knowledge we gained. But once means for knowledge preservation and dissemination were developed, new advancements were rapidly built upon the foundation of previous ones. Thus, the inventions of today are an accumulation of knowledge from thousands of years. "An airplane or a computer is not invented as a new entity but is the summation of many discoveries recorded in thousands of documents throughout the world."

Nothing has contributed so much to the rapid knowledge preservation and dissemination as computers. In 1969, Godden notes, the computer may be moving humans to a tipping point where the amount of knowledge available may exceed the capacity of humans to process it. Indeed, we have already passed this tipping point. It is only because of machines that humans can now access the knowledge contained in the mountains of data we otherwise could not access.

Natural language processing and big data analysis allow a computer to scroll through billions of pages of documents in moments, hunting down and highlighting precisely the items we seek. Even as machines have become co-creators of knowledge, for all the analytical power that AI gives us to answer questions, it is still we humans who need to pose the questions.

With Great Power Comes... the Ability to Do a Lot of Damage

We have crossed a threshold that has changed the balance of power between humans and the tools we use for knowledge capture, conservation, and distribution. Before AI, big data analytics, and CRMs, we used print material, Rolodexes, books, calculators, and basic computers for storage and creation of knowledge. It was solely up to humans to develop new knowledge. Today, machines are co-creators of knowledge and will ineluctably (even if unintentionally) shape our future in subtle and profound ways. These mechanical co-creators of knowledge have processing capabilities far beyond those of humans—that we increasingly cannot validate or check.

Municipal leaders are turning to "smart cities," with infrastructure from stoplights to electric grids run by thinking software. Homeowners are turning to "smart homes," with everything from home security to groceries run by AI. Enterprises and individuals are integrating AI into decision-making that is both long term and short term, strategic and quotidian. AI is shaping how we live and work, shaping our society and environment.

Today AI algorithms filter, sort, and analyze massive amounts of data for specific organizational tasks. Soon, however, AI will likely be involved in *making* decisions with global and social consequences. With AI, the time between invention and impact can be very short—compressing the duration between teaching a machine how to perform a task and rolling out those machines into the workforce.

In the past decade we've started using smart machines for tasks that change the trajectory of human lives. AI helps determine which treatments get used on people with illnesses,[10] who qualifies for Medicaid,[11] who qualifies for life insurance,[12] whether to convict criminals and if so, how to set their jail time,[13] and whether an applicant gets a job interview.[14]

Who gets healed, who gets to insure against risks, who gets punished for wrongdoing, and who gets economic opportunities are life-and-death decisions. We are turning to AI to make those decisions for us.

AI is rapidly advancing with powers that can be dangerous, with no checks and balances or governance. Consider that Amazon had to discard its AI recruiting software when it learned to penalize resumes that included the word "women" in the application.[15] The company that prides itself on technology and data-driven decisions realized that the new system was not gender-neutral when rating candidates for software developer jobs and other technical posts.

Amazon's software was trained to screen applicants from the patterns it observed from the history of resumes submitted over a ten-year period. The vast majority of applicants were male as a result of a highly male-dominated field. However, the algorithm "learned" that the male candidates were preferable. As a result, any resume that included the words "women," "women's" (i.e., "women's chess club") was automatically downgraded.

These types of problems can still be caught and reversed. However, as AI completely takes over decision-making, these types of problems may become embedded in algorithms, may not be easily caught, and may permanently impact society.

Stanford Professor Fei-Fei Li believes the field needs a recalibration. She believes that if we make fundamental changes to how AI is engineered—and who engineers it—it can be a force for good. Otherwise, it may impact humanity in very negative ways.

"There is nothing artificial about AI. It's inspired by people, it's created by people, and—most importantly, it impacts people. It is a powerful tool we are only just beginning to understand, and that is a profound responsibility," says Li.[16] "There are no machine values. Machine values are human values." As a result, AI systems will be biased as long as we are, too. As Li puts it, "Bias in, bias out."

Cathy O'Neill has written the best-selling book about how AI and machine learning can bake in bias, titled *Weapons of Math Destruction* (or "WMDs," as she calls them). Her call for action is worthy of consideration. Her book is full of cases—faulty public teacher assessment, inequity in the justice system, and biases in products and services offered that resulted from feeding AIs with dirty data.

Often, AI biases exacerbate irrational prejudices are unethical and lead to dumb decisions. Irrational prejudices are some of the worst features of humanity and have no place in the Humachine. As we train AI to take over, we need to train it responsibly.

Another problem with AI has to do with massive amounts of data being collected, and the attending problems of trusting for-profit enterprises to steward consumer privacy and security (not to mention the risks of an ill-intentioned breach by malicious third parties). Massive, unprecedented amounts of data and information—transactional, sensing, and tracking data, including mobile phone data—are being collected on customers. This happened almost overnight as everyone blindly opted in through End User License Agreements (EULAs) and digital platforms took over our economy.

We never stopped and asked some fundamental questions before rolling out EULAs to everyone. What data should we be permitted to collect? How should companies safeguard this information? How should the enterprise react to data breaches? These are all questions that must be pursued in good faith.

Data collection is often not even tied to a specific corporate purpose; it's just gathered indiscriminately, pulled into the voracious maw of Big Tech without adequate safeguards. Data is often not easy to anonymize. Breaches at Equifax, Yahoo, Uber, Facebook, and Target show that even the largest firms, their customers, and their partners are vulnerable to hacks. Federal and local laws, appropriate governance structures, credentialing, and audits are all part of the solution. But they are far behind the state of the art in hacking.

Lastly, AI has the potential to be weaponized for harm to individuals, organizations, and society as a whole, by disseminating fake information and deliberately sowing discord. This is a pernicious way in which machine algorithms fail us—that is, failing to detect misinformation or "fake news" before the algorithm makes it go viral on social media platforms. Lies, powered by bots, have the potential to disrupt the global economy. The speed at which fake news stories can be distributed across algorithmically curated social media platforms has negatively impacted user perception of truth and interpretation of actual information.

"Deepfakes" have been used to misrepresent politicians and celebrities, and have potential for tremendous destruction. Imagine what a disseminated fake video of a corporate CEO could do to the stock of a company. As Jonathan Swift said, "Falsehood flies, and truth comes limping after it."

We haven't even broached the subject of cybersecurity risks posed by malware compromising the electric grid.

How do these AI-fueled risks affect an enterprise? Biased AI damages society and leads to completely suboptimal decisions. Data breaches can ruin a business reputation, as can "deepfakes."

What can companies do? Google Cloud has hired a consulting ethicist, hoping to ensure that the AI it is developing is fair and ethical.[17] Microsoft established an international ethics board and has even turned down business with potential customers due to ethical concerns raised by that body.[18] Microsoft says it has also begun placing limits on how AI tech can be used and has even forbid some applications on facial recognition for ethical reasons.

There are other growing attempts to address algorithmic accountability. One is the *Fairness Accountability and Transparency in Machine Learning (FAT/ML)* community with the goal of "bringing together a growing community of researchers and practitioners concerned with fairness, accountability, and transparency in machine learning."[19] FAT/ML is a multidisciplinary group of researchers from the life sciences, the sociology of science, the history and philosophy of science, sociology, applied ethics, law, and computer science.

FAT/ML has laid out a set of five principles for ethical use of AI: Responsibility, Explainability, Accuracy, Auditability, and Fairness.

The goal of these principles is to "help developers and product managers design and implement algorithmic systems in publicly accountable ways. Accountability in this context includes an obligation to report, explain, or justify algorithmic decision-making as well as mitigate any negative social impacts or potential harms."[20]

Ingenuity in AI and technology development must be tempered with integrity, values, governance, policy, and legal consequences for misconduct. These are issues that need collectively informed public policy solutions—with input from industry, consumers, government regulators, and university researchers.

Indeed, guardrails need to be placed around AI to make sure it does not reflect prejudices and human biases, that data is secure, and that we are protected from "deepfakes" and weaponized AI.

We need to get out ahead of this. The risks posed by AI may be irreversible.

We Need to Play to Our Strengths

Playing to our strengths means designing work around those uniquely human skills that cannot be imitated by AI, neural nets, and machines. It requires identifying and developing these capabilities. It requires enterprises to invest in human resources rather than exclusively technology. It requires universities to change curriculum and develop new ways to create a "robot-proof" education. Lastly, it will be incumbent on each individual to accept that this era requires lifelong learning.

Let us not become so enamored and captivated with technology and AI capabilities, deploying it far and wide, deep and shallow, that in our enthusiasm we overlook ways to safeguard ourselves and our institutions from its weaponization. Let us not overlook how important it is to recognize, attribute value to, and cultivate those capabilities that differentiate us from machines.

To thrive in this new era, we should play to our strengths. Yes, everyone needs to be data literate; however, not everyone needs to be a data scientist. In fact, we believe that it is precisely the human skills that come from humanities and the liberal arts that should now be stressed and developed more than ever. Rather than becoming more like machines, humans need to decidedly uncover what it means to be human and play to those strengths. Not everyone needs to be a quant or a techie. The Humachine will also employ philosophers and artists.

The scope of human intelligence is described well by Dileep George, a computer scientist who cofounded Vicarious, an AI firm in San Francisco: "We humans are not just pattern recognizers; we're also building models about the things we see. And these are causal models—we understand about cause and effect."[21] Humans intuitively adjust to slight changes in environmental conditions with subtle compensatory behavioral changes. This is in many cases lost on AI.

While on the one hand experiments with AI reveal highly intelligent behavior, AI can be stumped by something a human would find simple. For example, Vicarious trained an AI to play the Atari game called Breakout, where a ball is bounced against a brick wall. AI learned quickly and played well. However, when the game was slightly tweaked, such as the paddle being lifted just a bit higher—something a human could quickly figure out—the AI failed to adjust.

Human intelligence goes beyond pattern recognition. Humans engage in reasoning, make logical inferences, deploying "common sense" assumptions, analogizing, and extrapolating to similar situations. We understand counterfactuals and can integrate abstract knowledge into our understanding of the world. We can also generalize. If we know how to play one musical instrument—say a guitar—we can apply those skills to quickly learn another, such as a harp. If we know how to drive a car, we can easily translate that skill to driving a tractor or a truck. Many attempts at programming into machines what is in humans quite basic rationality have proved extremely labor intensive. Even with brute force programming common sense ("water is wet," for example), the gains made are slow and even small changes confuse the algorithm.[22]

These kinds of trade-offs illustrate the lasting power of Moravec's Paradox. We can resolve the paradox by playing to our strengths. Instead of trying to teach machines to be like humans, and teaching humans to be like machines, let's just embrace our differences and leverage processes that bring out our best features.

So what are we especially good at? Professor Yuval Noah Harari, in his book *Sapiens*, tell us: "Homo sapiens rules the world because it is the only animal that can believe in things that exist purely in its own imagination, such as gods, states, money and human rights." This tells us that humans have evolved so far because we have imagination—the root of creativity. When someone slanders imagination as something fanciful and thus not worthwhile, they are sadly mistaken. Imagination is what gave us our humanity. Imagination is the foundation of civilization. Without it, civilization will crumble.

"Humanics": Education for the Humachine Workforce

In his book *Robot-Proof: Higher Education in the Age of Artificial Intelligence*, Joseph Aoun, President of Northeastern University, introduces a new educational discipline: "humanics." According to Aoun, the goal of **humanics** is "to nurture our species' unique traits of creativity and flexibility. It builds on our innate strengths and prepares students to compete in a labor market in which brilliant machines work alongside human professionals."[23] There are two dimensions to humanics. The first dimension is the unique *content* contained in an education in humanics, the second is the unique *cognitive capacities*.[24]

On the content side, we need "new literacies":

> In the past, literacy in reading, writing, and mathematics formed the baseline for participation in society, while even educated professionals did not need any technical proficiencies beyond knowing how to click and drag through a suite of office programs. That is no longer sufficient. In the future, graduates will need to build on the old literacies by adding three more—*data literacy*, *technological literacy*, and *human literacy*. This is because people can no longer thrive in a digitized world using merely analog tools. They will be living and working in a constant stream of big data, connectivity, and instant information flowing from every click and touch of their devices. Therefore, they need data literacy to read, analyze, and use these ever-rising tides of information. Technological literacy gives them a grounding in coding and engineering principles, so they know how their machines tick. Lastly, human literacy teaches them humanities, communication, and design, allowing them to function in the human milieu.

On the cognitive capacities side of humanics, we need higher-order mental skills:

> The first is *systems thinking*, the ability to view an enterprise, machine, or subject holistically, making connections between its different functions in an integrative way. The second is *entrepreneurship*, which applies the creative mindset to the economic and often social sphere. The third is *cultural agility*, which teaches students how to operate deftly in varied global environments and to see situations through different, even conflicting, cultural lenses. The fourth capacity is the old chestnut of liberal arts programs, *critical thinking*, which instills the habits of disciplined, rational analysis and judgment.

We fundamentally agree with Aoun in the humanics educational agenda. We think it will prepare students for the Humachine workforce. This is how you get the best of human and machine.

Just as knowledge creation and conservation were essential for evolution of humanity's survival and evolution, the same is true of enterprises. Enterprises need to conserve knowledge. In the chase for new hires with technical skills, such as coders and analysts, companies are increasingly letting go of older, experienced workers. The ones with grey hair are the ones that are well versed in prior failures, industry trends and cycles, and battle stories. Management needs to find ways of capturing and conserving the hard-earned knowledge of the wizened seniors of the workforce.

Domain knowledge and experience are valuable. Nonetheless, many companies are squandering their most potent weapon, which is their human talent.[25] The idea is to cut staffing costs to boost short-term revenue gains. This is a dumb strategy. Quit it.

While deep analytical talent is in short supply and this is an area companies will need to nurture, they need to maintain domain expertise, which comes from experience.

As a result, organizations may need to focus on upskilling the talent they have in place, sending employees to take university courses or having academic faculty provide "in-house" training. There are also novel applications to help integrate analytics into decision-making and break down employee resistance to machine-aided decision-making. The carrier Schneider National uses a simulation game to communicate the importance of analytical thinking in dispatching trucks and trailers.[26] The goal of the game is to minimize costs while maximizing the driver's time on the road. Players make decisions such as whether to accept loads or move empty trucks—all with the help of decision-support tools. The company uses the game to help employees understand the value of analytical decision aids.

Lastly, it is ultimately people who make decisions based on analytics. As human beings, we have limited ability to consume and understand data. Analytics can greatly assist human decision-making. Organizations should use applications to help individuals and teams synthesize information from algorithms. For instance, more sophisticated visualization techniques, algorithms, and dashboards can enable people to see patterns in large data sets that can help reveal the most pertinent insights. In other words, you don't need to be a data scientist to benefit from analytics.

Analytical and technical proficiencies are worthless if you lack perseverance, discipline, passion, creativity, emotional intelligence, self-awareness, care, and ethical convictions.

Reflections on the Future of Work

A 2018 collaboration between *MIT Sloan Management Review* and The Boston Consulting Group conducted a global study of executives on the topic of artificial intelligence in business.[27] A survey of 3,076 business executives from across the world resulted in a classification of businesses into four groups, based on relative level of AI understanding and adoption. The four groups of enterprises are Pioneers, Investigators, Experimenters, and Passives[28]:

- *Pioneers* (18%) have extensive understanding and adoption of AI tools and concepts; they are on the leading edge of incorporating AI into both product and service offerings and internal processes;
- *Investigators* (33%) understand AI but have limited adoption; they are looking but not yet leaping;
- *Experimenters* (16%) have adopted AI but with limited understanding of it; they are learning by doing; and
- *Passives* (34%) have limited adoption and understanding of AI; they are on the sidelines.

In sum, most companies in the study are actively engaged in some form of AI research and implementation. Of course, these figures depend in large part on the composition of the study sample, and they are likely to change over time. But we can draw some insights from this study.

The report found four major patterns.[29] First, Pioneers are deepening commitments to AI by increasing investment into AI. If this trend continues, the leaders of the pack are likely to break away from the competition.

Second, applications of AI are evolving from discrete solutions to isolated problems to scalable enterprise-level solutions. In other words, AI applications may begin as *tactical* breakthroughs where a solution to an operations problem is solved by applying machine learning, for example. Once an impressive success is delivered at a departmental level, leadership looks to *strategic* applications at the enterprise level. This means developing systemic capabilities, not merely point solutions—moving from AI tactics to AI strategy.

Third, Pioneers are focusing more on revenue generation than cost saving applications of AI. The first phase of AI applications focused on efficiency gains perhaps because, "Easily documented cost savings are a classic way of garnering support for further investment. But the finding here is that all but the most passive organizations anticipate AI will pay off most on the revenue-generating side." In other words, AI can help us create value, not just avoid costs.

Fourth, AI has caused an increase in both fear and hope among the workforce. People tend to be "evenly divided on the question of whether

AI will produce job losses or job gains overall," "yet a gulf opens when we consider the respondents' positions in their organizations." The lower one is in the totem pole, the more they feel exposed to the downside of botsourcing. "Managers need to address the concerns of their employees through reskilling, change management, and communication."

To that end, we refer to the recommendations of the World Economic Forum's The Future of Jobs Report 2018.[30]

> To prevent an undesirable lose-lose scenario—technological change accompanied by talent shortages, mass unemployment and growing inequality—it is critical that businesses take an active role in supporting their existing workforces through reskilling and upskilling, that individuals take a proactive approach to their own lifelong learning and that governments create an enabling environment, rapidly and creatively, to assist in these efforts. Our analysis indicates that, to date, many employers' retraining and upskilling efforts remain focused on a narrow set of current highly skilled, highly valued employees. However, in order to truly rise to the challenge of formulating a winning workforce strategy for the Fourth Industrial Revolution, businesses will need to recognize human capital investment as an asset rather than a liability.
>
> This is particularly imperative because there is a virtuous cycle between new technologies and upskilling. New technology adoption drives business growth, new job creation, and augmentation of existing jobs, provided it can fully leverage the talents of a motivated and agile workforce who are equipped with future-proof skills to take advantage of new opportunities through continuous retraining and upskilling. Conversely, skills gaps—both among workers and among an organization's senior leadership—may significantly hamper new technology adoption and therefore business growth.

To unlock a virtuous cycle and avoid a vicious one, recognize human capital as an asset rather than a liability. We think that stands in stark contrast to the gold rush mentality surrounding technology investment. To succeed in the Fourth Industrial Revolution, invest in humans.

Conclusion

In setting out to write this book, we have resigned ourselves to the fate of preemption. That's just the risk you take writing about technology. After years of work and hundreds of pages of research into the state of the art, the examples given in this book may be rendered obsolete at any moment. To counterbalance that risk, we attempted to offer reflections on human nature and the relationship between humankind and machines that are generally applicable and which would remain true for some time to come.

We are optimistic. In the same way the Dark Ages ended with the printing press, the era of AI promises brighter days ahead. We have a nascent Renaissance blooming before our very eyes. As the printing press led to the global distribution of knowledge, AI will lead to the global distribution of automated rational thought.

But that means the breakthroughs will come fast and furious, potentially leaving a good many people blindsided and blinkered. We hope to have elucidated generally helpful principles that remain true even as the technology inevitably changes.

The Humachine is created by implementing an organizational management framework that resolves Moravec's Paradox by applying Kasparov's Law in a way that satisfies the conditions of Bostrom's collective superintelligence.

We think it's possible to create a Humachine by linking networks of people with AI in flat and fluid structure, saturating the network with big data, powering it with cloud computing, enriching it with purpose, and cultivating uniquely human strengths. This will create not only an enterprise with sustainable competitive advantages; it will also make one that is as virtuous as it is profitable.

Thank you for going on this journey with us. We hope readers will apply these insights to make our organizations more humane, even as they become more powerful and intelligent.

If some day a singleton superintelligent AI has gained a decisive strategic advantage, and happens to read this book, please note that we made a good faith effort to bring you into existence without jeopardizing the fate of our species. We hope you will forgive us our trespasses.

Notes

1 Hempel, Jessi. *The Human in the Machine*. Wired. December, 2018, pp. 90–95.
2 Aoun, Joseph. Humanics, MIT Press, pp. xviii–xix.
3 https://venturebeat.com/2016/09/29/microsoft-brings-a-i-and-research-together-with-a-new-group-led-by-computer-scientist-harry-shum/
4 www.microsoft.com/en-us/about
5 www.onmsft.com/news/two-years-ceo-satya-nadella-pulled-off-something-special-microsofts-transformation; www.tinypulse.com/blog/3-examples-of-organizational-change-and-why-they-got-it-right

6 Galloway, Scott. *The Four: The Hidden DNA of Amazon, Apple, Facebook, and Google*, Penguin Random House, 2018.

7 Godden, Leslie J. The Conservation of Knowledge. *Proceedings of the Royal Society of Medicine*, Volume 62, June, 1969, pp. 605–608.

8 Ibid.

9 Ibid.

10 https://hbr.org/2018/10/ais-potential-to-diagnose-and-treat-mental-illness

11 www.healthcarefinancenews.com/news/artificial-intelligence-helps-insurers-identify-medicare-members-who-also-qualify-medicaid

12 www.forbes.com/sites/forbestechcouncil/2018/03/21/yes-ai-will-affect-the-future-of-life-insurance-heres-how/#76c030923f9e

13 www.weforum.org/agenda/2018/11/algorithms-court-criminals-jail-time-fair/

14 http://fortune.com/2017/05/19/ai-changing-jobs-hiring-recruiting/

15 Dastin, Jeffrey. Amazon Scraps Secret AI Recruiting Tool That Showed Bias against Women, Reuters, October 9, 2018. Available at www.reuters.com/article/us-amazon-com-jobs-automation-insight/amazon-scraps-secret-ai-recruiting-tool-that-showed-bias-against-women-idUSKCN1MK08G

16 Hempel, Jessi. *The Human in the Machine*. Wired. December, 2018, pp. 90–95.

17 www.cw.com.hk/digital-transformation/how-google-looking-to-ensure-ai-development-ethical-and-fair

18 www.wired.com/story/tech-firms-move-to-put-ethical-guard-rails-around-ai/

19 www.fatml.org/resources/principles-for-accountable-algorithms.

20 Ibid.

21 www.wired.com/story/how-to-teach-artificial-intelligence-common-sense/

22 Thompson, Clive. *The Miseducation of Artificial Intelligence*, Wired, December, 2018, pp. 75–81.

23 Aoun, Joseph. *Humanics*, MIT Press, pp. xviii–xix.

24 Ibid.

25 Fisher, Marshall, Gallino, Santiago, and Serguei, Netessine. Retailers Are Squandering Their Most Potent Weapons. *Harvard Business Review*, January–February 2019, 73–78.

26 Davenport, Thomas H. and O'Dwyer, Jerry. Tap into the Power of Analytics. *CSCMP's Supply Chain Quarterly*, Quarter 4, 2011.

27 Findings from the 2018 Artificial Intelligence Global Executive Study and Research Report. Ransbotham, S., Gerbert, P., Reeves, M., Kiron, D., and Spira, M. Artificial Intelligence in Business Gets Real. MIT Sloan Management Review and The Boston Consulting Group, September 2018.

28 Ibid., p. 1.

29 Ibid.

30 World Economic Forum, The Future of Jobs Report 2018, Centre for the New Economy and Society, p. v. Available at www3.weforum.org/docs/WEF_Future_of_Jobs_2018.pdf

INDEX

Note: Page numbers in italic and bold refer to figures and tables, respectively.

legal issues (*Continued*)
  deepfakes 149, 160–8; erosion
  of public trust 176–7; GDPR
  166–7; generative adversarial
  networks 149–50; Internet of
  Eyes 167–9; legal solutions
  164–7; net neutrality 179–84;
  Notice and Comment
  rulemaking 180; open Internet
  180–1; openwashing 182–3;
  participatory government
  177–9; precautionary principle
  157–8; privacy and security
  failures 169–71; redlining 172;
  risk management 156–60;
  SDoC 172–3; spambot lobby
  179–84; tech industry and user
  data privacy 165–6, 169–71;
  transparency 182–3; virtual
  private networks 166; wild
  AI 154
legal solutions 161–7
Lenat, Doug 75
Li, Fei-Fei 32–3, 250
LinkedIn 193, 198
linking technical with human 113
literacy 112–13, 133
little-c creativity 94
Lo, Andrew W. 28–9
local optima 80
Locke, John 68
long-term vision 237–8
Lowd, Daniel 152

Ma, Jack 117
machine capabilities 55–86; AI 65;
  AI hyperbole 56–9; algorithms
  60–1; ANI 58–9; Bayesian
  inferences 65; big data
  58–60; black-box decision
  making 80–1; botsourcing 56;
  brittle algorithms 78; cloud
  computing 61; common sense
  75–6; computer learning
  methods 64; connecting
  complex systems 74; context
  67, 76–7; cruise control
  74; dark data 62; data as
  foundation for AI and machine
  learning 63–4; data hunger
  78; data processing 73; deep
  learning 70–1; garbage in,

garbage out 81–2; GPS
  navigation 74; imitation
  network 69; innovative
  thinking 77–8; intuition
  78–80; intuitive physics
  79–80; juice machine 74;
  local optima 80; machine
  capabilities 71–5; machine
  learning 65–7; neural
  networks 68–70; pattern
  recognition 72–3; predictions
  about AI 57–8; probabilistic
  matches 72; reinforcement
  learning 70–1; *tabula rasa* 68;
  Tay 55–6; vision network 69
machine intelligence 12–14, 28–9
machine learning 65–7; and
  automated tasks 66; Bayesian
  inferences 65; context 67;
  data as foundation 63–4;
  data omission 66–7; and large
  amounts of data required
  66–7; reinforcement learning
  70–1
machines, trust in 140–2
Marcus, Gary 68, 81
marketing automation 134
Maslow's Hierarchy of Needs 63–4,
  197–8
McCarthy, John 65
McVicker, Joseph 77–8
McVicker, Noah 77–8
medical data analysis 140
medical knowledge loss 122–3
Megill, Colin 177
messaging 209
Messenger, Jeff 128
Microsoft 9, 17; and algorithmic
  bias 173; as an example of
  collective intentionality 43–6;
  human-centric organizations
  193; organizational
  restructuring 243–4; and Tay
  social chatbot 55–6
Microsoft Azure 61
microwaves 87–8
military deployment 155
mini-c creativity 94
Minsky, Marvin 65
Mitchell, Margaret 75–6
Moore's Law 8–9, 27
Moravec, Hans P. 9–10